THE BRIGHTWELL FAMILY Of Alabama

Including
family connections to the
Bedgood – Parker
Perdue – Nix
Families.

GENEALOGY & HISTORY

*Compiled and Researched
by Lanette Hill*

Brightwell Enterprises, Inc.

INTRODUCTION

Civilization had its beginning around an open fire. Here at its warmth gathered the family group to find safety, comfort, and companionship. In tracing the word "fireplace" one finds it definitely related to the Latin word "Focus". There is the explanation of what home has always meant; for home is the center of life, no mere residence of the body but the axis of the heart; the place where affections develop themselves, children love and learn, where two toil together to make life a blessing.

Ones ancestors are the flagstones that have led to the home you now have. As each babe begins a new life from the warmth of a mother's lullaby to the adventures of adulthood, the days slip away as each flagstone is set in place; some carefully, some hastily--but all record the path, it seems to fade and become obscured in the distance. It is hard to visualize the battles fought, the seas spanned, the wilderness braved, deserts walked, fields cleared, houses built, homes made and families loved and raised--each event a stone in the path unseen on the other side of the rolling hills.

I saw behind me those who had gone, and before me those who are to come. I looked back and saw my father, and his father, and all our fathers, and in front to see my son, and his son, and the sons upon sons beyond.

And their eyes were my eyes.

As I felt, so they had felt and were to feel, as then, so now, as tomorrow and forever. Then I was not afraid, for I was in a long line that had no beginning and no end, and the hand of his father grasped my father's hand, and his hand was in mine, and my unborn son took my right hand, and all, up and down the line that stretched from Time That Was to Time That Is, and Is Not Yet, raised their hands to show the link, and we found that we were one, born of Woman, Son of Man, made in the Image, fashioned in the Womb by the Will of God, the Eternal Father.

Note by: Lanette Hill

Descendants of THE BRIGHTWELL FAMILY HISTORY

Generation No. 1

1. THE BRIGHTWELL FAMILY[1] HISTORY

Notes for THE BRIGHTWELL FAMILY HISTORY:
BRIGHTWELL

Coats of Arms: Appeared for the first time in France in the 11th Century. The need arose from joisting tournaments for the Lords to have an identification. Only Lords were allowed in these tournaments. It was visible proof of their nobility; then they started wearing the coats of arms on shields, armors, or banners.

Brightwell, meaning bright or clear spring or well, is a small village in ENGLAND on the old Woodbridge to Felixstowe road, just to the south of Martlesham. One source suggests that it was one of Suffolk's holy wells, said to have healing powers for ophthalmic problems. Bronze Age barrows in the north are part of a chain built across Foxhall to Waldringfield.

The village is centred around a wooded valley where Mill river flows east, then south-east to Kirton creek and the river Deben. The old vicarage, built about 1830, now known as Brightwell House, looks over the valley from the south with the church opposite on the north hill. The church is dedicated to St John the Baptist and its beauty lies in its simplicity and the furnishings made by local craftsmen. Both the church and the churchyard are well cared for. It dates from about 1300 and was extensively repaired in about 1656 by Thomas Essington, of Brightwell Hall. There are two pathetic but beautiful monuments in the chancel commemorating two of his children — Thomas, who died in 1656 aged five years and Anna, who died in 1660 aged 17 years.

Brightwell Hall was extensively altered and rebuilt in about 1663 by its new owner, Sir Samuel Barnardiston MP, leader of the Suffolk Whigs and a deputy Governor of the East India Company. His family hatchments are in the church today. The Hall was demolished in about 1755. Terraces mark the parterres and garden walks still.

At the bottom of the valley the stream formed a 'splash' or ford, with a pedestrian walkway on one side. The bridge and road were built in the late 1920s, curving past the old smithy. A painting of the church and village by John Constable, painted in 1828 or 1829 but looking much as it does today, was rediscovered in Essex in 1980.

Many tons of sand were removed from the hill behind the village hall in the 1960s for use in building Felixstowe docks. Another link between the village and the port is the choice of the name Brightwell, in 1986, for a powerful new tug.

Several folk have heard of a ghost who rides through the valley with his head under his arm.., but no one admits to having seen him. A more recent reality was the discovery in July 1983 of the body of Mrs Diane Jones of Essex in the north of the parish, an unsolved murder to this day.

1634 RICHARD BRIGHTWELL - FIRST COLONISTS to MARYLAND
This is a recreation of one of the original ships, the Dove and the ARK, to bring the first colonists to Maryland [see pictures] in 1634. My Richard Brightwell (later to become Captain of the Horse Rangers of Prince George's County and grandfather of William Kinnick who served in the Revolutionary War), entered America in 1663 as an indentured servant on a ship very much like this one.

These ships could both cross the Atlantic and sail up many of the rivers off the Chesapeake Bay and load up on hogsheads of tobacco as well as leave off settlers and manufactured goods from England. Records say that Richard Brightwell was brought to Maryland by Captain Thomas Trueman. After serving his time as an indentured servant, he earned his freedom, and acquired land, married, and had five children who reached adulthood. He also worked for the state and county government, as early as 1674, as a Ranger. As settlers moved inland, the local Indians were less friendly than they had been in the St. Mary's area. Rangers, both on foot and on horseback, "ranged" out along the frontier to report Indian activity and assist settlers they met along the way. When Prince George's County was created in 1696, Captain Richard Brightwell was appointed one of two Captain of the Horse Rangers, for the county, patrolling the western and northern frontiers, from the Potomac River on the west to the Patuxent River on the east. Although Richard Brightwell patented several parcels of land, he died just a few years later, leaving five young children, three sons and two daughters, under the oversight of his friends, William Watson and Thomas Greenfield, then Sheriff of Prince George's County, a common practice.

Richard Brightwell born in England in the mid 1640's; in 1680 married in England, Katherine Lashley, born in England, one of five sisters. Katherine, along with her mother, Elizabeth, and sisters, lived at Poplar Hill, a plantation owned by one of the sisters, Mary, by way of her late husband, John Boague, who had patented the land in 1666. Katherine' parents were Robert Lashley born abt 1620 in England/traveled to America and lived in Calvert Co. Maryland. His wife was Elizabeth born in England. Elizabeth's WILL of 11-13-1681-Calvert Co. Maryland lists Katherine Brightwell.
[more info] Richard Brightwell married, Katherine, one of five sisters. Katherine, along with her mother, Elizabeth, and sisters, lived at Poplar Hill, a plantation owned by one of the sisters, Mary, by way of her late husband, John Boague, who had patented the land in 1666. Richard moved there and they began their family at Poplar Hill. Their family included Richard, Peter and John Brightwell. They also had two daughters,
one whose name we do not know, and Elizabeth, who became the mother of William Kinnick. His father, Jasper, died in 1733, when William was 14 years old. In the Prince George's Orphans Court, he chose his uncle, John Brightwell as his guardian.
It appears that shortly after William reached the age of majority, he and his brother, also named Jasper, served in the War of Jenkin's Ear.

Richard moved there and he and Katherine began their family at Poplar Hill. Their family included Richard (1687), Peter (1691), Elizabeth (Abt 1693) and John Brightwell (1694). They also had two daughters, one whose name we do not know, Elizabeth, who became the mother of William Kinnick. William's father, Jasper, died in 1733, when William was 14 years old. In the Prince George's Orphans Court, William chose his uncle, John Brightwell, as his guardian.

Poplar Hill land was granted to Richard Brightwell in 1690 and patented as Brightwell's Hunting Quarter which consisted of 1,086 Acres on 10/10/1695. He also owned Blackwell, 160 Acres 9-20-1683. He also owned Brightwell's Landing of 47 Acres 2-1-1695; and he also owned Brightwell's Range 100 Acres 12-12-1688. Later in 1780's this land was sold to Robert Peter; then John Clarke Curtis inherited it. This land had a Seneca Red Stone on it and it was quarried and used in several building projects through the years. The quarrie closed down, but the remains are still there today, overgrown with weeds. There are historical societies trying to get this historical quarrie restored and have as a national park.

On their return to Maryland, they spent the rest of their years in Charles County, about five to ten miles south and west of Poplar Hill, in the Bryantown area.

ffeb: 25th 1677.
     Richd Brightwell Ridgely Attorney for Bernard Johnson Cooper of
        Calvert County, that the said Bernard Johnson be
admitted defendt who shall forthwith appear by his Attorney afore
said, & receive a declaracon & shall plead thereunto the generall issue
as of this Court And att the tryall thereupon to be had, the said
Bernard shall appeare in his proper person or by his Councel or At

torney, & shall confesse lease entry & Ejectmt or in default thereof Judgemt shall be entred thereupon agt the said Richard Brightwell the casuall Ejector But further prosecucon shall be stayed agt him untill he shall make default in any the prmisses And itt is further ordered by this Court by consent aforesaid that the said Bernard shall not take any advantage agt the plaintiffe for not presecuteing his tryall occasioned by such default But that the said Bernard John son shall pay unto the plaintiffe such costs as shall be by this Court taxed for the same. contd.

According to a deed recorded in 1785 in Prince George's County, MD, Richard Brightwell gave two slaves to his granddaughter Rhoda Cave. This convinces me that the Mary Brightwell who married Thomas Cave in 1782 in Prince George's County, MD, was the daughter of Richard Brightwell and the mother of Rhoda Cave. Mary likely died about that time because Thomas Cave married Elizabeth Peirce [sic] on November 18, 1786.

It appears that shortly after William; Richard's son reached the age of majority, he and his brother, also named Jasper, served in the War of Jenkin's Ear (1741-3). On their return to Maryland, they spent the rest of their years in Charles County, about five to ten miles south and west of Poplar Hill, in the Bryantown area. Poplar Hills was located in Bryantown Maryland. In 1697; Richard Brightwell donated a few acres of land for a Chapel for the southern portion of the parish.(Church of England in the Colonies; became the Episcopal Church). A couple miles down the road there is a St. Mary's Episcapal Church which is the modern version or (very near) on land that was set aside by Richard Brightwell.

Early Immigrants to America :
Name: Richard Brightwell
Year: 1663
Place: Maryland
Source Publication Code: 8510
Primary Immigrant: Brightwell, Richard
Annotation: Index from manuscript by Arthur Trader, Chief Clerk in the Maryland Land Commission, 1917. And see nos. 4507-4511, Land Notes.
Source Bibliography: SKORDAS, GUST, editor. The Early Settlers of Maryland: an Index to Names of Immigrants, Compiled from Records of Land Patents, 1633-1680, in the Hall of Records, Annapolis, Maryland. Baltimore: Genealogical Publishing Co., 1968. 525p. Repr. 1986.
Page: 59

RICHARD BRIGHTWELL is found in Colonial Soldiers of the South; by M. J. Clark. Muster Roll of Soldiers under the command of Captain James Wilson ---Price George's Co. Maryland #50 Rank --Soldier. Along with Richard (Jr) Brightwell #63; Rank Soldier.
John Jr. Brightwell, Muster Roll of Captain Joshua Beall's Co.-Prince George Co. Maryland. Militia Rank #23 Captain Brightwell Thomas.

Richard Brightwell of Maryland was brought over to become part of the landed gentry. Richard served as Captain of Rangers for which he was well "paid" for by the powers that be in the State of Maryland. Richard married the daughter of a wealthy widow. Richard Brightwell married Betty Howard 12/6/1787 Maryland. Richard Brightwell was able to "live off" his family and friends while he accummuled his own holdings. Richard's holdings were several, but not terribly large --- a few hundred acres, at most. not thousands. Richard Brightwell cultivated powerful friends who allowed him some leeway in building some land ownership. Richard owned 1,000 acres on the banks and a Hunting Lodge with wild land; earned as Captain of the Rangers who patrolled the land for Indians.

King William County, Virginia was established in 1704.
Establishment: By enabling act of Virginia General Assembly effective on April 11, 1702; created from Pamunkey Neck section of King & Queen County (Town of West Point incorporated on July 11, 1870)
Namesake: William III; King of England, Scotland and Ireland from April 11, 1689 to March 19, 1702

1677 May 29 - A peace treaty between the remnants of six Indian tribes and English King Charles II, acting through Governor Herbert Jeffreys and the Council of State, required the tribes to avow allegiance to the queen of the Pamunkey and the English crown. The treaty effectively reaffirmed the existence of the Mattaponi and Pamunkey Indian lands, later called reservations, and stipulated payment each March of an annual quitrent to the governor. The Mattaponi and Pamunkey Indian reservations are the only reservations in Virginia and two of the oldest reservations in the United States.

1691 King & Queen County was created from New Kent County. The new county, which was named after the ruling English monarchs, King William III and Queen Mary II, encompassed lands lying north of the Pamunkey and York Rivers including Pamunkey Neck. The legislative enabling act that created the new county contained the first official reference to English town lands at West Point in Pamunkey Neck

1692 The House of Burgesses, the lower house of the General Assembly, rejected a petition from inhabitants of King & Queen County requesting legalization of titles and possession of lands that they acquired from the Indians in the Pamunkey Neck section of the county.

1693 King William III and Queen Mary II granted the College of William & Mary its royal charter, which included an endowment of 10,000 acres in the upper part of Pamunkey Neck. The land was sold to lessees by 1830.

1695 May 4 - William Leigh and Joshua Story, burgesses for King & Queen County, introduced the first legislative petition to divide King & Queen County and to create a new county. The bill was passed by the House of Burgesses but was defeated by the Council, which was the upper chamber of the legislature.

1699 June 21 - The Council-appointed a commission to meet at King & Queen County Court House in September and to examine the validity of private land claims in the Pamunkey Neck section of the county.

1701 August - The General Assembly passed the act that established a regional port town called Delaware (or Del la War), the predecessor of the Town of West Point. The new town was situated on land conveyed by John West III and three siblings to King & Queen County for establishment of a regional port.

September 4 - The Council-appointed commission submitted its report to the General Assembly. The legislature adopted the report's recommendations, approving patents for 50 settlers and denying patents for 16 other settlers.

September 5 - The bill to establish a distinct county from King & Queen County was introduced in the legislature by Robert Beverley, a burgess from Jamestown who held the clerkship for King & Queen County.

October 2 - The General Assembly passed and Governor Frances Nicholson assented to the enabling act creating a distinct county from the Pamunkey Neck section of King & Queen County. The new county was named for the reigning English monarch, King William III. Queen Mary II had died in 1694.

King William County Virginia esta. 1704.

Maryland Historical Accounts: RICHARD BRIGHTWELL LAND GRANT in 1690.
Mongomery County, Maryland
The settlement at the mouth of Seneca Creek has a history older than Montgomery County or the Union itself. In days before roads were common, the creek provided a route of transport from the rich farmlands for several miles up its course. The small falls just down the Potomac River from the mouth of the creek were an impediment to river traffic, which at times of low water required a portage.

There are four points of interest in the area: The Seneca Sandstone quarries from whence the stone was cut, the Quarry Master's House, the stone cutting facility where the stone was reduced into building blocks, and the loading basin in the canal from which the mill obtained a supply of water and where barges were loaded with stone blocks for shipment to Georgetown.

The land was granted to Richard Brightwell in 1690 and patented as Brightwell"s Hunting Quarter. In the 1780's Robert Peter, the mayor of Georgetown, bought it and, at that time, there was a quarry on the site. The property was inherited by John Parke Custis Peter who built Montevideo Mansion from seneca stone. In 1967 the Potomac Red Sand Stone Company incorporated to operate the quarries, which it did with success until the interests were sold to the Seneca Stone Company, which worked the quarries until the early 1900's when the quality of the stone became poor.

In the latter part of the 17th century, the Potomac Rangers under the command of Colonel Mason ranged through the Seneca Section to the headquarters of Captain Richard Brightwell, whose land grant stretched along the river's edge above Seneca.

St. Pauls Parish's History   Connection to RICHARD BRIGHTWELL
Part One - The Beginning

The origin and most of the early history of St. Paul's Church has been lost in colonial obscurity, but it is known that St. Paul's Church at Mt. Calvert was built long before the establishment in 1692 of the Church of England in the Maryland colony. Some historians think it is possible that St. Paul's was organized under the ministration of the Reverend William Wilkinson who served as Church of England clergyman in St. Mary's County from 1650 to 1664.

In 1692, 'the Act for the Service of Almighty God and the Establishment of the Protestant Religion Within the Province' was passed by the General Assembly. This Act established the Church of England in Maryland and divided the colony into thirty parishes. St. Paul's Parish, located in what was then Calvert County, was one of the original parishes and the church, which had already been erected, became the parish church.

In 1696, Prince George's County was created from parts of Calvert and Charles Counties and St. Paul's Parish, became part of Prince George's County. Mt. Calvert became the county seat as well as an official port of entry. The commissioners had the area surveyed and plans for the town were drafted. Port and warehouse facilities were erected; streets were built; and stores and inns were opened to meet the needs of the growing community. A court house was built in 1698 but until that time, St. Paul's Church was also used to hold court. The town was known both as Mt. Calvert and Charles Town until the court officially named it Charles Town.

In 1693, Captain Richard Brightwell of Popular Hill, located in the south-eastern part of the parish, gave three acres of his plantation to St. Paul's and a chapel was built there for the convenience of communicants in that part of the parish. It is thought that this chapel was used for about forty years.

Richard Brightwell of England died August 1698, Prince George Co. Maryland. His wife; Katherine was also born in England and died in 1698 Calvert, Maryland USA.

COURT RECORDS, Prince George Co. Maryland; 1696-1699 has:
Richard Brightwell is listed several times and numerous records as well as a Robert Brightwell.
Assembly Proceedings: May 10-June 9, 1692:
Captain Richard Brightwell and his rangers; found a mare belonging to Richard Thompson with an Indian arrow shot into her heart and dead near Charles Carters house.

JOHN BRIGHTWELL RECORDS Frederick Co.Maryland.
1749 Frederick Co, MD Petition. "This [1749] petition thus marked the beginning of the Liberty Road, Maryland State Route 26, from Mt. Pleasant... to Taylorsville (Burnt House Woods.)... But the large number of others signing this petition shows how rapidly after 1743 the settlement grew. These included Joseph WOOD of Linganore... John PHILLIPS... John HOWARD, son of Gideon, and Philip HOWARD...Stephen RICHARDS... Patrick HOLLIGAN... James BROWN... Matthias STALCAP... Robert BIRCHFIELD... Solomon SPARKS... Charles WOOD ("Charles' Choice, 1748, beginning 'in the forks between Linganore and Comb's Woolpit Branch.' one mile east of Unionville), John BRIGHTWELL... Richard COMBS, Sr., Richard COMBS, Jr., and Dennis ENSEY (all on "Coomes His Inheritance" 1749 one mile east of Unionville)..." (Excerpted from PIONEERS OF OLD MONOCACY; THE EARLY SETTLEMENTS OF FREDERICK COUNTY, MD, 1721-1743; Tracy and dern; Gen. Pub. Co.; Balt. 1987 (and other sources) by Combs Researcher Thom Mont)

There was another Brightwell family member named JOHN BRIGHTWELL who was an imigrant who arrived abroad the ship Baltimore, PASSENGER #1070; DATED jUNE 1749 WITH HIS WIFE; ONE BOY AND TWO GIRLS. oCCUPATION: tAYLOR; ARRIVING FROM hALIFAX, nOVA sCOTIA.

Marriages in MARYLAND in 1778-1800.
John Brightwell, August 16, 1799 wife Polly Pitay.
John Brightwell, Jan. 4, 1785; wife Mary Dobson or Marg. Dobson.
Richard Brightwell Dec. 16, 1787; wife Betty Howard.
William Brightwell August 20, 1785; wife Mary Waddle.

In Maryland State Archives (Chauncey Papers Index) 1797; it reads:
January 20, 1797 - 392: Ralph Briscoe, Sarah Briscoe, and Samson Trammel vs. John Young; Martha
Howard, Cornelius Howard, Ellis Hart, RICHARD BRIGHTWELL, ELIZABETH BRIGHTWELL,
Margaret Young Howard, and Richard Howard. FR. ESTATE of JOHN TRAMMEL. Dukes - Woods.

DEED - Prince George Co Maryland LIBER FF Book 2, page 242 (1780-1785): At the request of Rhoda
Cave, the following deed of gift was enrolled May 14, 1785 by Richard Brightwell of Prince George Co.
MD in that he gave to his grand-daughter Rhoda Cave; (2) negroes-Jane and her increase-daughter of Ciller
and; (2) George-son of Platt. So ordered.

Richard Brightwell remained in the Maryland State but members of the Brightwell family began moving
into the State of Virginia.

The connection between Richard Brightwell and Reynolds Brightwell has not been determined at this time.
There are several researchers continuing to study and research this matter to connect our Reynolds
Brightwell to the Maryland Richard Brightwell.

Here's the link to the Brightwell section just so you don't have to look it up again:

http://freepages.genealogy.rootsweb.com/~sassytazzy/family/surnames/brightwell/brightwell.html

Have a great day!

Susan :)
Sassytazzy's Online Genealogy Research Library
http://freepages.genealogy.rootsweb.com/~sassytazzy/index.html

ID: I23
Name: Richard BRIGHTWELL
Sex: M
Death: AUG 1698 in Prince George's Co, MD
Note:

Will written 21 Aug, probated 29 Aug 1698.
Thos. Greenfield and Wm. Watson, exs., to hold estate in trust until majority of eld. son Richard.
Change Date: 31 MAY 2001

Marriage 1 Katherine
Children
 female BRIGHTWELL b: ABT 1683 in Charles Co, Maryland
 Richard (2) BRIGHTWELL b: 1687
 Peter BRIGHTWELL b: 1691 in Charles Co, Maryland
 Elizabeth BRIGHTWELL b: ABT 1693
 John BRIGHTWELL b: 1694
ID: I25

CHILD:
Name: Richard (2) BRIGHTWELL

Sex: M
Birth: 1687
Death: 1775
Note:

Taxable in Mattapany Hundred 1719 and 1733
Michelle has born abt 1678, Charles Co, MD....died in Prince George's Co.
Change Date: 30 SEP 2001

Father: Richard BRIGHTWELL
Mother: Katherine

Marriage 1 Mary LAWSON
Children
 Richard (3) BRIGHTWELL b: abt 1720-25
 John Lawson BRIGHTWELL
 Elizabeth (R) BRIGHTWELL
 Rebeckah BRIGHTWELL

CHILD:
ID: I26
Name: Peter BRIGHTWELL
Sex: M
Birth: 1691 in Charles Co, Maryland
Death: 1747 in Prince George's Co, MD
Note:

Peter was one of the heirs of Robert Kent, Calvert Co. 1693 (MCW II.54 & 66)
Taxable in Mattapany Hundred 1719 and 1733
Michelle has born in Charles Co, MD.
Change Date: 30 SEP 2001

Father: Richard BRIGHTWELL
Mother: Katherine

Marriage 1 Ann
Children
 Elizabeth (P) BRIGHTWELL
 Catharine (P) BRIGHTWELL

CHILD:
ID: I28
Name: John BRIGHTWELL
Sex: M
Birth: 1694
Death: 1774
Note:

Alfred Tomerlin has born about 1694 (WorldConnect)
1694 also on Michelle Justice gedcom (27 May 2000) downloaded from ancestory.com via john shelly
Early Families had bef 1698.
Change Date: 30 SEP 2001

Father: Richard BRIGHTWELL
Mother: Katherine

Marriage 1 Elizabeth COLEMAN
Children
 John (2) BRIGHTWELL b: 1720 in Prince George's Co, MD
 Catherine (J) BRIGHTWELL b: 1722
 Ursala BRIGHTWELL b: ABT 1725
 Sarah BRIGHTWELL b: 1728
 Priscilla BRIGHTWELL b: ABT 1730
 Eleanor BRIGHTWELL b: ABT 1732
 Martha BRIGHTWELL b: ABT 1733
 Thomas Coleman BRIGHTWELL b: ABT 1735

A marriage record for the following in Prince George Co. Maryland:
Richard Brightwell marrying Mary Pearce May 31, 1785
Richard C. Brightwell marrying Fanomi Thomas Dec. 16, 1794.

REVOLUTIONARY WAR SERVICE:
Anderson Brightwell Private Virginia
John Brightwell Private Virginia Reg. 13, 5 & 7
Leonard Brightwell Virginia
Robert Brightwell Private in John Reed's Command PA Volunteers
 William Brightwell 7th Virginia Regiment.

1830 Census a Richard Brightwell lived in Spottsylvania Co. Virginia.[no further information] See
Sassytazzy Records.

Child of THE BRIGHTWELL FAMILY HISTORY is:
2.   i.   REYNOLDS OR RANDALL[2] BRIGHTWELL, b. Bet. 1664 - 1666, READ NOTES King William
            Virginia; d. 22 Jan 1702/03, King William Virginia Will.

Generation No. 2

2. REYNOLDS OR RANDALL[2] BRIGHTWELL *(THE BRIGHTWELL FAMILY[1] HISTORY)* was born Bet. 1664 -
1666 in READ NOTES King William Virginia, and died 22 Jan 1702/03 in King William Virginia Will.
He married ELIZABETH 1683 in Marriage-King William Co. Virginia. She was born 1670 in King William
Co. Virginia/1704 Quit Claim Roll 300.

Notes for REYNOLDS OR RANDALL BRIGHTWELL:
Reynold BRIGHTWELL was born 1664 in King William Co., VA. He died 22 Jan 1702/1703 in King
William Co., VA.
Abstract of REYNOLDS BRIGHTWELL'S will in King William Co, VA.

Wife: Elizabeth, Son: Thomas Brightwell - land on the line of Matthew Toler; Son: Reynolds Brightwell;
Son: John Brightwell; Daughter: Rebecca Grackwitt (?); Daughters: Elizabeth & Anne Brightwell.
Probated February 1702/3.
Witnesses: Henry Lower, Fergus Maghekey, Robert Alvey.

Reynold married Elizabeth UNKNOWN on 1683.

There is a REYNOLDS BRIGHTWELL is found on a 1790 Tax Lists for Virginia-Henrico Co. Virginia.
along with John Brightwell; King William Co. Virginia and
John (Jr) Brightwell of King William Co. Virginia.

This Reynolds Brightwell is found on the 1793 Census of Prince Edward Co. Virginia - with six family members, no black. The other two Brightwells were Charles Brightwell with only himself and Barnet Brightwell.

In the 1795 Only Barnard Brightwell shows with three members in the family and 1 female no blacks.
Reynold Brightwell 1664 King William Co. Va. Spouce: Elizabeth

Elizabeth Brightwell is listed in 1704 and she is in King William Co., Virginia with 300 Acres of Property owned/rented.
Reynolds Brightwell has a Daughter: Lucy Brightwell born before 1795 who married Samuel Thaxton (1789-1828) Jan. 26, 1811 - Prince Edward Co. Virginia

Rent Roll of Virginia 1704/05
Brightwell Elizb   King William County

ID: I575200569
Name: Reynold BRIGHTWELL
Given Name: Reynold
Surname: Brightwell
Sex: M
Birth: 1692 in King William Co., VA
Change Date: 20 Mar 2004

Father: Reynold BRIGHTWELL b: 1664 in King William Co., VA
Mother: Elizabeth UNKNOWN

Marriage 1 Spouse Unknown
Note: _UID502C8F194716B746B548FCF1C4A844082062
Children
 Reynold BRIGHTWELL b: 1735 in King William Co., VA
  He appears in the 1768, 1769, and 1770 tax Records for Louisa Co, VA.
In 1771 he has a land record in Prince Edward Co, VA and appears in
the 1783 and 1785 census for Prince Edward Co, VA.

LAST WILL & TESTAMENT:
Abstract of REYNOLDS BRIGHTWELL'S will in King William Co, VA.
Wife: Elizabeth, Son: Thomas Brightwell - land on the line of
Matthew Toler; Son: Reynolds Brightwell; Son: John Brightwell;
Daughter: Rebecca Grackwitt (?); Daughters: Elizabeth & Anne
Brightwell. Probated February 1702/3. Witnesses: Henry Lower, Fergus
Maghekey, Robert Alvey

Notes for ELIZABETH:
On 1704 Quit Claim Roll King William Co. Virginia with 300 Acres. The only Brightwell listed on the roll.

More About REYNOLDS BRIGHTWELL and ELIZABETH:
Marriage: 1683, Marriage-King William Co. Virginia

Children of REYNOLDS BRIGHTWELL and ELIZABETH are:
3.   i.   REYNOLDS[3] BRIGHTWELL, b. Bef. 1735, King William Co., VA./Rev. War Private Virginia; d. 15
                  Aug 1804, Prince Edward Co Va./Granville N.C. Records.
            ii.   REBECCA BRIGHTWELL, b. 1684, King William Co. Virginia; m. (1) GRACKWITT(??); m. (2) JOHN
                  BEANE, 10 Mar 1784, Prince George Co. Maryland.

            More About JOHN BEANE and REBECCA BRIGHTWELL:
            Marriage: 10 Mar 1784, Prince George Co. Maryland

iii.   THOMAS BRIGHTWELL, b. 1690, King William Co. Virginia.

iv.   JOHN BRIGHTWELL, b. 1694, King William Co. Virginia/Rev. War Private Virginia; d. 1796, King William Co. Virginia.

v.   ELIZABETH BRIGHTWELL, b. 1696, King William Co. Virginia.

4.   vi.   MARY BRIGHTWELL, b. 1698, King William Co. Virginia.

vii.   AMY OR ANNE BRIGHTWELL, b. 1700, King William Co. Virginia.

Generation No. 3

3. REYNOLDS[3] BRIGHTWELL *(REYNOLDS OR RANDALL[2], THE BRIGHTWELL FAMILY[1] HISTORY)* was born Bef. 1735 in King William Co., VA./Rev. War Private Virginia, and died 15 Aug 1804 in Prince Edward Co Va./Granville N.C. Records. He married (1) MARY 1756 in Married in VA. lst Wife.. She was born 1741 in born Va. alive in 1811, moved to Edgefield Co., S. Carolina., and died Aft. 1811 in Her Will in Edgefield S. Carolina.. He married (2) DRUCILLA ALLMAND 25 Feb 1771 in Louisa Co., Va. Marriage Record./Thomas Allmand signed doc., daughter of THOMAS ALLMAND. She was born 1749 in of Prince Edward Co. Virginia READ her notes..

Notes for REYNOLDS BRIGHTWELL:
Reynolds Brightwell is said to have also gone by the name of Leonard in records. More research to be done on this.

Event: Tax Records 1768 Louisa Co., Va.
Event: Tax Records 1769 Louisa Co., Va.
Event: Tax Records 1770 Louisa Co., Va.
Event: Land Record 1771 Prince Edward Co., Virginia
Census: 1783 Prince Edward Co., Virginia - had only Reynold Brightwell and his son; Barnet Brightwell listed living in the county at that time.
Census: 1785 Prince Edward Co., Virginia

1783-1790 Census Prince Edward Co. Virginia lists the following:
    Charles Brightwell White (1) Black (0)
    Reynold Brightwell   White(6) Black (0)
    Barnet Brightwell White (2) Black (0)

1785   Renard Brightwell White (9) Dwelling/Other 1   0

1790 Tax Lists - Virginia
    Reynolds, Brightwell. White Henrico Co. Virginia 1790 Personal Property B 03
    Black-above 16 (2); Black under 16 (5) Homes Acres (100) Carriage Wheels (4)
    along with:
    John Brightwell King William 1787 Personal 04 -
    John Brightwell King William 1787 Personal   14
1782 - 1787 - Virginia TAX PAYERS List:
    John Brightwell of King William County, Virginia

1790 - FIRST CENSUS of FREDERICK CO. Maryland; has John Brightwell listed; which indicates that he also must have land and/or had holdings in the State of Maryland. October 9, 1757 - November 8, 1758 - John Brightwell was a Private in Capt. Ware's Co. of Frederick County, Maryland. Revolutionary Service.

John Brightwell, Arrived aboard Ship Baltimore, passenger #1070, June 1749 with wife, 1 boy, 2 girls, occupation taylor.Arriving Halifax, Nova Scotia.

1787 Census in Virginia lists the following Brightwells:
    Anderson Brightwell
    Barnard Brightwell
    Charles Brightwell

John Brightwell
Reynold Brightwell
Reynolds Brightwell
Thomas Brightwell

1787 - Additional information for the Year 1787 is that Reynolds Brightwell, is also listed on a per personal property Tax List for Henrico Co. Va. and Thomas Brightwell is again listed in Orange Co. Va.

1800 Tax Lists for State of Virginia lists:
    Thomas Brightwell - Nansemond Co VA
    Aaron Brightwell (estate) Nansemond
    Edward Brightwell - Shenandoah Co.
    James Brightwell - Isle of Wight Co.
    Martha Brightwell - Norfolk Co.
    Thomas Brightwell (estate) - Nansemond Co..
    (2) Williams Brightwell - Caroline Co. Va and (1) William Brightwell in Isle of Wight

1803/12-30 Thomas Brightwell died in Orange Co. Virginia; born 11-17-1777; connection not known at this time. He had two sons listed; Thomas (Jr) Brightwell and a Richard Brightwell. More research on him to be done.

1810 Census of PRINCE EDWARD County, VIRGINIA:
Barnett Brightwell
Charles Brightwell
William (Sr) Brightwell born 1806 Elizabeth B. 1808; Mary Ann B. 1807
                    Mary Young
Drucilla Brightwell [Head of Household] Prince Edward Co. VA.
William (Jr) Brightwell - Prince Edward Co. Va.
Anderson Brightwell - Prince Edward Co. VA.

NOTE: Reynolds Brightwell is not found in the 1810 Census of Prince Edward Co. Virginia; his wife Drucilla Brightwell is shown as a Head of Household along with his children.

These same men; except for Drucilla; who apparently died in Prince Edward Co. Virginia --remained in Prince Edward County Virginia up until 1840 Census records. Some of the Brightwell family decided to remain in Virginia.

However; a group of the BRIGHTWELL family left Virginia and headed for the State of Alabama on a wagon train heading south down through North Carolina. Reynolds Brightwell and William Brightwell had received a Land Grants in Alabama for his service in the Revolutionary War and so he, and family left Virginia and headed south on a wagon train along the Appalachian Mountainous Terrian stopping over in Grandville, North Carolina. Granville, N. Carolina is where his father Reynolds Brightwell died and is buried. Reynolds Brightwell's WILL is in Grandville, N. Carolina and Mary Olive Brightwell's WILL was found in Edgefield, S. Carolina. Reynolds son; William Brightwell was traveling with him. So many people died on wagon trains heading to their promised new land. Illnesses and harsh weather, terrerous weather, no food, so many things to combat caused many not to make it and they died along the way. So, we ask, "Why would they have tried to make it so far?" It was the promise of a new life, a chance for land of their own, a new beginning for their families. They wanted to live to see their children in the new land and didn't want to get left behind. Families stuck together back then, where one went, they all went. Families helped each other through hard, hard times. So it was on to the new land that encouraged them to travel so far.

After William Brightwell's father died; he and his mother, William Brightwell left the area and continued south towards the Land Grant in Alabama and lived in Edgefield, S. Carolina where Mary's Last Will and Testament is found. After she died William Brightwell and the rest of family left the area and continued traveling south with the Wagon Train in order to avoid the mountaineous terrain. They needed to head west towards Alabama and had to go through the State of Georgia to get there. William Brightwell arrived in Barnwell, S. Carolina and had to remain there awhile before the family could continue towards Alabama. A passport was required to travel through the Indian Territoriy and land to go west towards Alabama. This Passport had to be issued by the Governor of the State of Georgia and it took time to get this passport approved. It also took time to form wagon trains and get a train master to head the trip west. The wagon train master had to know the way to travel, areas to avoid. Be experienced and trained to watch for Indian Raids, and skirmishes [which were still happening].

Reynolds Brightwell and Mary Olive of Grandville NC.
{See will of Reynolds Brightwell in Grandville and Mary's will in Edgefield SC}.
Reynolds Brightwell in Grandville NC. had Mitchell kin to move to E. Texas.x. [per Martha Brightwell]
1)_Mary _Olive(b.pre.1741-d.pre.1771) died Edgefield S. Carolina.
2)1771 Louisa Co Va to Drucilla Almand (b.pre.1756-liv 1810 Prince Edward Co VA)

CHILDREN OF REYNOLD'S 1ST WIFE
1.Charles Brightwell (SR) (b.ca.1756 King Wm Co VA-d.1847 Pr.Edw.Co VA) md Nancy _____.
Received Revolutionary War Pension. He left a will.
a.William Brightwell (JR) (b.ca.1784-liv 1850) md 1804 Pr.Edw.Co.VA to his 1st cousin Nancy Brightwell
(d/o Barnett)
b.Barnett U Brightwell (b.ca.1787-d.1855) md 1812 Buckingham Co VA to Judith W Boatwright
c.Rachel Brightwell md 1804 Pr.Edw.Co.VA to Samuel Roberts
d.Rhoda Brightwell md 1805 Pr.Edw.Co.VA to Obadiah Lumpkin
e.Polley Brightwell
f.Elizabeth A Brightwell md 1819 Pr.Edw.Co.VA to William M Jenkins
g.Peggy Brightwell
2.Barnett Brightwell (SR) (b.pre.1762-d.ca.1830 Pr.Edw.Co. VA) md 1782 Pr.Edw.Co.VA to Mary Guill
(d/o Alexander Guill SR). Barnett's estate (1830) was administered by his son-in-law William Brightwell
(JR); Mary's estate (1839) was administered by her son Charles Brightwell (JR).
a.Alexander Brightwell (b.ca.1785-liv 1850TN) md: 1)1807 Pr.Edw.Co.VA to Mrs Sally Carter and 2)1840
Wilson Co TN to Adaline Pitlow.
b.John Brightwell (b.ca.1786VA-d.ca.1835GA) md 1811 Cumberland Co Va to Frances H Glenn. He
moved to Clarke Co Ga about 1822.
?c.Charles Brightwell (JR) (b.ca.1789VA-d.1847VA) md 1811 Pr.Edw.Co.VA to Hopy W Boatwright
(b.ca.1791-liv 1850)
?d.Josiah Brightwell (b.ca.1791-liv 1850) md 1819 Pr.Edw.Co.VA to Jane P Hill.
e.Reuben Brightwell (b.ca.1798-liv 1850) md 1822 Pr.Edw.Co.VA to Mary J Hill.
f.Nancy Brightwell (b.ca.1789-liv 1850) md 1804 Pr.Edw.Co.VA to her 1st cousin William Brightwell (JR)
(s/o Charles SR)
???g.SAMUEL BRIGHTWELL (b.ca.1783GA-d.184_GA) md:
1)1803 Pr.Edw.Co.VA to Betsy A Moon/Moore
2)1808 Oglethorpe Co Ga to Frances BErry
???h.Barnett Brightwell (b.179_-d.pre.1840) md 1815 Pr.Edw.Co.VA to Nancy Matthews
i.others???
3.Nancy Brightwell (b.ca.1767-liv 1839 Pittsylvania Co VA) md 1786 Pr.Edw.Co.VA to Anderson
BRIGHTWELL (b.ca.1766-d.1837)-probably a cousin-he received a Rev.War Pension.
?a.Jesse Brightwell (b.ca.1789-liv 1850) md 1811 Pr.Edw.Co.VA to Rhoda Dodson
b.Betsy Brightwell (b.ca.1798-liv 1821)
c.Dicey Brightwell (b.ca.1800-liv 1821)
d.Sally Brightwell (b.ca.1803-liv 1821)
e.Milley Brightwell (b.ca.1806-liv 1821)
f._____ Brightwell (b.ca.1809-liv 1821)
g.others???
CHILD OF REYNOLD'S 1ST OR 2ND WIFE?
4.Elizabeth Brightwell (b.pre.1774-d.(1789-1794) md 1789 Pr.Edw.Co.VA to William Guill.
CHILD OF REYNOLD'S 2ND WIFE-DRUCILLA
5.William Brightwell (SR) (b.ca.1779VA-d.183_Pr.Edw.Co.VA) md 1800 Pr.Edw.Co.VA to Mary Young
(b.ca.1785VA-liv 1850)
a.Henry Brightwell (b.ca.1820-liv 1850)
b.Richard Brightwell (b.ca.1822-liv 1850)
c.Willie Ann Brightwell (b.ca.1824-liv 1850)

d.Mary Brightwell (b.ca.1825-liv 1850)

e.others.

6.Amy Brightwell (b.ca.1782) md 1803 Pr.Edw.Co.VA to Robert Martin

7.others???

NOTE: JR and SR meant "the older one" and "the younger one" not necessarily father/son.

William Brightwell Sr was an uncle to William Brightwell Jr and SR was only about 5 years older than Jr

Barnett Brightwell Sr (b.pre.1762-d.abt.1830) md 1782 Mary Guill (b.176?-d.abt.1836). Nine children (from tax, deed & estate records):

Children

1.   Reynold BRIGHTWELL b: 1692 in King William Co., VA

" ID: I524764465

" Name: Reynold BRIGHTWELL

" Given Name: Reynold

" Surname: Brightwell

" Sex: M

" Birth: 1692 in King William Co., VA

Marriage 1 UNKNOWN UNKNOWN b: 1741 in Virginia

"   Married: 1756 in Virginia 1

Children

1.   Barnett BRIGHTWELL b: 1757 in Prince Edward Co., VA

2.   Charles BRIGHTWELL b: 1757 in King William Co., VA

3.   Lucy BRIGHTWELL b: Bef 1795

Marriage 2 Druscilla ALLMAND

"   Married: 25 Feb 1771 in Louisa Co., Va 1

Children

1.   Nancy BRIGHTWELL b: 1767

2.   William BRIGHTWELL b: 1779

3.   Amy BRIGHTWELL b: 1782 in Prince Edward Co., VA

4.   Elizabeth BRIGHTWELL b: 1789

" ID: I524759127

" Name: Reynold BRIGHTWELL

" Given Name: Reynold

" Surname: Brightwell

" Sex: M

" Birth: 1735 in King William Co., VA 1

" Death: 1806 in Prince Edward Co., VA

" Note:

[janet skelton.FTW]

Event: Tax Records 1768 Louisa Co., Va.

Event: Tax Records 1769 Louisa Co., Va.

Event: Tax Records 1770 Louisa Co., Va.

Event: Land Record 1771 Prince Edward Co., Virginia

Census: 1783 Prince Edward Co., Virginia

Note: With 6 white souls.

Census: 1785 Prince Edward Co., Virginia

:

Listed as: Renard

With 9 white souls and 1 dwelling.

Event: Publick Claims 17 MAY 1784 Prince Edward Co., VA

Note: For two bu wheat, pg 39

Event: Publick Claims 28 JAN 1782 Prince Edward Co., VA

More About REYNOLDS BRIGHTWELL:
Burial: Also listed as Renard Brightwell White (9) Dwelling (1)

Notes for MARY:
Reynolds Brightwell and Mary ? of Grandville NC.
{See will of Reynolds Brightwell in Grandville and Mary's will in Edgefield SC}.

Other records indicate that a Runnell Brightwell was born About 1740. Runnell died After August 1781 in Granville, North Carolina. He was married to a lady named Mary {?} last name not known but it is known he married After 1755. They had a daughter named Salley Brightwell who was born About 1760.

I saw a posting that Mary's last name was OLIVE. born 1741 Virginia; alive in 1811 moved to Edfield Co. S. Carolina. Her WILL Edgefield South Carolina. The last name OLIVE is currently being investigated whether it is accurate or not.

More About REYNOLDS BRIGHTWELL and MARY:
Marriage: 1756, Married in VA. lst Wife.

Notes for DRUCILLA ALLMAND:

 Reynold Brightwell was also shown as Leonard on many records in Virginia as can be seen in this marriage record.
     Leonard Brightwell was born 1820 and married Drusilla (Blackwell(?) Calvert, MD

More About REYNOLDS BRIGHTWELL and DRUCILLA ALLMAND:
Marriage: 25 Feb 1771, Louisa Co., Va. Marriage Record./Thomas Allmand signed doc.

Children of REYNOLDS BRIGHTWELL and MARY are:
5.   i.   CHARLES (SR)[4] BRIGHTWELL, b. Abt. 1756, Born King William Co. Virginia; d. 1847, Prince Edward Co. Va. He left a WILL..
6.   ii.   BARNETT (SR) BRIGHTWELL, b. 1762; d Abt. 1830, Prince Edward Co. Va..
7.   iii. SAMUEL BRIGHTWELL, b. 1783, born GA of Clark Co. Ga. READ HIS NOTES; d. 1840, 184(?) Georgia died [in Elbert Co. Ga. 1805].

Children of REYNOLDS BRIGHTWELL and DRUCILLA ALLMAND are:
8.   iv.   NANCY[4] BRIGHTWELL, b. 1767, Liv in Pittsylvania Co VA.; d. 1839, Pittsylvania Co. Va..
        v.   ELIZABETH "BETSEY" BRIGHTWELL, b. 1774, King William County Virginia Rent Roll 1704/05; d. Bet. 1789 - 1794, 300 Acres of Property ONLY Brightwell in King William Co. VA; m. WILLIAM GUILL, 15 Jan 1789, Prince Edward Co. Va. Marriage Records..

              More About ELIZABETH "BETSEY" BRIGHTWELL:
              Burial: Died Prince Edward Co. Virginia.

              More About WILLIAM GUILL and ELIZABETH BRIGHTWELL:
              Marriage: 15 Jan 1789, Prince Edward Co. Va. Marriage Records.

        vi.   LUCY BRIGHTWELL, b. Bef. 1775, Prince Edward Co. Virginia; d. Her father was decd when she got married.; m. SAMUEL THAXTON, 26 Jan 1811, Prince Edward Co., Va. Marriage Records.; b. Bet. 1789 - 1828, of Prince Edward Co., VA..

Notes for SAMUEL THAXTON:
Reynolds Brightwell - born before 1775 in Prince George Co.,Virginia has a
   Daughter: Lucy Brightwell born before 1795 who married Samuel Thaxton (1789-1828) Jan. 26,
1811 - Prince Edward Co. Virginia

More About SAMUEL THAXTON and LUCY BRIGHTWELL:
Marriage: 26 Jan 1811, Prince Edward Co., Va. Marriage Records.

9.	vii.	BARNETTE BRIGHTWELL, b. 1778, Prince Edward Co. Virginia.
10.	viii.	WILLIAM BRIGHTWELL, b. Bet. 1774 - 1779, Born Pr Edw Co VA./mvd w/fam afr 1820 Cen. to N. Carolina; liv in the 1830 Edgefield, S.Carolina cen.; d. Aft. 1866, Alabama-Moved w fam.1850 Cen./ Covington Co. Ala..
	ix.	AMY BRIGHTWELL, b. 1782, Prince Edward Co. VA.Amy was 21 yrs old at marriage. Prince Edward Co. VA; m. ROBERT MARTIN, 09 Dec 1806, Married Prince Edward Co. Va..

More About ROBERT MARTIN and AMY BRIGHTWELL:
Marriage: 09 Dec 1806, Married Prince Edward Co. Va.

4. MARY³ BRIGHTWELL *(REYNOLDS OR RANDALL², THE BRIGHTWELL FAMILY¹ HISTORY)* was born 1698 in King William Co. Virginia. She married THOMAS CAVE 15 Apr 1782 in Prince George Co. Maryland.

More About THOMAS CAVE and MARY BRIGHTWELL:
Marriage: 15 Apr 1782, Prince George Co. Maryland

Child of MARY BRIGHTWELL and THOMAS CAVE is:
        i.   RHODA⁴ CAVE.

Generation No. 4

5. CHARLES (SR)⁴ BRIGHTWELL *(REYNOLDS³, REYNOLDS OR RANDALL², THE BRIGHTWELL FAMILY¹ HISTORY)* was born Abt. 1756 in Born King William Co. Virginia, and died 1847 in Prince Edward Co. Va. He left a WILL.. He married NANCY. She was born in She rec'd Rev. War Pension for him..

Notes for CHARLES (SR) BRIGHTWELL:
ID: I575202774
Name: Charles BRIGHTWELL
Given Name: Charles
Surname: Brightwell
Sex: M
Birth: 1757 in King William Co., VA 1
Death: 1847 in Prince Edward Co., VA
Change Date: 19 Apr 2004 1 2
Note:
Virginians in the Revolution, pg 94
Brightwell, Charles, of Prince Edward, 78, mpl.(Militia pension list,1835)
Brightwell, Charles, Prince Edward, saw service at Williamsburg,dmp(declarations of militia pensioners).
Event: Pension Application JAN 1833 Prince Edward Co., VA
Note: Rev. and other record of Prince Edward County, pg 73.

In the name of God Amen. I Charles Brightwell Senr being of sound mind domake this my last will hereby revoking all others. 1st It is my desirethat at my death that all my just debts should be paid. I also wish thatall my estate remain in the hands of my beloved wife Nancy if she choosesto keep it during her life if she survives me. 2nd I wish to give to thechildren or bodderly [sic] heirs of my daughters Rachel, Rhoda & Pollythat may be liveing [sic] at my death fifty dollars each. 3d I wish theballance [sic] of my estate both real and personal to be equally dividedamongst the ballance [sic] of my children except my daughter Elizabeth A.Jenkins which I desire to have one hundred dollars [_____] to be given toher and the lawful heirs of her boddy [sic]. 3d The negroes which I havebefore given to my children at valuation say to my son William one Negroboy Pleasant at one hundred & fifty dollars to my son Barnett U one negrogirl Crecy at one hundred and forty dollars, to my daughter Peggy onenegro girl Mahaly at Two hundred and seventy five dollars. to my daughterElizabeth A one negro girl Cely at one hundred and fifty dollars (carred[sic] over) each to have them at the valuation as above in making adivision of my estate. I appoint my sons William & Barnett U. Brightwellmy executors with orthority [sic] to sell all my lands for a division.

Given under my hand this the 19th January 18 hundred & thirty seven.

Charles [his X mark] Brightwell Sr.

signed in the presents [sic] of
by his marke

Robert Venable
Charles Brightwell
John B. Davis

At a court held for Prince Edward County February the 15th 1847. Thislast will and testament of Charles Brightwell Senr decd. was presented incourt, and Robert Venable and Charles Brightwell witnefses thereto, beingboth dead, and John B. Davis another witnefs thereto, having removed fromthis state. Henry B. Brightwell and John J. Brightwell being sworn, eachsaid they were acquainted with the hand writing of the said RobertVenable and Charles Brightwell the witnefses thereto, and that theirsignatures are in their proper hand writing and that they are both dead,ordered that the said will be recorded. On the motion of WilliamBrightwell executor herein named, he with Thomas H. Venable, Anthony W.Gilliam and Henry Hubbard his securities entered into and acknowledgedtheir bond for the purpose in the penalty of six Thousand dollarsconditioned according to law, and Took the oath required by law.certificate for obtaining a probat [sic] Thereof in due form is grantedhim.

Teste

B [___] Worsham CC

Source: Prince Edward Co., VA Will Book 9, Page 177.

Appraisement & Inventory
Inventory of the Estate of Charles Brightwell Senr. decd. taken byWilliam Brightwell Exor and appraised by Samuel [L] Venable, Joel Elam &Anthony W. Gilliam after being sworn according to law. This 18th day ofDecember 1847.

Negro Woman Polly $00.00
do do Anaka 175.00
negro man Jack 550.00
do do Archer 600.00
one woman Jane & two children, Florance & Mary 850.00
one boy Peyton 600.00
do do John 700.00
do do Wyatt 575.00
one tract of land 170 acres $1.25 pr acre 212.50
one feather bed, two pair sheets, yarn cover, blanket, bedstead & cord11.00
one small trunk .75
one chest & two small boxes 1.00
$4275.25

Pursuant to an order of May court 1847. to us directed we have this dayviewed and appraised the estate of Charles Brightwell Sr decd. and findthe same to amount to the sum of four Thousand two hundred and seventyfive dollars and twenty five cents as for above inventory. Given underour hands this eighteenth day of December 1827

Joel Elam
A. W. Gilliam Commr

Children of CHARLES BRIGHTWELL and NANCY are:

11. i. BARNETT U.[5] BRIGHTWELL, b. 1787, Born Prince Edward Co., VA.; d. 13 Jul 1855, Prince Edward Co. Virginia.

  ii. RACHEL BRIGHTWELL, b. (her brother William witnesssed marriage).; m. SAMUEL ROBERTS, 14 Aug 1804, Prince Edward Co., Va. Marriage Records..

   More About SAMUEL ROBERTS and RACHEL BRIGHTWELL:
   Marriage: 14 Aug 1804, Prince Edward Co., Va. Marriage Records.

  iii. POLLEY BRIGHTWELL.
12. iv. ELIZABETH (BETSY) ANN BRIGHTWELL.
  v. PEGGY BRIGHTWELL, m. JOHN BUCHANAN, 29 Nov 1819, Married Prince Edward Co. Virginia..

   More About JOHN BUCHANAN and PEGGY BRIGHTWELL:
   Marriage: 29 Nov 1819, Married Prince Edward Co. Virginia.

13. vi. WILLIAM B. (JR) BRIGHTWELL, b. Abt. 1784, Prince Edward Co., Va.; d. 25 Jul 1861, Still Living 1850Prince Edward Co. Va..

  vii. RHODA BRIGHTWELL, m. OBEDIAH LUMPKIN, 14 Apr 1808, Prince Edward County, Virginia Marrige Bond.

   More About OBEDIAH LUMPKIN and RHODA BRIGHTWELL:
   Marriage: 14 Apr 1808, Prince Edward County, Virginia Marrige Bond

6. BARNETT (SR)[4] BRIGHTWELL *(REYNOLDS[3], REYNOLDS OR RANDALL[2], THE BRIGHTWELL FAMILY[1] HISTORY)* was born 1762, and died Abt. 1830 in Prince Edward Co. Va.. He married MARY (MOLLY) GUILL 21 Feb 1782 in Prince Edward Co. Va., daughter of ALEXANDER (SR) GUILL. She was born in Mary's estate 1839; admin. by her son Charles Brightwell JR..

Notes for BARNETT (SR) BRIGHTWELL:
Barnette Brightwell, son of Reynold Brightwell and Drucilla Allmand, birth date unknown. He married Mary (Molly) Guill in Prince Edward Co, VA, February 21, 1782.

Barnette Brightwell and Mary (Molly) Guill had the following children:

i. Alexander Brightwell was born in Prince Edward Co, VA 1783.
ii. Barnett Brightwell was born in Prince Edward Co, VA ca 1785. He married Nancy Mathews in Prince Edward Co, VA, November 15, 1815.
iii. Nancy Brightwell was born circa 1787. Married William Brightwell (see below)
iv. Charles Brightwell was born in Prince Edward Co, VA ca 1789.
 Charles Brightwell (iv) s/o Barnette Brightwell and Mary (Molly) Guill born circa 1789 in Prince Edward County eventually married a Hoppy (or Happy) Boatwright Nov. 18th, 1811 in Prince Edward County
v. Josiah W. Brightwell was born in Prince Edward Co, VA ca 1791.
vi. Mary Brightwell was born in Prince Edward Co, VA ca 1793.
vii. Reuben Brightwell was born in Prince Edward Co, VA ca 1798. He married Mary J. Hill in Prince

Edward Co, VA, December 22, 1822.
viii. Ann Brightwell was born in Prince Edward Co, VA ca 1800.
ix. John Brightwell was born in Prince Edward Co, VA ca 1802.
x. Archibald Brightwell was born in Prince Edward Co, VA ca 1805.

BARNETTE BRIGHTWELL's Descendants as LISTED:
Second Generation

Nancy Brightwell, parents Barnette Brightwell and Mary (Molly) Guill, was born circa 1787. Nancy died May 1865 in Prince Edward Co, VA, at 77 years of age. She married William Brightwell in Prince Edward Co, VA, December 6, 1804. William, parents unknown, was born before March 1, 1784 (chr. date) in Prince Edward Co, VA. William died July 25, 1861 in Prince Edward Co, VA, at 77 years of age. He was christened in Prince Edward Co, VA, March 1, 1784.

Nancy Brightwell and William Brightwell had the following children:

i. dau Brightwell. dau died before 1861. She married Asher.
ii. Martha (Nan) Brightwell was born in Prince Edward Co, VA March 10, 1809. Martha died December 1849 at 40 years of age. She married Clayborn Hill in Prince Edward Co, VA, February 1, 1831.
iii. Frederick A. Brightwell was born in Prince Edward Co, VA June 11, 1812. Frederick died March 7, 1887 in Cambridge Twp, Saline Co, MO, at 74 years of age. His body was interred March 8, 1887 in Good Hope Cem, Saline Co, MO. He married twice. He married Elizabeth A. Reynolds in Saline Co, MO, January 5, 1848. Elizabeth was born October 6, 1822 in VA. Elizabeth died November 13, 1863 in Saline Co, MO, at 41 years of age. He married Eliza (Mary Jane) in Saline Co, MO, July 31, 1866. Eliza was born February 23, 1828 in VA. She married Baker before 1862. Eliza died June 7, 1892 in TX, at 64 years of age. Her body was interred in Henrietta Cem, Clay Co, TX.

The following biographical note is found on page 603 of the History of Saline County, Missouri, Missouri Historical Co, St. Louis, 1881.
Frederick A. Brightwell, P.O. Cambridge. Mr Brightwell was born in Prince Edward county, Virginia, on the 11th of June, 1812, and came to this county from Virginia, in an ox wagon, in 1837, and taught school for about two years. In the spring of 1839, he moved to Howard county, and clerked in a store in Glasgow, and afterwards sold goods on his own account until the year 1844. He then returned to Saline county, and was the first post-master in Cambridge, and had the honor of giving that town its name. He sold goods in Cambridge, for some years, and suffered greatly from the overflow of 1844, in his generous efforts to assist those who lost their all in the waters. On the 13th of January, 1848, he married Miss Elizabeth Reynolds, and had four children, two boys and two girls. After the death of his first wife he married a second time - this time to Mrs. Mary J. Baker, of Hanover county, Virginia, and widow of a confederate soldier, killed at the battle of Pea Ridge. By this marriage he has two children, one boy and one girl. At present Mr. Brightwell is occupied in farming, his farm lying between Cambridge and Gilliam station.

The Saline County Progress, Marshall, MO, Saturday, March 12, 1887, Gilliam Items.
Frederick Brightwell
Died -- At his residence, near Good Hope church, on Tuesday morning, Mr. Frederick Brightwell an old citizen of the county, the remains were interred at the Good Hope cemetery the following day.

iv. Mercer Brightwell was born in Prince Edward Co, VA circa 1813. He married Julia Ann Brightwell in Prince Edward Co, VA, December 15, 1834.

v. Arabelle Brightwell was born circa 1816. She married Jerman Gilliam in Prince Edward Co, VA, October 23, 1872.

vi. Albert Gallatin Brightwell was born in Prince Edward Co, VA September 8, 1822. Albert died September 18, 1909 at 87 years of age. He married Elizabeth Belle Harvey in Prince Edward Co, VA, November 21, 1849.

vii. Therett Brightwell was born in Pamplin, Prince Edward Co, VA November 4, 1823. Therett died July 4, 1883 in Saline Co, MO, at 59 years of age. His body was interred July 5, 1883 in Saline Co, MO, Good Hope Cemetery. He married twice. He married Florinda Ann Scott Hawkins in Cambridge Twp, Saline Co, MO, October 9, 1849. Florinda was born October 10, 1830 in VA. Florinda died April 7, 1863 in Saline Co, MO, at 32 years of age. Her body was interred in Good Hope Cem, Saline Co, MO. He married Catherine Ann Thorpe in Saline Co, MO, December 13, 1863. Catherine was born November 7, 1842 near Slater, Saline Co, MO. Catherine was the daughter of Dennis Thorp and Emily. She married James Stokley Anderson. Catherine died November 22, 1920 in Kansas City, Jackson Co, MO, at 78 years of age. Her body was interred in Kansas City, Jackson Co, MO, Elmwood Cemetery.

The Saline County Progress, Marshall, MO, Friday, July 12, 1883, Gilliam Items.
Mr. Third Brightwell
Mr. Third Brightwell, an old resident and respected citizen died at his home about two miles north of this point on last Friday morning at three o'clock, his remains were interred at the Good Hope cemetery the following evening.

viii. Addison Brightwell was born in Prince Edward Co, VA circa 1828. Addison died June 1865 in Prince Edward Co, VA, at 36 years of age. He married Adaline.

ix. Laura Maud Brightwell was born in Prince Edward Co, VA circa 1830. Laura died April 26, 1860 in Prince Edward Co, VA, at 29 years of age.

His estate was administered by his son in Prince Edward Co. VA. He
appears in the 1783 and 1785 census for Prince Edward Co, VA.
He had military service about 1776 in Brooks Co., 38th Infantry and
applied a military warrant to purchase land 11 May 1818 in Illinois.

More About BARNETT (SR) BRIGHTWELL:
Burial: Barnett's estate 1830 admin. by son-in-law William Brightwell JR

More About BARNETT BRIGHTWELL and MARY GUILL:
Marriage: 21 Feb 1782, Prince Edward Co. Va.

Children of BARNETT BRIGHTWELL and MARY GUILL are:

i. ALEXANDER[5] BRIGHTWELL, b. Abt. 1785; d. 1850, Liv Tenn. Prob. Wilson Co. (Weakley ???); m. (1) SALLY CARTER, 06 Aug 1807, Prince Edward Co. Va. lst Wife.; b. [Widow of Joseph Carter]; d. Bet. 1832 - 1840; m. (2) ADALINE PITLOW, 1840, Wilson Co. Tenn..

More About ALEXANDER BRIGHTWELL and SALLY CARTER:
Marriage: 06 Aug 1807, Prince Edward Co. Va. lst Wife.

More About ALEXANDER BRIGHTWELL and ADALINE PITLOW:
Marriage: 1840, Wilson Co. Tenn.

14.   ii. JOHN M. BRIGHTWELL, b. Abt. 1786, 1820 Cumberland Co. Virginia censsus; d. 1835, moved 1822 GA. in Clark Co. 18 32 Cen. Ga.
        iii. CHARLES (JR) BRIGHTWELL, b. Abt. 1789, VA. He received 58 acres from Barnetts estate.; d. 1847, VA.; m. (1) HOPY W. BOATWRIGHT, 18 Nov 1811, Prince Edward Co. Va. Marriage Record.; b. 1791, Liv in 1850 Buckingham Co. Va.; m. (2) HOPY W. BRIGHTWELL, 18 Nov 1811, Married cousin. by consent Prince Edward Co. Va..

More About CHARLES BRIGHTWELL and HOPY BOATWRIGHT:
Marriage: 18 Nov 1811, Prince Edward Co. Va. Marriage Record.

More About CHARLES BRIGHTWELL and HOPY BRIGHTWELL:
Marriage: 18 Nov 1811, Married cousin. by consent Prince Edward Co. Va.

iv. JOSIAH W. BRIGHTWELL, b. Abt. 1791, Liv 1850; d. Bet. 1863 - 1864, VA.; m. JANE P. HILL, 15 Dec 1819, Prince Edward Co. Va. Marriage Record.; b. Abt. 1799, VA.; d. 13 Aug 1878, VA. Received 49 acres from Burnetts estate..

More About JOSIAH BRIGHTWELL and JANE HILL:
Marriage: 15 Dec 1819, Prince Edward Co. Va. Marriage Record.

15. v. BARNETT (JR) BRIGHTWELL, b. Abt. 1794, Born in Prince Edward Co. Va; d. Bet. 1821 - 1827, Died in VA..

16. vi. REUBEN BRIGHTWELL, b. Abt. 1798, Liv in 1850 found in Buckingham County, Virginia..

vii. NANCY BRIGHTWELL, b. Abt. 1798, Liv 1850 Received 48 acres from Barnett's Estate.; d. May 1865, Died in VA. Marriage Prince Edward Co. Virginia.; m. WILLIAM BRIGHTWELL, 05 Dec 1804, Marriage to cousin consented by Barnett Brightwell..

More About WILLIAM BRIGHTWELL and NANCY BRIGHTWELL:
Marriage: 05 Dec 1804, Marriage to cousin consented by Barnett Brightwell.

viii. MARTHA BRIGHTWELL, b. READ hERNOTES.

Notes for MARTHA BRIGHTWELL:
found this in The Library of Virginia Archieves and Manuscripts(Bible Records) at the Library of Virginia web sit:
Accession # 26933
Jenkins Family Bible record, 1792-1881
Martha Patsy Brightwell was the daughter of Barnet Brightwell and Mary Guill.

Martha Patsy Brightwell, B: 10 June 1795 Pr. Ed. Co., Va., M: 15 Jan 1818 in Pr. Ed. to Henry Y. Jenkins, B13 Oct. 1792, Pr. Ed. , D: before 1862 while serving for the CSA near Richmond, Va. Martha died 16 May 1868.
They had the following children:

1, Mary E. Jenkins, B: 25 oct 1818, Pr Ed, D: 7 june 1864,M: W.N. Davis.They had:
2. Willie S. Davis, B: 15 jan 1858
2. Henry F. Davis, B: 9 Feb 1861
1. Sarah Ann Jenkins, B: aft 1818, D: 15 jan 1824
1. James Jenkins, B: aft 1820,D:30 june 1862(also Known as Thos James Jenkins- he was killed at Malvern on 30 Jun 1862 while serving the CSA)
1. Henry Jenkins, B:aft 1820, D:?
1.Patsy Jenkins, B: aft 1820
1. Abraham Jenkins, B: aft 1820, M: Feb 1856 to Martha Parkinson. They had:
2. Louis Jenkins, B: 10 Feb 1857
2. Natahnial A. Jenkins, B: 5 Sept 1858
2. Betty Young Jenkins, B: 19 Feb 1861
2. Clara Jenkins, B: 2 March 1863
2. Pattie Jenkins, B: 21 Jan 1867
2. Asa D. Jenkins, B: 15 Feb 1869
1. Jane W. Jenkins, B: 15 Jan 1832, D: 10 April 1871, M: 22 Dec 1852 to R.B. Jenkins(male), B:? They had:
2. Addie N. Jenkins, B: 10 sept 1855, M: 1 Oct 1872 to Thoms W. Porter They had :
3. Magg B. Porter B: 6 Dec 1881
2. Nannie E. Jenkins, B: 16 Nov 1858
2. Charles W. Jenkins, B: 29 Aug 1860
2. Sally Joe(Jane?) Jenkins, B: 21 May 1863
2. Mary Jenkins, B: 18 Sept 1866
1. Benjamin Jenkins, B: 10 Dec 1834

7. SAMUEL[4] BRIGHTWELL *(REYNOLDS[3], REYNOLDS OR RANDALL[2], THE BRIGHTWELL FAMILY[1] HISTORY)* was born 1783 in born GA of Clark Co. Ga. READ HIS NOTES, and died 1840 in 184(?) Georgia died [in Elbert Co. Ga. 1805]. He married (1) BETSY A. MOORE 25 Apr 1803 in Prince Edward Co. Va. lst Wife., daughter of PLEASANT MOORE. She was born in Her father was Deceased at the marriage., and died in Moon???. He married (2) FRANCES BERRY 1808 in Oglethorpe Co. Georgia, daughter of WILLIAM BERRY and SUSANNAH TAYLOR. She was born 1803 in born Ga., and died in widow in 1870 Census of Morgan Co. Ga..

Notes for SAMUEL BRIGHTWELL:
 Samuel Brightwell and Betsy were married in 1803 Prince Edward County Virginia.
 Samuel is shown in 1820 Census of Oplethorpe County Georgia with the following living in his home:
2 males shown 10 yrs. one male between 16-18 yrs of age; one male 26-45;
    3 females 10 and one female between 26-45.

ID: I56427
Name: Samuel Brightwell
Sex: M
Birth: ABT 1780 in VA
Change Date: 24 JAN 2005

Father: Reynold Brightwell b: ABT 1735 in VA, King William Co.
Mother: Drucilla Allmand b: ABT 1756

Marriage 1 Friend

Marriage 2 Betsy Moore
Married: ABT 1803 in VA, Prince Edward Co.
Children
 Archibald Runnels Brightwell b: ABT 1804 in VA

Marriage 3 Frances Berry b: ABT 1793 in VA
Married: 29 AUG 1809 in GA, Oglethorpe Co.
Children
 Marshall F. Brightwell b: ABT 1813 in GA, Oglethorpe Co.
 William Barnett Brightwell b: 30 DEC 1816 in GA, Oglethorpe Co.
 Harriett Brightwell b: ABT 1829 in GA
 Ophelia Brightwell b: ABT 1831 in GA
 Amanda Caroline Brightwell b: ABT 1838 in GA
 Frances Susan Brightwell
 Mary Brightwell

More About SAMUEL BRIGHTWELL and BETSY MOORE:
Marriage: 25 Apr 1803, Prince Edward Co. Va. lst Wife.

More About FRANCES BERRY:
Burial: Clark Co. Ga. 1850 57 yrs old WIDOW

More About SAMUEL BRIGHTWELL and FRANCES BERRY:
Marriage: 1808, Oglethorpe Co. Georgia

Children of SAMUEL BRIGHTWELL and BETSY MOORE are:
17.   i.   MOSES[5] BRIGHTWELL, b. 1802, born Virginia of 1840/NEWTON Co. Ga; 1850 Cen.; d. Oglethorpe Co. Ga. 1824.
         ii.   ARCHIBALD RUNNELLS BRIGHTWELL, b. 1805; d. Runnells could be Reynolds????; m. (1) HARRIETT H. HILL; m. (2) HARRIET H. HILL, 19 Jan 1835, Prince Edward Co. Va. Marriage..

More About ARCHIBALD BRIGHTWELL and HARRIET HILL:
Marriage: 19 Jan 1835, Prince Edward Co. Va. Marriage.

Children of SAMUEL BRIGHTWELL and FRANCES BERRY are:
     iii.   MARSHALL F.[5] BRIGHTWELL, b. 1813, born Ga. Bartow County Georgia; m. MARTHA HATCHER, 1844, Dekalb Co. Georgia.; b. born in S. Carolina her children born Georgia..

           More About MARSHALL BRIGHTWELL and MARTHA HATCHER:
           Marriage: 1844, Dekalb Co. Georgia.

     iv.   CAROLINE BRIGHTWELL, b. 1824.
     v.   AMANDA CAROLINE BRIGHTWELL, b. 1838; d. 1903, Died; unmarried in Kennesaw, Georgia Cobb Co..
     vi.   HARRIETT BRIGHTWELL, b. 1841, [partly insane] Clark Co. Georgia.
18.   vii.   WILLIAM BARNETT BRIGHTWELL, b. 1860, born in GA..
     viii.   OPHELIA BRIGHTWELL, b. 1831, born in GA. RE: Clarke Co. Ga. 1850 Cen.; d. 18 Aug 1892, Cobb Co. Kennesaw Georgia; m. IRVIN L. ROBERTSON, Abt. 1855, Married Georgia.; b. 11 Jun 1831, Born Georgia.

           Notes for OPHELIA BRIGHTWELL:
           ID: I11965
           Name: Ophelia Brightwell
           Sex: F
           Birth: ABT 1831 in GA
           Death: 18 AUG 1892 in GA, Cobb Co., Kennesaw
           Burial: GA, Cobb Co., Kennesaw
           ALIA: Ophila
           Change Date: 28 JAN 2005

           Father: Samuel Brightwell b: ABT 1780 in VA
           Mother: Frances Berry b: ABT 1793 in VA

           Marriage 1 Irvin L. Robertson b: 11 JUN 1831 in GA
           Married: ABT 1855
           Children
           Francis Annia Robertson b: ABT 1859 in GA ?
           Mary Gevernia Robertson b: 13 JUN 1860 in GA
           Samuel Robertson b: ABT 1863 in GA
           James Edward Robertson b: 11 MAR 1870 in GA ?
           Jacob H. Robertson b: 11 JAN 1869 in GA ?
           John William Robertson b: 23 MAY 1873 in GA
           Daniel W. Robertson

           More About IRVIN ROBERTSON and OPHELIA BRIGHTWELL:
           Marriage: Abt. 1855, Married Georgia.

8. NANCY[4] BRIGHTWELL *(REYNOLDS[3], REYNOLDS OR RANDALL[2], THE BRIGHTWELL FAMILY[1] HISTORY)* was born 1767 in Liv in Pittsylvania Co VA., and died 1839 in Pittsylvania Co. Va.. She married ANDERSON BRIGHTWELL 04 Dec 1786 in Married Prince Edward Co. Va. Reynolds Consented to both.. He was born 1766 in He received Revolutionary War Pension Re. Nancy's Pen. Appl., and died 1837.

Notes for ANDERSON BRIGHTWELL:
Descendants of Mr ? Brightwell who was born pre-1735 and lived in King William Co VA. Bounty Warrant applications show that his 5 sons served in the Continental Line of the Revolutionary War:

1)Anderson Brightwell (b.ca.1766 King Wm Co VA-d.1837 Pittsylvania Co VA) md 1786 Prince Edward Co VA to Nancy Brightwell (1767-living 1839) dau of Reynold Brightwell.

2)Leonard Brightwell (died after the War but before 1828)-no children.
3)William Brightwell (died abt 1805 King Wm Co VA)-no children.
4)Jesse Brightwell -killed at the Revolutionary Battle at Charleston. Not married.
5)John Brightwell (died 1796 King William Co VA) married Elizabeth _____ (she was born in the 1760's and was alive in 1830 in Chesterfield Co VA)
6)Lucy Brightwell (living 1823 King Wm Co VA) md Barnard Powers.

Children of Anderson & Nancy Brightwell:
1)Jesse Brightwell (b.1789)
2)James Brightwell (b.abt.1793)
3)Claybrook Brightwell (b.abt.1795)
4)Betsy Brightwell (b.abt.1798)
5)Dicy Brightwell-Phelps (b.abt.1800)
6)Sarah "Sally" Brightwell-Smith (b.abt.1803)
7)Mildred "Milly" Brightwell-Kendrick (b.abt.1806)
8)Leonard Lemuel Brightwell (b.abt.1809)

Children of John (d.1796) & Elizabeth (living 1830):

1)William Brightwell (b.1780's King Wm Co VA-d.1820's Chesterfield Co VA) md Mrs Sally Turner in 1807 Chesterfield Co VA. Sally was born abt 1785 and was living 1850 Chesterfield Co VA. Two sons.

2)Jason Brightwell (b.pre.1794 King Wm Co VA-d.1829 Pittsylvania Co VA) md a)1812 Henrico Co VA to Sally Frayser b)1817 Mecklenberg Co VA to Jane G Poindexter. Jane was born 1794-1800 and was alive in 1840 Pittsylvania Co VA. Five girls & one boy.

More About ANDERSON BRIGHTWELL and NANCY BRIGHTWELL:
Marriage: 04 Dec 1786, Married Prince Edward Co. Va. Reynolds Consented to both.

Children of NANCY BRIGHTWELL and ANDERSON BRIGHTWELL are:
   i.   JESSE[5] BRIGHTWELL, b. 1789, liv 1850; m. RHODY DODSON, 05 Oct 1811, Prince Edward Co. Va. Marriage Record..

        More About JESSE BRIGHTWELL and RHODY DODSON:
        Marriage: 05 Oct 1811, Prince Edward Co. Va. Marriage Record.

   ii. BETSY BRIGHTWELL, b. 1798, liv 1821.
   iii. DICEY BRIGHTWELL, b. 1800, liv 1821.
   iv. SALLY BRIGHTWELL, b. 1803, liv 1821.
   v.   MILLEY BRIGHTWELL, b. 1806, liv 1821.

9. BARNETTE[4] BRIGHTWELL (REYNOLDS[3], REYNOLDS OR RANDALL[2], THE BRIGHTWELL FAMILY[1] HISTORY) was born 1778 in Prince Edward Co. Virginia. He married MARY POLLY GUILL 21 Feb 1782 in Prince Edward Co. Va..

More About BARNETTE BRIGHTWELL and MARY GUILL:
Marriage: 21 Feb 1782, Prince Edward Co. Va.

Child of BARNETTE BRIGHTWELL and MARY GUILL is:
   i.   BARNETTE JR.[5] BRIGHTWELL, b. Prince Edward Co Virginia; m. NANCY MATTHEWS, 15 Nov 1815, Prince Edward Co. Virginia Marriage Record..

10. WILLIAM[4] BRIGHTWELL *(REYNOLDS[3], REYNOLDS OR RANDALL[2], THE BRIGHTWELL FAMILY[1] HISTORY)* was born Bet. 1774 - 1779 in Born Pr Edw Co VA./mvd w/fam afr 1820 Cen. to N. Carolina; liv in the 1830 Edgefield, S.Carolina cen., and died Aft. 1866 in Alabama-Moved w fam.1850 Cen./ Covington Co. Ala.. He married (1) MARY "POLLY" YOUNG Bet. 20 - 30 Dec 1800 in Prince Edward Co. Va. Marriage[Barnette Brightwell Gives Consent], daughter of HENRY YOUNG and ELIZABETH. She was born Bet. 1785 - 1786 in Born Prince Edward Co. Virginia liv in 1850, and died 30 Nov 1861 in Prince Edward Co. Virginia. He married (2) SARAH WINDSOR/WINDZER Bef. 1825 in Married In Barnwell Co. S. Carolina, daughter of ANDERSON WINDOR. She was born 1814 in (see Will of Anderson Windsor, Barnwell, S.C.), and died 1886 in She is found 1880 Webster Co Cen. Ga..

Notes for WILLIAM BRIGHTWELL:

WILLIAM BRIGHTWELL

1750's -- William Brightwell's first record I have found proving that he was in Granville/Edgefield N. C. is the following excerpt from the Camden Archives of S. Carolina state; Muster Roll of Edgecombe Co. Militia North Carolina (1750s) under Capt. Jacob Whiteheads Co. #5 Rank Serjant WILLIAM BRIGHTWELL. Granville Co. N. C. was formed from Edgecombe Co. North Carolina.

This William Brightwell born 1779 in Prince Edward County, Virginia. Other Brightwell researchers have stated that Sarah Windsor was his wife.,,It is known that this William's son; John Jackson Brightwell also married a Sarah Windsor. Did Sarah live in the home of her step-son; or did she marry him later? William Brightwell's other wife's name was Mary Young. This is confusing; as to just which man Sarah Windsor was married to; or was there two different Sarah Windsors? More research to be done of this.
     In 1811 Anderson Winzer who lived in Barnwell, SC wrote a will naming 2 of his 6 children. In addition he named a daughter Sary Brightwell for whom he had earlier provided.
     As far as we know William 1 Brightwell(Barnwell SC) was the ONLY Brightwell living in South Carolina that could be married to Sarah Winzer. Further research proves this statement as true. The only census that William Brightwell lived in South Carolina was in 1810 and in the Barnwell area. Before that and after that census no Brightwells remained in South Carolina. In 1870 there are Brightwells that are Black listed living in South Carolina, and these were probably the freed slaves left behind in South Carolina.

As a Revolutionary Soldier WILLIAM BRIGHTWELL was given a land grant.
ALABAMA FEDERAL LAND GRANT Brightwell   William   Butler County 15E 8N   6   1858

     It is clear from records that William Brightwell received land as a result of his service in the Revolutionary War. Travel back in those days took years, months and weeks to do; travel was by wagons and horse or with river streams; as is seen by this families records, they resided in South Carolina for a time during their travels before finally reaching Alabama where the land grant was awarded.

1790 - S. Carolina NO Brightwell Family is listed - they live in Virginia.

1800 Census Edgefield, South Carolina. lists one; WILLIAM BRIGHTWELL (16-26 yrs old) and wife (16-26 yrs old) with no children.

Marriages in Prince Edward Co. Virginia:
1807 / August 3rd. Alexander Brightwell to Sally Carter
1803 / April 25th. Samuel Brightwell to Betsy Moore [Moon?]

In the year 1810; the Brightwell family is seen living in the State of Virginia as follows:
     Absolom Brightwell Spottsylvania County Virginia - married Winnefred Pines 2/24/1800 Orange

County Virginia

Anderson Brightwell Prince Edward Co. Va. -[He received a Rev. Soldier Pension of $200} U.S. Treasury Rev. Land Scrip 6,511

Charles Brightwell Prince Edward Co. Va.

Drucilla Brightwell Prince Edward Co. Va.

Mary Brightwell Spottsylvania Co. Va.

Thomas Brightwell Spottsylvania Co.Va.

William Brightwell Spottsylvania Co. Va.

-There is a marriage record dated 12/30/1800 to Mary Young Prince Edward Co. Va.-

William Brightwell, Senior Prince Edward Co. Va. - he married a Nancy Brightwell [prob. cousin] in Prince Edward Co. Virginia 12/5/1806 [re: marriage record.]

William Brightwell Chesterfield Co. Va. [see Rather]

He married Sally Turner in Chesterfield Virginia 4/15/1807 re: [marriage record]

Settlers are restricted from Indian Territory prior to the end of the American Revolution by decree of the English King.

It was during the year 1810 that the BRIGHTWELL FAMILY began their travels toward Alabama. To do so required them traveling down along the Apalachian Mountains to the flatter lands of South Carolina first before heading West. This is the way most wagon trains traveled and there are also Indian pathways which led the same way. As the White Man expanded and moved into lands with new hunting grounds, fresher streams and less population it enfringed upon the Cherokee Indians of North Carolina. As the White man moved south, so the did the Tribes of the Cherokee Indians, pushing them away from their lands and homes. In the first 15 years of the 18th century over a million pelts are shipped from the port of Charleston, South Carolina. The impact on the environment forces the braves to hunt further from home and competition from white hunters depletes these resources. With the encroachments of the whites beginning in 1721(South Carolina), border wars with neighboring Indians, and disease, the Cherokee face a new life. To the Cherokee the world is crumbling.

Sometime before 1810 - The BRIGHTWELL packed their families and set out on a long journey towards the land and State of Alabama. Traveling that far took several years to complete and so the journey is found living in various areas before finally settling in Alabama. The first state they are found residing in is South Carolina as seen in census records below.

1810 Barnwell Co SC census
p.098
Brightwell, William
3 males under 10, 1 male 26-45, 1 female under 10, 1 female 16-26
1820 Barnwell Co SC census
p.
Britewil, William
4 males under 10, 1 male 10-16, 1 male 45+
2 females under 10, 2 females 10-16, 1 female 26-45

1810
Thomas Brightwell - living in Abbe Co. Barnwell, S. Carolina
The BRIGHTWELL families did not remain in South Carolina very long. The Brightwell family began to make their trek towards Alabama West through the State of Georgia.

1820 Census of S. Carolina through 1850 Census has NO Brightwell family listings. This family as of 1820 had started on their travels through the Indian Lands of State of Georgia. Passports were issued from 1810 - 1820 which was a time of the Creek Indian Uprisings and no one could travel without the passport.

1820 - Georgia Census records do NOT have any Brightwell Family members listed.[the family was traveling at this time].

It was while living in Barnwell, S. Carolina that William Brightwell had a son named; Len Reynolds

Brightwell b. 1825.

The Wagon Train loaded up; William Brightwell would have had to get a Passport from the Governor of Georgia in Bulloch Co. Ga. before heading West towards Alabama. The Passport was required to pass through Indian Lands. It was during the wait for the Passport from the Governor of Georgia that this family lived in Barnwell, S. Carolina as seen on census records. These trips were extremely dangerous. There was still much rivalry from the Indians during this time and lots of folks didn't live to make it to their land grants. But we know William Brightwell did make it. William Brightwell and his family would have had to travel with a small baby in a wagon pulled by horses across treacherous terrain. We know that William and his family made it though as they are found in further census records in Alabama. William Brightwell claimed the land grant his father had earned as a Revolutionary Soldier in Virginia. And, he purchased land himself in Alabama as seen in later land deeds in Alabama.

In 1830 Census records; S. Carolina has some BRIGHTWELL family members who decided to remain in S. Carolina and not travel any further west; and they were:
    1830 Edgefield Co SC census - p.197
Britewell, William
1 male under 5, 2 males 10-15, 1 male 40-50, 1 female 10-15, 2 females 15-20, 1 female 30-40
    1830 Barnwell Co SC census p.156
Britewell, John 1 male 20-30, 1 female under 5, 1 female 15-20

The BRIGHTWELL families between 1810 and 1820 are not found in S. Carolina or Georgia census records as they are traveling thorugh the State of Georgia towards Alabama. Each time the family stopped and lived in an area they eventually left some family members behind with their new families. Daughters were left with their new husbands.

State of Georgia 1830 Census Records now show the BRIGHTWELL family arriving and settling in Clarke Co. and Jackson Co.'s. Brightwell Family is also found in Stewart Co. Georgia. There were several BRIGHTWELL family members who did not travel further and decided to stay in Clarke and Stewart Co. Georgia - where they were.

1830 - John Brightwell - Clark Co. Georgia Census
    Also; found on Court Record dated 1828,Clark Co. Ga.
1830 Samuel Brightwell - Jackson County Georgia Census
    Also; found on Court Record dated 1824 for Clark Co. Ga.
    then; Samuel Brightwell must have left the area as he didn't pickup letters at post office; Fri. May 3, 1839, Sept. 1839, May 1840, June 1840 or July 1840. No further mention.
    Samuel Brightwell married Frances Berry Clarke Co. Ga. 8/29/1809.
    Samuel Brightwell died Abt. 1842 as Frances is seen on records by herself in 1850. Both Frances and Samuel Brightwell are found in Church Records of Mars Baptist Church Clark Co. Georgia.
    1850 Census of Clarke Co. Alabama lists: Frances Brightwell 57 years old-Female with:
        Harriet age 20 years female
        Ophila Brightwell 19 years old Female
        Caroline Brightwell age 17 yrs. female
        Henry Brightwell age 17 years - Male
        Mary Brightwell age 13 yrs. Female

    Estate Records of Clark Co. Georgia:
Andrew J. Brightwell (ward) 1835 and; also listed on Court Record 223rd Dist. 1840 & 12/20/1845 Clark Co. Ga.
    Signed a Property Deed for Thomas Preston Clark Co. Ga. 450 Acres, Fri. Sept. 24, 1841.
    Andrew J. Brightwell's wife is Cynthia Patman; daughter of Rev. Patman [whose home they lived in for awhile in Bunscombe District (Clark Co. Ga.} By 1850; A. J. Brightwell and family moved to Texas.
Francis A. Brightwell 1845
John Brightwell   1835-44
John M. Brightwell   1842
Ann C. Brightwell marriage to Samuel Simonton May 12, 1831, Clark Co. Ga.

William Barnett Brightwell and wife; Paulett; - Court Record dated 1814; 1840 & 1841
    children: Jesse C. Brightwell, Barnett Brightwell, Nathan C. Brightwell are listed on Deed.
    William B. Brightwell owned Losts # 68 & 69 in Watkinsville; 6 Acres and it was levied upon to
satisfy execution,
    Friday, June 12, 1840.
    William B. Brightwell; (1) negro man named Frederick; levied to satisfy excution, May 1, 1839-1840.
    There is an additional marriage record for William B. Brightwell to Mary Cain in Clarke Co. Ga.
    William Barnett Brightwell is also the SON of Samuel Brightwell and Frances [Berry] Brightwell
Marshal F. Brightwell, didn't pickup letters at post office: Jan. 1841 or Feb. 1840.

    Clarke County Georgia wasn't exactly a good financial experience for some of the branches of the
Brightwell family during this time period. But for the Brightwells who had made roots; they didn't want to
leave. The other Brightwells left and headed for their promised land in Butler County, Alabama. Clarke
County, Georga proved to be a good decision for those who remained as in later years, written in history
records for Clark Co. Ga. a Descendant of the Brightwells - W. T. Brightwell was a Prominent
Citizen/Banker - on Board of Directors for the Georgia National Bank.

In 1850 Census of Stewart Co. Georgia there are (2) Windsor families living next to William Brightwell
and wife Pamela Bush and children. A Lucinda Windsor married a John Bush who moved over to Butler
Co. Alabama where William (2) Brightwell; his brother L. Reynolds Brightwell and Reynolds inlaws
Daniel C. Parker lived.

Home At Last to Alabama: The BRIGHTWELL family travels finally came to an end when they arrived in
Alabama in the 1850's; before that census there are no other Brightwells listed on any census records for
the State of Alabama.

PROP: Father left him all his land, 220 a., in his will 1806 1
PROP: Sold 6 a. of the 220 a. he recd from his father 1820S 1
PROP: Land remained in family until this time. 1892 - 1894 1 2 6

State of Alabama CENSUS Records for BRIGHTWELL family.
1820 - NO Brightwell listed.
1830 - No Brightwells Listed.
1850 - No Brightwells Listed - on Mortality Schedule

Initially; this Brightwell family is found settling in Butler Co. Alabama; then Crenshaw County and also
Covington Co. Alabama as seen in the records.

Just which William Brightwell initially made it to Alabama or did both the brother of Len Reynolds
Brightwell and father both make it to Alabama? More research on this to be done.

1860 Census Records reflect a: WILLIAM BRIGHTWELL, age 47 - born 1813; male Farmer in Butler
Co. Alabama. His wife's name is P. Brightwell age 33 shown born in Georgia; William Brightwell is
shown as being born in South Carolina.
Their children listed were: M. J. Brightwell age 14 female 1846
        S. C. Brightwell age 12 female1848
        A. E. Brightwell age 10 female1850
        Jno. P. Brightwell age 7 male born 1853
        William H. Brightwell age 5 male - 1855
        Sand{??} couldn' read Brightwell age 3 Male
The names of the children were not spelled out. Was the P. Brightwell Polly?? More research to be done
on this information. I believe this is the brother to Len Reynolds Brightwell.

Name: WILLIAM BRIGHTWELL
Land Office: GREENVILLE , ALABAMA LAND PURCHASE
Document Number: 4857

Total Acres: 337
Signature: Yes
Canceled Document: No
Issue Date: November 01, 1858
Mineral Rights Reserved: No
Metes and Bounds: No
Statutory Reference: 3 Stat. 566
Multiple Warantee Names: No
Act or Treaty: April 24, 1820
Multiple Patentee Names: No
Entry Classification: Sale-Cash Entries
Land Description: 1 N½ ST STEPHENS No 8N 15E 6

1856 - Butler County, Alabama.
When William Brightwell first arrived in Alabama; he settled with his family in Butler County, Alabama as can be seen in Butler Co. Al. Church Records of Mt. Olive Church. He was listed first in History of the Church as Founder. Mt Olive East Baptist Church - Butler Co., AL

The following is an excerpt from Rev. J. W. Joyner's book, A History of the Baptists in Butler County (1819-1957). Surnames have been capitolized for easier visualization.

MT. OLIVE EAST BAPTIST CHURCH, Butler Co. Alabama
In my research into the history of Baptist in Butler County, seeing the part they have had in moulding religious influences, in this section, I have come across many things of interest. In reading the old records of this church I found some things that gave to me a personal pride. This is one of the oldest churches in the county, having been organized in the year 1856 with seventy-one members. The first name on the record is that of WILLIAM BRIGHTWELL.
WILLIAM BRIGHTWELL'S mother's name was Mary Olive and this is why the name Mt. Olive came about. When the Brightwell family first arrived in Maryland; their church name they attended was also named Mt. Olive. Others are DICKENS, PARKER, BENNETT, BUST, TURNER, BAILEY, PENNY, and HITES.
This church for many years was one of the strongest churches, but, because of economic conditions, now has only a few members.

William (2) Brightwell owned 337 Acres of land next door to Mt. Olive East Baptist Church that was organized in 1856 w/71 members. [This is definitely Len Reynolds Brightwell's brother]

William Brightwell must have moved with his family to Covington County, Alabama as can be seen from the census record. But; he and his family helped form the Mt. Olive Baptist Church above in 1856; so his family must have still attended the church. William Brightwell is most likely buried at Mt. Olive Baptist Church Cemetery (more research to be done on this).

1850 Covington Co. Alabama Census records
946/946 William BRIGHTWELL 28 m farm laborer   GA

WILLIAM BRIGHTWELL Purchased Land AL 2050_pg 238 Document # 48570
Greenville, Alabama N 1/2 Section # 6 - Township # 8 North
Range 15 East --- St. Stephens Meridian
It was a Cash sale on November 1, 1858 for $ 337.00

1860 - No BRIGHTWELL's listed on Mortality Schedule for the State of Alabama.
William Brightwell was the father of John Jackson Brightwell who married Sarah Windsor; daughter of John Windsor who preached from 1820-1830 at the Dry Creek Church near Red Bank, Alabama. Sarah (Sally) Windsor (1814-1886); wife of John Jackson Brightwell (b 1802 SC) apparently moved with John to Georgia about 1830 along with his brothers and father; as written in Webster Co. Ga. History Book.

Franklin Brightwell, Henry Brightwell, Jonathan Brightwell, William Brightwell, James Glenn Owens, Robert K. Parker, Robert T. Parker and William D. Owens were all in the 17th Reg, Company A Webster Rifles CSA. William D. Owens is father of Sarah Clay who married W. H. Mitchell.

1860 Census Alabama:
Also note: There was a William Brightwell who was 47 years old; male Farmer making him born in the year 1813 in Butler Co. Alabama with his wife: P. Brightwell age 33. Their children listed were M. J. Brightwell female age 14; S. C. Brightwell daugh age 12; A. E. Brightwell female age 10; Jno. P. Brightwell 7 yrs old male; William H. Brightwell, age 5 male and lastly Sand Brightwell age 3 yrs. male.

    NOTE: I am not sure how this next group fits into the Brightwell family at this time. However; I didn't want to leave out the information just in case someone can match it with the BRIGHTWELL family lines.

Children of John French Brightwell (1839-1900) & wives Lottie _____ & Sarah E "Sally" Darby; grandchildren of ????? Brightwell & Mary _____;
Census: 1870 Webster Co GA; 1880-1900 Pike Co AL
1)Sarah J Brightwell (b.Sep 1865GA-living 1900)
2)H Ettia Brightwell (b.abt.1869GA-living 1880)
3)R E Brightwell (b.abt.1872-living 1880AL)
4)George Franklin Brightwell (b.30 Jan 1876-d.12 Aug 1929)
5)Georgia E (b.abt.1877-living 1880)
6)John W Brightwell (b.Aug 1880-liv 1900)
7)Homer Brightwell (b.Jan 1886-liv 1900)
****

More About WILLIAM BRIGHTWELL:
Burial: Found in 1866 Covington Co. Alabama Census.
Military: 7th Virginia Regiment Revolutionary War Service.

More About WILLIAM BRIGHTWELL and MARY YOUNG:
Marriage: Bet. 20 - 30 Dec 1800, Prince Edward Co. Va. Marriage[Barnette Brightwell Gives Consent]

Notes for SARAH WINDSOR/WINDZER:
In 1811 Anderson Winzer who lived in Barnwell, SC wrote a will naming 2 of his 6 children. In addition he named a daughter Sary Brightwell for whom he had earlier provided. I am trying to deduce who her husband was. There is a Sarah Winzer married to a Jackson Brightwell in Stewart Co., GA where the family was found in 1850 but this Sarah is too young to be the one mentioned in Anderson's will. I thought you Brightwell people might know. The two families were quite close apparently from SC to GA.

How do you know that John Jackson Brightwell's wife Sarah in Stewart Co.Ga.was a Winzer?
William Brightwell in Edgefield/ Barnwell SC. was the only Brightwell living in SC at the time.William was John Jackson Brightwell's Father. In book history of Edgefield co. sc. chap xxviii Baptist Churches - page 308 under Dry creek Church--stanton S.Burdett,William B. Villard, Prescott Bush, and JOHN WINDSOR preach from 1820-1830. At a church named RED BANK mumford perryman clerk at red bank died 1820. He was the grandfather of General Perryman of Tx. The Perrymans and the Travises were related,COURNEL WM.BARRETT TRAVIS,massacred at the Alamo (onced belonged to Red bank). The travis family moved to Al. when Barrett (the family call him that) Travis was 12 yrs. old near where the Brightwell, Prescott Bush family, and Parker families moved in 1850s.as you know luncinda Winzer married John Bush and moved over also. The Travis family still live in the area and William Barrett Travis's younger brother is buried on hiway between Andalusis al. and evergreen Al.

On 1850 census of Stewart Co.Ga. there are two Winzer families living next William(2) Brightwell ,wife

Pamelia Bush Brightwell, and children . William (2) is beleived to be a brother to John Jackson Brightwell. A LUCINDA WINZER is listed in home of Falby Winzer age 60 SC. A Lucinda Winzer married John Bush and moved over to Butler Co. Al. where William(2) Brightwell, His brother L.Reynolds Brightwell and Reynolds inlaws Daniel C.Parker lived. You can find Lucinda and John Bush's names on the 1st. church roll of Mt. Olive East Baptist church organized 1856 with 71 members. The 1st. name on the roll was William Brightwell. William and a P.Bush names are on the deed at court house. Other names on roll are Prescott Bush, John Bush, Daniel C. Parker, wife Mary Mitchell Parker ,her mother Mary Mitchell.There are many other names also. John and Lucinda Winzer Bush are both buried at Ft.Dale cemetery in Greenville Alabama. Their graves are unmarked. I hope some one will mark the graves. The church still stands today south of Greenville Al. and there is a cem. next to it with some SC. names. William (2) Brightwell own 337 acres of land next door to the church. Daniel C. Parker own 168.50 acres a few yrs. down the rd. The Bush family own land just a few miles down another rd.If you are ever in Greenville Al. you can find a history of Mt. Olive east Baptist Church in the reasearch Lib.(you can find a little info. on internet also).In the Bush folder you can find John and Lucinda Winzer Bush 's obituaries.

Sarah (Sally) Winzer (1814-1886), wife of John Jackson Brightwell(b 1802 SC). John apparently moved to Ga about 1830 with his brothers. You can find the information in "The History of Webster County"

In 1811 Anderson Winzer who lived in Barnwell, SC wrote a will naming 2 of his 6 children. In addition he named a daughter Sary Brightwell for whom he had earlier provided.

As far as we know William 1 Brightwell(Barnwell SC) was the ONLY Brightwell living in South Carolina that could be married to Sarah Winzer.

More About WILLIAM BRIGHTWELL and SARAH WINDSOR/WINDZER:
Marriage: Bef. 1825, Married In Barnwell Co. S. Carolina

Children of WILLIAM BRIGHTWELL and MARY YOUNG are:
19.   i.   NANCY[5] BRIGHTWELL.
20.   ii.   JOHN JACKSON BRIGHTWELL, b. 1802, born in S. Carolina.; d. Abt. 1829, die Webster Co Ga. Fd Mt. Olive Bapt Church Stewart Co. Ga..
        iii.   AMY BRIGHTWELL, m. ROBERT MARTIN, 1803, Prince Edward Co. Virginia.

          More About ROBERT MARTIN and AMY BRIGHTWELL:
          Marriage: 1803, Prince Edward Co. Virginia

21.   iv.   WILLIAM THOMAS BRIGHTWELL, b. 1815, Born in S. Carolina READ HIS NOTES; d. 1884, 1870 Cen of Preston GA/Died Terrell Co Ga..
        v.   HENRY BARNETT BRIGHTWELL, b. Abt. 1820, In 1820 Cen. Pr Edward Co. Va./Liv in 1850; m. ELIZABETH FOREST MOORE, 16 Dec 1843, Marriage Prince Edward Co. Va.; b. William Brightwell consented to marriage BOND Dec. 20th..

          More About HENRY BRIGHTWELL and ELIZABETH MOORE:
          Marriage: 16 Dec 1843, Marriage Prince Edward Co. Va.

        vi.   RICHARD BRIGHTWELL, b. Abt. 1822, Liv 1850.
        vii.   WILLIE ANN BRIGHTWELL, b. Abt. 1824, Liv 1850.
        viii.   MARY ANN BRIGHTWELL, b. Abt. 1825, Liv 1850; m. JAMES HILL, 28 Jan 1828, Marriage Prince Edward Co. Virginia.; b. of Prince Edward Co. Virginia.; d. 27 Jun 1862, Died Battle of Richmond/Civil War.

          More About JAMES HILL and MARY BRIGHTWELL:
          Marriage: 28 Jan 1828, Marriage Prince Edward Co. Virginia.

Child of WILLIAM BRIGHTWELL and SARAH WINDSOR/WINDZER is:
22.   ix.   LEN REYNOLDS[5] BRIGHTWELL, b. 1825, Bn. Barnwell, S.C. Conf. Soldier/ Co. C. Ala. - 37th CIVIL

WAR; d. 20 May 1863, Believed buried Covington Co., Alabama - due to Civil War.

Generation No. 5

11. BARNETT U.[5] BRIGHTWELL *(CHARLES (SR)[4], REYNOLDS[3], REYNOLDS OR RANDALL[2], THE BRIGHTWELL FAMILY[1] HISTORY)* was born 1787 in Born Prince Edward Co., VA., and died 13 Jul 1855 in Prince Edward Co. Virginia. He married JUDITH W. BOATWRIGHT 10 Dec 1812 in Buckingham Co. Va. Marriage. She was born Abt. 1794 in New Canton Buckingham Co. Virginia, and died Oct 1875 in New Canton Buckingham Co. Virginia.

Notes for BARNETT U. BRIGHTWELL:
JUDITH W. BOATWRIGHT (REUBAN BAKER6, JOHN5, JOHN4, JOHN3, JOHN2, JOHN1) was born Abt. 1794 in New Canton, Buckingham County, Virginia, and died Oct 1875. She married BARNETT U. BRIGHTWELL 10 Dec 1812 in Buckingham County, Virginia, son of CHARLES BRIGHTWELL and NANCY. He was born Abt. 1787 in Prince Edward County, Virginia, and died 13 Jul 1855.

Notes for JUDITH W. BOATWRIGHT:
Census: 1850 Prince Edward Co., VA

Children of JUDITH BOATWRIGHT and BARNETT BRIGHTWELL are:

243.   i. JULIA ANN BRIGHTWELL, b. 1813; d. Aft. 1880.
    ii. THOMAS J. BRIGHTWELL, b. Abt. 1815; d. Feb 1878.
244.   i. ELIZA JANE BRIGHTWELL, b. 1816; d. 1888.

More About BARNETT BRIGHTWELL and JUDITH BOATWRIGHT:
Marriage: 10 Dec 1812, Buckingham Co. Va. Marriage

Children of BARNETT BRIGHTWELL and JUDITH BOATWRIGHT are:
23.   i.   JULIA ANN[6] BRIGHTWELL, b. 1813; d. Aft. 1880.
    ii.   THOMAS J. BRIGHTWELL, b. Aft. 1815; d. Feb 1878.
24.   iii.   ELIZA JANE BRIGHTWELL, b. 13 Oct 1816, Buckingham CO. Virginia; d. 1888.

12. ELIZABETH (BETSY) ANN[5] BRIGHTWELL *(CHARLES (SR)[4], REYNOLDS[3], REYNOLDS OR RANDALL[2], THE BRIGHTWELL FAMILY[1] HISTORY)* She married WILLIAM M. JENKINS 21 Jan 1819 in Prince Edward Co. Virginia Marriages.

Notes for WILLIAM M. JENKINS:

More About WILLIAM JENKINS and ELIZABETH BRIGHTWELL:
Marriage: 21 Jan 1819, Prince Edward Co. Virginia Marriages

Child of ELIZABETH BRIGHTWELL and WILLIAM JENKINS is:
    i.   R. R.[6] JENKINS, b. 1838, He was 30 at marriage; Bk 1m, Pg. 14.; m. LOUISA MARIE BRIGHTWELL, 23 Jan 1868, Married Prince Edward Co. Virginia. married age 22.; b. 1846, Buckingham Co. Va.; d. Nov 1860.

    More About R. JENKINS and LOUISA BRIGHTWELL:

Marriage: 23 Jan 1868, Married Prince Edward Co. Virginia. married age 22.

13. WILLIAM B. (JR)[5] BRIGHTWELL *(CHARLES (SR)[4], REYNOLDS[3], REYNOLDS OR RANDALL[2], THE BRIGHTWELL FAMILY[1] HISTORY)* was born Abt. 1784 in Prince Edward Co., Va., and died 25 Jul 1861 in Still Living 1850Prince Edward Co. Va.. He married NANCY BRIGHTWELL 06 Dec 1804 in Prince Edward Co. Va. Married his 1st Cousin., daughter of CHARLES BRIGHTWELL. She was born in Daughter of his Uncle Barnett Brightwell. liv in 1850.

More About WILLIAM BRIGHTWELL and NANCY BRIGHTWELL:
Marriage: 06 Dec 1804, Prince Edward Co. Va. Married his 1st Cousin.

Children of WILLIAM BRIGHTWELL and NANCY BRIGHTWELL are:

    i. MARTHA[6] BRIGHTWELL, m. CLAIBORNE HILL, 01 Feb 1831, Prince Edward Co.Virginia..

     More About CLAIBORNE HILL and MARTHA BRIGHTWELL:
     Marriage: 01 Feb 1831, Prince Edward Co.Virginia.

    ii. LOUISA MARIE BRIGHTWELL, b. 1846, Buckingham Co. Va.; d. Nov 1860; m. R. R. JENKINS, 23 Jan 1868, Married Prince Edward Co. Virginia. married age 22.; b. 1838, He was 30 at marriage; Bk 1m, Pg. 14..

     More About R. JENKINS and LOUISA BRIGHTWELL:
     Marriage: 23 Jan 1868, Married Prince Edward Co. Virginia. married age 22.

25. iii. MERCER BRIGHTWELL, b. 1813, Prince Edward Co. VA.
    iv. N. BRIGHTWELL, b. Abt. 1815, Prince Edward Co Va..
    v. ISABELLA OR ARIBELLA BRIGHTWELL, b. 1822, Prince Edward Co Va..
    vi. ALBERT G. BRIGHTWELL, b. 1824, Prince Edward Co Va..
   vii. R. W. BRIGHTWELL, b. 1826, Prince Edward Co Va..
   viii. ADDISON BRIGHTWELL, b. 1828, Prince Edward Co Va.; d. 1865.
    ix. ELIZABETH BRIGHTWELL, b. 1831, of Buckingham Co. Va..

14. JOHN M.[5] BRIGHTWELL *(BARNETT (SR)[4], REYNOLDS[3], REYNOLDS OR RANDALL[2], THE BRIGHTWELL FAMILY[1] HISTORY)* was born Abt. 1786 in 1820 Cumberland Co. Virginia censsus, and died 1835 in moved 1822 GA. in Clark Co. 18 32 Cen. Ga. He married FRANCES H. GLENN 09 Dec 1811 in Cumberland Co. Va. Marriage bond Issued, daughter of WILLIAM GLENN. She was born Bet. 1785 - 1790, and died 1842 in Died GA. Clarke Co..

More About JOHN M. BRIGHTWELL:
Burial: He received 52 acres from Barnett's estate.

More About JOHN BRIGHTWELL and FRANCES GLENN:
Marriage: 09 Dec 1811, Cumberland Co. Va. Marriage bond Issued

Children of JOHN BRIGHTWELL and FRANCES GLENN are:
26. i. WILLIAM B.[6] BRIGHTWELL, b. 1818, born in Virginia Oglethorpe Co. Georgia; d. 1860 census shows 42 yrs VA..
    ii. NATHANIEL "NATHAN" G. BRIGHTWELL, b. 1822, READ his noteS born in Virginia.

     Notes for NATHANIEL "NATHAN" G. BRIGHTWELL:
     Brightwell, Nathan G 48 VA
     NOTE: unmarried son of John Brightwell & Frances H Glenn

27. iii. JOHN BRIGHTWELL, b. 1825, READ his notes; d. 36 yrs old 1870 Ga Census.

15. BARNETT (JR)[5] BRIGHTWELL *(BARNETT (SR)[4], REYNOLDS[3], REYNOLDS OR RANDALL[2], THE BRIGHTWELL FAMILY[1] HISTORY)* was born Abt. 1794 in Born in Prince Edward Co. Va, and died Bet. 1821 - 1827 in Died in VA.. He married NANCY MATTHEWS 15 Nov 1815 in Prince Edward Co. Va. Marriage Record..

More About BARNETT BRIGHTWELL and NANCY MATTHEWS:
Marriage: 15 Nov 1815, Prince Edward Co. Va. Marriage Record.

Child of BARNETT BRIGHTWELL and NANCY MATTHEWS is:
      i.   MARTHA[6] BRIGHTWELL, m. HENRY Y. JENKINS, 15 Jan 1818, Prince Edward Co.Virginia. Marriages; b. READ THEIR NOTES..

          Notes for HENRY Y. JENKINS:
          MISCELLANEOUS Brightwell Family Information:

          There was a Martha Brightwell who married Henry J. Jenkins . They lived in Prince Edward Co., Virginia. She was born June 10, 1795 and she died May 16, 1868.
          They were married January 15, 1818
          The children from this union were:
             Mary E.Jenkins, Sarah Ann Jenkins, James Jenkins, Henry B.Jenkins, Martha F. (Patsy Jenkins, Abraham (Louis) Jenkins, Jane W. Jenkins, Benjamin Jenkins.

          Brightwell's Mill: Located on Stovall Creek on
             Virginia 633, the mill has been owned by the Brightwell
             family since the early 1920s. It was rebuilt after it
             washed away in a flood in 1942.
          http://www.newsadvance.com/Almanac%20Items/amherst1.html
          Noteworthy places and festivals in Amherst County (Virginia?)

          Included in the Domesday Book of Oxford were strange sounding villages, some of which survived, such as
          Ducklington, Brightwell Baldwin
          Oxfordshire, England and the Domesday Book of 1086
          http://www.infokey.com/oxford/Welcome.html

          More About HENRY JENKINS and MARTHA BRIGHTWELL:
          Marriage: 15 Jan 1818, Prince Edward Co.Virginia. Marriages

16. REUBEN[5] BRIGHTWELL *(BARNETT (SR)[4], REYNOLDS[3], REYNOLDS OR RANDALL[2], THE BRIGHTWELL FAMILY[1] HISTORY)* was born Abt. 1798 in Liv in 1850 found in Buckingham County, Virginia.. He married MARY J. HILL 22 Nov 1822 in Prince Edward Co. Va. Marriage Record..

More About REUBEN BRIGHTWELL and MARY HILL:
Marriage: 22 Nov 1822, Prince Edward Co. Va. Marriage Record.

Child of REUBEN BRIGHTWELL and MARY HILL is:
      i.   HOPY W.[6] BRIGHTWELL, m. CHARLES (JR) BRIGHTWELL, 18 Nov 1811, Married cousin. by consent Prince Edward Co. Va.; b. Abt. 1789, VA. He received 58 acres from Barnetts estate.; d. 1847, VA..

          More About CHARLES BRIGHTWELL and HOPY BRIGHTWELL:
          Marriage: 18 Nov 1811, Married cousin. by consent Prince Edward Co. Va.

17. MOSES[5] BRIGHTWELL *(SAMUEL[4], REYNOLDS[3], REYNOLDS OR RANDALL[2], THE BRIGHTWELL FAMILY[1] HISTORY)* was born 1802 in born Virginia of 1840/NEWTON Co. Ga; 1850 Cen., and died in Oglethorpe Co. Ga. 1824. He married MARGARET "PEGGY" ADALINE PHILLIPS 1841 in Newton County, Georgia. She was born 1811.

More About MOSES BRIGHTWELL:

Burial: Clark Co.1830-32/Newton Co. Ga. by 1835

More About MOSES BRIGHTWELL and MARGARET PHILLIPS:
Marriage: 1841, Newton County, Georgia

Children of MOSES BRIGHTWELL and MARGARET PHILLIPS are:
  i.   AMANDA[6] BRIGHTWELL, b. 1842.
  ii. BENNETT BRIGHTWELL, b. 1844.
  iii. MARY BRIGHTWELL, b. 1846.
  iv. EUGENIUS BRIGHTWELL, b. 1849.

18. WILLIAM BARNETT[5] BRIGHTWELL *(SAMUEL[4], REYNOLDS[3], REYNOLDS OR RANDALL[2], THE BRIGHTWELL FAMILY[1] HISTORY)* was born 1860 in born in GA.. He married MARY ADALINE CAIN in Married. She was born 1824 in born in GA..

More About WILLIAM BRIGHTWELL and MARY CAIN:
Marriage: Married

Children of WILLIAM BRIGHTWELL and MARY CAIN are:
  i.   MARY[6] BRIGHTWELL, b. 1850.
  ii.   WILLIAM BRIGHTWELL, b. 1851.
  iii. MARTHA BRIGHTWELL, b. 1854.
  iv.   JOHN BRIGHTWELL, b. 1861.
  v.   ANN BRIGHTWELL, b. 1867.
  vi.   NATHAN BRIGHTWELL, b. 1868.
28. vii. GEORGE BRIGHTWELL, b. 1839, born in GA. in other records he is called "Charles"???; d. Was George middle name or census error????.

19. NANCY[5] BRIGHTWELL *(WILLIAM[4], REYNOLDS[3], REYNOLDS OR RANDALL[2], THE BRIGHTWELL FAMILY[1] HISTORY)* She married WILLIAM HENRY MITCHELL 1835 in Married Webster Co or Baldwin Co. Georgia, son of HENRY MITCHELL and MARY LASSITER. He was born Abt. 1800, and died in Memb of Hopewell Bapt Ch. Jones Co. Ga..

Notes for WILLIAM HENRY MITCHELL:
Henry MITCHELL, b. c1800 GA and wife Nancy BRIGHTWELL. They married 1835 in Webster County, GA. Their children are: John A.; Vandance (died young) and William Henry (my gg grandfather), b. 18 Jan 1842 in Webster and married Sarah Clay OWENS, daughter of William Dow OWENS & Martha Ann WILSON (all in GA 1870 census). My gg grandfather is on the list of soldiers General Lee surrendered to Grant at Appomatox, VA. His brother John A. MITCHELL had two sons: William Henry & John. They went to Alabama c1880, per deed records and no one has ever heard from them again.

Henry is a member of the Hopewell Baptist Church in Jones County Ga.. They have 2 sons that I know about. John and William Henry.

Nancy Brightwell Mitchell who married Henry Mitchell is beleived to be sister to William Brightwell who moved from Stewart co. Ga. to Butler Co. Al. 1800s. Henery Mitchell is son of Mary Mitchell mother Mary Mitchell Parker (Mrs. Daniel C. Parker)living in Mt. Olive East area of Butler co. Al. Daniel C. Parker own land door to New Prossspect Meth. Church down the road from Mt. Olive East baptist Church. William Brightwell,s name is 1st. name on the first roll of Mt. Olive East. Also William Brightwell,s name on deed to Mt. Olive East Baptist Church

More About WILLIAM MITCHELL and NANCY BRIGHTWELL:
Marriage: 1835, Married Webster Co or Baldwin Co. Georgia

Children of NANCY BRIGHTWELL and WILLIAM MITCHELL are:

29.   i.   JOHN A.[6] MITCHELL, b. 1835, Liv 1850.
       ii.   WILLIAM HENRY MITCHELL, b. 18 Jan 1842, Liv 1850; d. on the list of soldiers General Lee surrended to Grant at Appomatox, VA.; m. SARAH CLAY OWENS.
      iii.   VANDANCE MITCHELL, b. Abt. 1850, Liv 1850; d. Died young..

20. JOHN JACKSON[5] BRIGHTWELL *(WILLIAM[4], REYNOLDS[3], REYNOLDS OR RANDALL[2], THE BRIGHTWELL FAMILY[1] HISTORY)* was born 1802 in born in S. Carolina., and died Abt. 1829 in die Webster Co Ga. Fd Mt. Olive Bapt Church Stewart Co. Ga.. He married SARAH WINDSOR/WINDZER 1829 in Married Barnwell S. Carolina, daughter of ANDERSON WINDOR. She was born 1814 in (see Will of Anderson Windsor, Barnwell, S.C.), and died 1886 in She is found 1880 Webster Co Cen. Ga..

Notes for JOHN JACKSON BRIGHTWELL:

Children of John Jackson Brightwell (1802-1859) & Sarah (Winzer?) (1815-living 1880):

1)Falby Brightwell (b.abt.1830-liv 1850) md 185_ Stewart Co GA to _____Slaton.
2)William Brightwell (b.1832GA-d.1881 Terrell Co GA) md Mary _____ (b.abt.1839GA-living 1880 Terrell Co GA)
3)Mary Missouri Brightwell (b.abt.1835GA-living 1860) md 1853 Stewart Co GA to J Francis McClendon (b.abt.1832-liv 1860)
4)Jonathan Brightwell (b.2 Apr 1837GA-d.9 Jan 1894) md Sarah Elizabeth _____ (b.abt.1844GA-d.1903). Buried Westview Cemetery, Atlanta, Fulton Co GA.
5)Andrew Jackson Brightwell (b.1847-d.1924) md Barbara Ann _____(living 1920)
6)Samuel Brightwell (b.1850-d.1887) md Mary "Molly" E Jenkins (b.1849-living 1900 Webster Co GA)
7)Elijah Leonard Brightwell (b.1853GA-d.1911ARK) md a)1871 Mary Shepherd b) 1883 Nevada City ARK toSusan Barnham
8)George Powell Brightwell (b.1854-d.1929) md: a)Georgia Ann Durham (1852-1891) b)Arrie Belle Barrentine
9)Julia Brightwell (b.1857-d.193_)
   grandchildren of John Jackson Brightwell & Sarah (Winzer).
   Census: 1870 Bullock Co AL, 1880 BArbour Co AL; 1900 Fulton Co GA

1)Frank E Brightwell (b.19 Dec 1870-d.23 Oct 1894)-buried WEstview Cemetery, Atlanta, Fulton Co GA
2)Annie Brightwell (b.abt.1875AL-living 1903 Atlanta, Fulton Co GA

Children of William Brightwell (1832-1881) & Mary _____ (b.18__-living 1880); grandchildren of John Jackson Brightwell & Sarah (Winzer?)
Census: 1860-1870 Webster Co GA; 1880 Terrell Co GA

1)Sarah E Brightwell (b.Dec 1855GA-living 1910 Mitchell Co GA--dead by 1925) md 1878 Terrell Co GA to Eugene D Bolton (b.Jan 1856-living 1910)--No children.
2)John L Brightwell (b.Jan 1860-living 1900 Terrell Co GA--dead by 1925)) md 1886 Terrell Co GA to Elizabeth "Lizzie" Brightwell (b.1864-d.pre.1900), dau of William Brightwell (1815-1884)
3)James T Brightwell (b.1865GA-d.1925FL) md 14 Dec 1890 Terrell Co GA to Lela Stokes. Buried Moultrie, Colquitt Co GA
4)W L Alac Brightwell (b.abt.1867-living 1880)
5)Susie F Brightwell (b.Sep 1871-living 1925 Terrell Co GA) md 1885 Terrell Co GA to John F Leverette (b.Sep 1859-liv 1900)
6)George W Brightwell (b.abt.1874-living 1925 Atlanta GA)
7)Richard Edward Brightwell (b.1877-living 1925 Atlanta GA) md 28 May 1899 Terrell Co GA to Ellen Clements (b.1876-living 1910)

8)Eugene Linwood Brightwell (b.1880GA-d.1944 Hillsborough Co FL) md Dora Lastinger (b.18__-d.1980FL)

William Jackson Brightwell 1871-1948 son of Andrew Jackson Brightwell 1847-1924 . g-son of John Jackson Brightwell b. Barnwell SC > Stewart Co. Ga.

Jonathan Brightwell and William3 Brightwell are sons of John Jackson Brightwell. William Henry (W.H.) Mitchell was son of Nancy Brightwell & Henry Mitchell. Jonathan Brightwell , William3 Brightwell, and William Henry Mitchell are grandsons of William1 Brightwell of Edgefield / Barnwell S.C.

Notes for SARAH WINDSOR/WINDZER:
In 1811 Anderson Winzer who lived in Barnwell, SC wrote a will naming 2 of his 6 children. In addition he named a daughter Sary Brightwell for whom he had earlier provided. I am trying to deduce who her husband was. There is a Sarah Winzer married to a Jackson Brightwell in Stewart Co., GA where the family was found in 1850 but this Sarah is too young to be the one mentioned in Anderson's will. I thought you Brightwell people might know. The two families were quite close apparently from SC to GA.

How do you know that John Jackson Brightwell's wife Sarah in Stewart Co.Ga.was a Winzer?
William Brightwell in Edgefield/ Barnwell SC. was the only Brightwell living in SC at the time.William was John Jackson Brightwell's Father. In book history of Edgefield co. sc. chap xxviii Baptist Churches - page 308 under Dry creek Church--stanton S.Burdett,William B. Villard, Prescott Bush, and JOHN WINDSOR preach from 1820-1830. At a church named RED BANK mumford perryman clerk at red bank died 1820. He was the grandfather of General Perryman of Tx. The Perrymans and the Travises were related,COURNEL WM.BARRETT TRAVIS,massacred at the Alamo (onced belonged to Red bank). The travis family moved to Al. when Barrett (the family call him that) Travis was 12 yrs. old near where the Brightwell, Prescott Bush family, and Parker families moved in 1850s.as you know luncinda Winzer married John Bush and moved over also. The Travis family still live in the area and William Barrett Travis's younger brother is buried on hiway between Andalusis al. and evergreen Al.

On 1850 census of Stewart Co.Ga. there are two Winzer families living next William(2) Brightwell ,wife Pamelia Bush Brightwell, and children . William (2) is beleived to be a brother to John Jackson Brightwell. A LUCINDA WINZER is listed in home of Falby Winzer age 60 SC. A Lucinda Winzer married John Bush and moved over to Butler Co. Al. where William(2) Brightwell, His brother L.Reynolds Brightwell and Reynolds inlaws Daniel C.Parker lived. You can find Lucinda and John Bush's names on the 1st. church roll of Mt. Olive East Baptist church organized 1856 with 71 members. The 1st. name on the roll was William Brightwell. William and a P.Bush names are on the deed at court house. Other names on roll are Prescott Bush, John Bush, Daniel C. Parker, wife Mary Mitchell Parker ,her mother Mary Mitchell.There are many other names also. John and Lucinda Winzer Bush are both buried at Ft.Dale cemetery in Greenville Alabama. Their graves are unmarked. I hope some one will mark the graves. The church still stands today south of Greenville Al. and there is a cem. next to it with some SC. names. William (2) Brightwell own 337 acres of land next door to the church. Daniel C. Parker own 168.50 acres a few yrs. down the rd. The Bush family own land just a few miles down another rd.If you are ever in Greenville Al. you can find a history of Mt. Olive east Baptist Church in the reasearch Lib.(you can find a little info. on internet also).In the Bush folder you can find John and Lucinda Winzer Bush 's obituaries.

Sarah (Sally) Winzer (1814-1886), wife of John Jackson Brightwell(b 1802 SC). John apparently moved to Ga about 1830 with his brothers. You can find the information in "The History of Webster County"

In 1811 Anderson Winzer who lived in Barnwell, SC wrote a will naming 2 of his 6 children. In addition he named a daughter Sary Brightwell for whom he had earlier provided.

As far as we know William 1 Brightwell(Barnwell SC) was the ONLY Brightwell living in South Carolina that could be married to Sarah Winzer.

More About JOHN BRIGHTWELL and SARAH WINDSOR/WINDZER:
Marriage: 1829, Married Barnwell S. Carolina

Children of JOHN BRIGHTWELL and SARAH WINDSOR/WINDZER are:

i. FALBY[6] BRIGHTWELL, b. Abt. 1830, Liv in 1850 Stewart Co Ga.; m. SLATON.

30. ii. WILLIAM BRIGHTWELL, b. 1842, born in Georgia. Read ALL HIS NOTES. of Terrell Co. Ga.; d. Census 1860-1870 Webster Co. Ga.; 1880 Terrell Co. Ga..

31. iii. MARY MISSOURI BRIGHTWELL, b. 1846, Liv in 1860 Census..

iv. JONATHAN BRIGHTWELL, b. 02 Apr 1837, Liv in Atlanta, Fulton Co Georgia; d. 09 Jan 1894, Buried at Westview Cemetery; m. SARAH ELIZABETH; b. 1844, Born in Ga.; d. 1903, Buried at Westview Cemtery, Fulton Co. Ga. Atlanta.

32. v. ANDREW JACKSON BRIGHTWELL, b. 1848, born Georgia/Andrew found on Orphans List.; d. 1924, 22 yrs ld in 1870 Census Georgia..

vi. SAMUEL BRIGHTWELL, b. 1850, born in Georgia; d. 1887, 20 yrs old in 1870 Census of Georgia.; m. MARY "MOLLY" E. JENKINS, Married Georgia.; b. 1849, Liv in 1900 Webster Co. Georgia Census; d. She was born Georgia..

Notes for SAMUEL BRIGHTWELL:

More About SAMUEL BRIGHTWELL and MARY JENKINS:
Marriage: Married Georgia.

vii. ELIJAH LEONARD BRIGHTWELL, b. 1853, Born GA/In 1860 Cen.of Webster Co. Georgia; d. 1911, Died Arkansas Nevada City; m. (1) MARY SHEPERD, 1871, Married; b. 1883, Nevada City Arkansas; m. (2) SUSAN BARTRAM, 1883, 2nd Wife.; b. Nevada City Arkansas.

More About ELIJAH BRIGHTWELL and MARY SHEPERD:
Marriage: 1871, Married

More About ELIJAH BRIGHTWELL and SUSAN BARTRAM:
Marriage: 1883, 2nd Wife.

viii. GEORGE POWELL BRIGHTWELL, b. 1854; d. 1929; m. (1) GEORGIA ANN DURHAM, Married lst wife.; b. 1852; d. 1891; m. (2) ARRIE BELLE BARRENTINE.

More About GEORGE BRIGHTWELL and GEORGIA DURHAM:
Marriage: Married lst wife.

ix. JULIA BRIGHTWELL, b. 1857; d. 193___(?).

21. WILLIAM THOMAS[5] BRIGHTWELL (WILLIAM[4], REYNOLDS[3], REYNOLDS OR RANDALL[2], THE BRIGHTWELL FAMILY[1] HISTORY) was born 1815 in Born in S. Carolina READ HIS NOTES, and died 1884 in 1870 Cen of Preston GA/Died Terrell Co Ga.. He married (1) MANIVRY. She was born 1831 in Of Alabama, and died 1880 in Liv in 1880 Terrell Co Ga. Census. He married (2) PAMELA BUSH 1846 in Stewart Co Ga. died before 1870; he remarried, daughter of THE BUSH FAMILY HISTORY. She was born Abt. 1825 in Born GA READ HERNOTES, and died Bet. 1860 - 1870.

Notes for WILLIAM THOMAS BRIGHTWELL:
Children of William Brightwell (1815-1884) & his wives Pamela Bush (1825-186?) and Minervy _____ (1831-living 1880)
NOTE: between 1860 & 1870, 1st wife Pamela Bush died and William remarried to Manirvy _____. So at least 1st six of his children were Pamela's; not sure which wife was the mother of the last four.

1)Mary J Brightwell (b.abt.1846-living 1880)-unmarried as of 1880

2)Sarah C Brightwell (b.abt.1848-living 1880)-unmarried as of 1880
3)Amanda E Brightwell (b.abt.1850-living 1920 Terrell Co GA) md 1878 Terrell Co GA to James Hollis Stokes
(b.1858-living 1920)
4)John P Brightwell (b.abt.1853-living 1860AL)
5)William H Brightwell (b.abt.1855-living 1886) md 14 Sep 1886 Terrell Co Ga to Nannie Cain
6)Samuel Evans Brightwell (b.1857-living 1910 Cooke Co TX) md 26 Dec 1878 Terrell Co GA to Elmira Emeline Howell (b.1861-living 1900TX)
7)Saphrony Brightwell (b.abt.1862-liv 1880)
8)Elizabeth "Lizzie" Brightwell (b.abt.1864-d.(1887-1900)) md 1886 Terrell Co GA to John L Brightwell
(b.1860-living 1900)-son of William Brightwell (1832-1881)
9)Ellen Brightwell (b.abt.1867-d.1884 Terrell Co GA)
10)Robert "Bobby" L Brightwell (b.abt.1869-liv 1920 Mitchell Co GA) md 28 Feb 1892 Terrell Co GA Josie Hallman (b.abt.1871-living 1920)

Brightwell, William 55 SC born 1815 S. Carolina
, Manirvy 39 AL
, M J (f) 25 GA
, A E (f) 20 GA
, William 14 AL
, Samuel 12 AL
, Saphrony 8 AL
, Elizabeth 6 GA
, R L (m) 1 Ga
NOTE: William Brightwell (1815SC-1884GA), probable son of William Brightwell of Barnwell Co SC; Manirvy is a 2nd wife.

Notes for PAMELA BUSH:
PAMELA BUSH & the BUSH family notes.

The BUSH, Brightwell, Parker and Mitchell families all moved to Butler co. Alabama at the same time from Stewart Co. Ga. They lived near Mt. Olive East Baptist Church south of Greenville, Ala. William Brightwell's husband of Pamela Bush; his name is found first on the roll. and it shows he was married in Stewart Co. Ga.

Those BUSH family members and where they are buried in Butler Co. Alabama·

Bush	Agnes Y.	Pleasant Hill (offsite link)
Bush	Anna J. Harbin	Moriah Cemetery
Bush	Billy Kendrick, Sgt.	Morrow Schoolhouse Cemetery
Bush	C.Q.	Oakey Streek Cemetery
Bush	Cumi	Antioch East Cemetery
Bush	Danny Ellis	Providence Methodist Church
Bush	Ewing E.	Antioch East Cemetery
Bush	Fredrick Norman	Antioch East Cemetery
Bush	G.W.	Antioch East Cemetery
Bush	Georgia	Antioch East Cemetery
Bush	Gordon	Morrow Schoolhouse Cemetery
Bush	Green Burney	Oakey Streek Cemetery
Bush	Herman	Antioch East Cemetery
Bush	Ida V.	Antioch East Cemetery
Bush	Ila Mae	Antioch East Cemetery
Bush	Inf. son of Mr. & Mrs. H. E.	Perdue Cemetery
Bush	John	Fort Dale Cemetery
Bush	John Henry	Fort Dale Cemetery

Bush	John W. And Elizabeth G.	Antioch East Cemetery
Bush	Lafayette (Fate)	Little Brown Church
Bush	Leo Franklin	Morrow Schoolhouse Cemetery
Bush	Lourow	Oakey Streek Cemetery
Bush	Lucille	Antioch East Cemetery
Bush	Lucindor Windsor	Fort Dale Cemetery
Bush	Mark David	Providence Methodist Church
Bush	Mary	Antioch East Cemetery
Bush	Mary Coker	Little Brown Church
Bush	Mary Ola	Fort Dale Cemetery
Bush	Maude	Morrow Schoolhouse (Diard List)
Bush	Millie	Oakey Streek Cemetery
Bush	Milly A.	Oakey Streek Cemetery
Bush	Mollie Jewell	Liberty Methodist Cemetery
Bush	Myrtle Lee	Antioch East Cemetery
Bush	Nancy	Moriah Cemetery
Bush	Patricia Jane (Cricket)	Providence Methodist Church
Bush	Richard H.	Moriah Cemetery
Bush	Robert	Antioch East Cemetery
Bush	Ruth	Antioch East Cemetery
Bush	Sallie Mrs.	Antioch East Cemetery
Bush	Sidney O.	Antioch East Cemetery
Bush	Willie G.	Pleasant Hill (offsite link)

More About WILLIAM BRIGHTWELL and PAMELA BUSH:
Marriage: 1846, Stewart Co Ga. died before 1870; he remarried

Children of WILLIAM BRIGHTWELL and MANIVRY are:
    i.   M. J.[6] BRIGHTWELL, b. 1845, born Ga. shown as 25 yrs old Ga 1870 Census..
    ii.   R.L. BRIGHTWELL, b. 1869, born in Georgia.

Children of WILLIAM BRIGHTWELL and PAMELA BUSH are:
33.   iii.   MARY J.[6] BRIGHTWELL, b. 1849, born S. Carolina shown age 48 in 1870 Ga Census; d. Liv in 1880 census -unmarried as of 1880.
    iv.   SARAH BRIGHTWELL, b. 1849, Living in 1880 census - unmarried as of 1880; m. SWIFT CRUMLY; b. 1841.

    Notes for SARAH BRIGHTWELL:
    1870 Stewart Co GA
    p.43
    Brightwell, Sarah 21 GA
    w/Swift Crumly 29 GA
    NOTE: daughter of William Brightwell (1815SC-1884GA) & Pamela Bush

    v.   AMANDA E. BRIGHTWELL, b. Abt. 1850, Liv in Terrell Co Ga in 1920; m. JAMES HOLLIS STOKES, 1878, Married Terrell Co. Georgia; b. 1858, Of Terrell Co. Georgia; d. Liv in 1920.

    More About JAMES STOKES and AMANDA BRIGHTWELL:
    Marriage: 1878, Married Terrell Co. Georgia

    vi.   JOHN P. BRIGHTWELL, b. Abt. 1853, Liv in 1860 Ala Census.
34.   vii.   WILLIAM H. BRIGHTWELL, b. 1856, Liv in 1886 Census- Born Mississippi; d. 1880 Census of Precinct 4, Bell, Texas.
    viii.   SAMUEL EVANS BRIGHTWELL, b. 1858, Liv 1910 Cooke Co Texas Census; m. ELMIRA EMELINE HOWELL, 26 Dec 1878, Married Terrell Co. Ga.; b. 1861, Liv in 1900 Texas..

More About SAMUEL BRIGHTWELL and ELMIRA HOWELL:
Marriage: 26 Dec 1878, Married Terrell Co. Ga.

    ix.   SAPHRONY BRIGHTWELL, b. 1862, Liv in 1880 census.
    x.   ELIZABETH "LIZZIE" BRIGHTWELL, b. 1864; d. Bet. 1887 - 1900; m. JOHNNY L. BRIGHTWELL,
        1886, Married Terrell Co Ga. lst Cousin,; b. Jan 1860, Liv in 1900 Census son of William Brightwell
        (1832); d. Married his first cousin. dead by 1925.

        More About JOHNNY BRIGHTWELL and ELIZABETH BRIGHTWELL:
        Marriage: 1886, Married Terrell Co Ga. lst Cousin,

    xi.   ELLEN BRIGHTWELL, b. Abt. 1867; d. 1884, Terrell Co Georgia.
    xii.   ROBERT "BOBBY" L. BRIGHTWELL, b. Abt. 1869, Liv in 1920 Mitchell Co Ga. Census; m. JOSIE
        HALLMAN, 28 Feb 1892, Terrell Co. Ga.; b. Abt. 1871, Liv in 1920 Census..

        More About ROBERT BRIGHTWELL and JOSIE HALLMAN:
        Marriage: 28 Feb 1892, Terrell Co. Ga.

22. LEN REYNOLDS[5] BRIGHTWELL *(WILLIAM[4], REYNOLDS[3], REYNOLDS OR RANDALL[2], THE BRIGHTWELL FAMILY[1] HISTORY)* was born 1825 in Bn. Barnwell, S.C. Conf. Soldier/ Co. C. Ala. - 37th CIVIL WAR, and died 20 May 1863 in Believed buried Covington Co., Alabama - due to Civil War. He married ELIZABETH CAROLINE PARKER 13 Sep 1846 in Md Stewart Co., Ga. Box Ankel Dist/Now Richland Co. Ga., daughter of DANIEL PARKER and MARY MITCHELL. She was born 1828 in 1880 Census Sandy Ridge, Lowndes Co.,Ala. she was 52 yrs. old., and died Aft. 1900 in Liv in 1900 Crenshaw Co., Ala Census..

Notes for LEN REYNOLDS BRIGHTWELL:
Len Reynolds Brightwell ----

L. Reynolds Brightwell b. about 1825 Barnwell, S.C. [Census of 1820&30 has his father William Brightwell listed; but not after 1830 census.] L. Reynolds Brightwell died 5 20 1863 Covington County Alabama. He died while home on furlough and is believed to buried in Covington County, Alabama. His father, William Brightwell and family were still attending Mt. Olive Baptist Church in Butler Co. Ala while living in Covington County, Alabama. Checking cemetery records in Butler County, Alabama as well as Covington Co. Alabama

L.Reynolds Brightwell Born 1825 in S.C. L. Reynolds Brightwell is John Jackson Brightwell's brother. L.Reynolds and another brother named William Thomas Brightwell #2 moved from Stewart Co. Ga. to Butler Co.Al > Covington Co.Al. then L. Reynolds Brightwell died in1863 in Covington Co near Andalusia Al. and William Thomas Brightwell #2 moved his Family back to Preston Ga. You can find him on the 1870 census of Preston Ga. age 55 yrs.Also on same census you can find John Jackson's son William Brightwell#3 listed.

Our L. (Len) Reynolds BRIGHTWELL joined on May 20th, 1863 - was in Co. C. Al. 37th. they also lived near Pigeon Creek . His brother was William Brightwell 1st. name on roll of Mt. Olive East Baptist Church in Butler Co. Al.---Reynolds signed up at LEON Al.--Died Covington Co. Al. 1863 as a result of the war . Len Reynolds Brightwell met his future wife at the Mt. Olive Baptist Church as the PARKER FAMILY can be seen on the founding list of the church.

Brightwell, Len Reynolds Co C
Included in report of Covington Rifles, SCV Camp No. 1586 of Andalusia, AL entitled "Known Gravesites of Confederate Soldiers and Sailors Buried in Covington County, Alabama" as one "... buried on the battlefields or believed to be buried in unmarked graves in Covington County" with this entry: "Brightwell, L. Reynolds. Died in service 20 May 1863. Co. C, 37th Alabama Infantry. Believed to have died at home while on furlough ..."

L.Reynolds Brightwell Born 1825 in S.C. L. Reynolds Brightwell is believed to be John Jackson
Brightwell's brother. L.Reynolds and another brother named William Thomas Brightwell #2 moved from
Stewart Co. Ga. to Butler Co.Al > Covington Co.Al. then L. Reynolds Brightwell died in1863 in Covington
Co near Andalusia Al. and William Thomas Brightwell #2 moved his Family back to Preston Ga. You can
find him on the 1870 census of Preston Ga. age 55 yrs.Also on same census you can find John Jackson's
son William Brightwell#3 listed. The father of our William Brightwell#1 in Barnwell S.C. , Barnwell
District. found 1810 census records

L. (Len) Reynolds Brightwell was born 1825 in Barnwell SC. Son of William1 Brightwell and Sara
Windsor.Daughter of Anderson Windsor of Barnwell SC{see Will in Barnwell Sc for A.Windsor}.

WILLIAM Brightwell is believe to be son of Reynolds Brightwell and Mary ? of Grandville NC.{See will
of Reynolds Brightwell in Grandville and Mary's will (Deed left to grand daughter Fanny Green Brightwell
in Edgefield SC}.Also see paper where Francis Green Brightwell Brightwell GRAND DAUGHTER of
Mary Brightwell was bound over to Mary Brightwell till of age In Grandville NC.....L. Reynolds
Brightwell served during the Civil War in CO c AL.37th. died at home Cov. Co. Al. He is beleived to be
buried in an unmarked grave in or near Cov. Co. Al.

Caroline Elizabeth Parker Brightwell (wife of L.R.Brightwell) was the daughter of Daniel C. Parker and
Mary Mitchell of Stewart co. Ga.--See 1850 census of Stewart co. Ga and Butler co. al. 1860.--Caroline is
thought to be buried at Sawyer Cem at Sandy Ridge Al.with her son James H. Brightwell Sr.'s 1st. wife
Mary Elizabeth Bedgood/Belinger and 3 of their children. See Heritage of Alabama Series Books vol:
Butler co. Al., Crenshaw Co.,Al, Covington Co. Al. for much more infomation and pictures.Pub: 2002----
Martha Clark Brightwell-2002.
Password:

1850 Stewart Co. ensus: Len Reynolds Brightwell was located in Stewart Co. Ga. with his wife; Elizabeth
and one child a daughter named Sarah Brightwell.
YEAR 1850. L. Reynolds Brightwell's father; William Brightwell is found in Covington County, Alabama
in the 1850 Census as Head of Household.

1860 Census Record of BUTLER CO. ALABAMA has both Len Reynolds Brightwell and William
Brightwell listed owing land:
Brightwell, L. R. AL BUTLER CO. PRECINCT NO. 15 007 1860
    L. R. Brightwell was 33 yrs. in the census.
Brightwell, William AL BUTLER CO. PRECINCT NO. 15 007 1860

Reynolds Brightwell and his wife Elizabeth Caroline PARKER Brightwell also moved over with her
parents Daniel C. and Mary Mitchell Parker. Mary parker's mother Mary Mitchell can be found living next
door to the Daniel C. Parker family 1860.

L. Reynolds Brightwell moved to Stewart Co.Ga. where he married Elizabeth Caroline Parker Sept. 13th.
1846 .
Our L. (Len) Reynolds BRIGHTWELL was in Co. C. Al. 37th. they also lived near Pigeon Creek . His
brother was William Brightwell 1st. name on roll of Mt. Olive East Baptist Church in Butler co. al.---
Reynolds sign up at LEON Al.--Died Covington Co. Al. 1863 as a result of the war

Caroline Elizabeth Parker Brightwell (wife of L.R.Brightwell) was the daughter of Daniel C. Parker and
Mary Mitchell of Stewart Co. Ga.--See 1850 census of Stewart co. Ga and Butler co. al. 1860.--Caroline is
thought to be buried at Sawyer Cem at Sandy Ridge Al.with her son James H. Brightwell Sr.'s 1st. wife
Mary Elizabeth Bedgood/Belinger and 3 of their children. See Heritage of Alabama Series Books vol:
Butler Co. Al., Crenshaw Co.,Al, Covington Co. Al. for much more infomation and pictures.Pub: 2002----
Martha Clark Brightwell-2002.

" ID: I44632739
" Name: L. Reynolds BRIGHTWELL

" Given Name: L. Reynolds
" Surname: Brightwell
" Sex: M
" Death: 20 May 1863
" Change Date: 14 Oct 1999

Marriage 1 Caroline PARKER
Children
1.   Missouri BRIGHTWELL b: May 1854 in United States,Alabama

" ID: I15984
" Name: L. Reynolds BRIGHTWELL 1
" Sex: M
" Change Date: 16 OCT 2002

Marriage 1 Elizabeth Caroline PARKER
"   Married:
Children
1.   Hilery Albert BRIGHTWELL
" ID: I266
" Name: L. (Len) Reynolds Brightwell
" Sex: M
" Birth: 1825 in Barnwell, SC
" Death: MAY 1863 in Covington Co., AL
" Note: 1850 US Census: Brightwell, Reynolds (links to incorrect image) State: Georgia Year: 1850
County: Stewart Roll: M432_82 Township: Box Ankle District Page: 63 Image: 128 died as result of the
Civil War.Co c Ala. 37th.
" Change Date: 13 JUL 2003

Father: William Brightwell
Mother:

Marriage 1 Elizabeth Caroline Parker
Children of L Reynolds Brightwell & Elizabeth Caroline Parker

1)Sarah J Brightwell (b.1849 in Crenshaw Co Ala. GA-living 1870 AL)
2)Martha A Brightwell (b.abt.1851-liv 1870 AL)
3)Mary E Brightwell (b.abt.1853-liv 1870 AL)
4)Missouri E Brightwell (b,.1854 in Alabama -liv 1880 AL)
5)Matilda C Brightwell (b.abt.1857-liv 1870AL)
6)Hillary Albertus Brightwell (b.1859-liv 1900 AL) md Sallie _____ (b.Apr 1860-liv 1900 AL)
7)James H Brightwell (b.1861AL-living 1900 AL) md Mary _____ (b.May 1861-liv 1900)****
****

LEN REYNOLDS BRIGHTWELL CIVIL WAR MILITARY RECORDS.

Reynolds Brightwell (First_Last)
Regiment Name 37 Alabama Infantry.
Side Confederate
Company C
Soldier's Rank_In Private
Soldier's Rank_Out Private
Alternate Name
Notes
Film Number M374 roll 6

The Alabama 37th Regiment, CSA
Narrative History and Chronology
April - August 1862
". . .(L)et me say of the fruitless struggle made by the Thirty-Seventh Alabama Regiment. . . I believe no truer, braver soldiers were to be found in the Confederate army, and I ask that those noble sons of Alabama shall not be forgotten while the deeds of others are often sung in loudest praise."

CIVIL WAR SERVICE
37th Alabama Infantry Regiment
The 37th Alabama Infantry Regiment was organized at Auburn, in the spring of 1862, under the requisition of President Jefferson Davis for 12,000 more Alabamians. The members were recruited from Barbour, Chambers, Henry, Macon, Pike, Russell, and Tallapoosa counties. Ordered to Columbus, MS, after a short time, the regiment proceeded to Tupelo. There it was placed in Gen'l Henry Little's Division, and in the Brigade of Col. Martin of TN, with three Mississippi regiments. Gen'l Dabney Herndon Maury succeeded Gen'l Little when the latter was killed at Iuka, where the 37th was first engaged, with some loss. The regiment took part in the Battle of Corinth, losing heavily in casualties. The brigade commander fell at Corinth, and the 37th was thrown into a brigade with the 2nd TX, and 42nd AL, Gen'l John C. Moore commanding. The winter was spent in MS -- the regiment retreating from Holly Springs and taking part in the repulse of the invaders at Chickasaw Bayou. Early in 1863, the 37th was sent to the Sunflower River but went back in time to take part in the battles of Port Gibson and Champion Hill, where its losses were severe. The regiment was then assigned to the garrison of Vicksburg and was captured with the fortress. Exchanged soon after, the regiment was in parole camp at Demopolis. Ordered to the Army of Tennessee, it lost heavily at Lookout Mountain and quite a number at Mission Ridge. The winter passed at Dalton, GA, where Gen'l Alpheus Baker of Barbour took charge of the brigade. The regiment was then engaged at Chattanooga (73 casualties our of 407 men present), Resaca, Noonday Creek, Kennesaw, and the battles around Atlanta. In one charge at Atlanta, 22 July, the regimental commander and 40 men were killed outright, out of 300 men present. During the fall and winter, the 37th was on garrison duty at Spanish Fort but moved into NC. It broke the enemy line at Bentonville, and furled its colors a few days later, with 300 of its number present out of the 1100 who took the field originally.

Field officers: Col. James F. Dowdell (Chambers Co., captured at Vicksburg and retired). Lt. Cols. A. A. Greene (Chambers Co., wounded, Iuka, Mission Ridge; KIA, Atlanta); and W. F. Slaton (Macon Co.). Majors John P. W. Amorine (Pike Co., transferred); W. F. Slaton (wounded, Corinth; captured, Lookout Mountain; promoted); and Joel C. Kendrick (Covington Co.)

[The 37th Alabama Infantry Regiment, Consolidated, was organized on 9 April 1865 by combining the original 37th Alabama with the 42nd and 54th Alabama regiments, at Smithfield, NC. The unit(s) surrendered on 26 April 1865 at Durham Station, Orange County, NC. Field officers: Col. John A. Minter and Lt. Col. William D. McNeill.]

— Brigadier General John Creed Moore, C.S.A., retired1

In the spring of 1862, Confederate President Jefferson Davis put forth a requisition to the state of Alabama to recruit and train 12,000 more troops.2 Men of stature — lawyers, bankers, politicians — and others with the power of persuasion, immediately begin to criss-cross the region raising their own companies of men. As the raw recruits gather, regiments are organized by forming these independent companies into larger units. Auburn, Alabama is one of the places where large groups of these men assemble.

April 18, 1862 — Fifty-year-old John Parker, 1st Corporal of Moses B. Greene's Company of Volunteers, may well be the first casualty of the group of men who become the 37TH ALABAMA REGIMENT. He dies at Auburn after enlisting there on March 22. The circumstances surrounding his death are unknown.3

May 13, 1862 — The ALABAMA 37TH REGIMENT OF VOLUNTEER INFANTRY, which is eventually made up of 1,100 men, is organized and mustered into Confederate service for three years or the war at Auburn, Alabama. Captain Hamner's Volunteers now become COMPANY B of the regiment.12

Additional information: Franklin Brightwell, Henry Brightwell, Jonathan Brightwell, William Brightwell, James Glenn Owens, Robert K. Parker, Robert T. Parker and William D. Owens were all in the 17th Reg, Company A Webster Rifles CSA. William D. Owens is father of Sarah Clay who married W. H. Mitchell William Henry is son of Henry. William Henry Co. K 17th.
Company K, 17th. Ga. Regiment was in the Battle of Gettysburg. other members poss. related to Brightwell family. Parker, Gore.

The ALABAMA 37TH REGIMENT OF VOLUNTEER INFANTRY is to be commanded by Colonel James F. Dowdell of Chambers County, Alabama. Lieutenant Colonel Alexander A. Greene, also of Chambers County, is named second-in-command. Two officers of field rank are also assigned: Major John P. W. Amerine from Pike County and Major William F. Slaton of Macon. John C. Meadows of Chambers is named Adjutant.17 The unit is ordered to Columbus, Mississippi. From there, the regiment is to report to Brigadier General Lewis Henry Little at Tupelo, Mississippi for further deployment.18
Many of you are aware that there was concern expressed last year over the fate of the battle flag of the 37th AL CSA. It has been on public display for many years at Auburn University as part of its Special Collections Library. It, from a number of recent reports, had also fallen into a state of significant deterioration.

THE BATTLE FLAG of Co. C 37th
According to a fellow researcher of the 37th AL, the flag is currently in Maryland where it will be professionally conserved and carefully restored. The conservator there will establish a timeline for the work, and for when the flag will be returned to Alabama, this time, unless I'm mistaken, to the Alabama State Archive at Montgomery. Flag: 37th Alabama Infantry (Co.E) Catalogue No. 87.3975.1 (PN10117, PN10197) Provenance Reconstruction: No documentation concerning the manufacture or presentation of this flag has been found. The flag was preserved by J. W. Skipper, son of Captain Jacob L. Skipper, Co. E, 37th Alabama Infantry. It was presented to the Alabama Department of Archives and History on March 28, 1911 by Mrs. Silas Tyson widow of J. W. Skipper.

He signed up in Leon Alabama. L. Reynolds Brightwell served during the Civil War in CO c AL.37th. died at home Cov. Co. Al. He is believed to be buried in an unmarked grave in or near Cov. Co. Al. Brightwell, L. Reynolds. Died in service 20 May 1863. Co. C, 37th Alabama Infantry. Believed to have died at home while on furlough. Wife Caroline. Found on Cemeteries of Confederate Soldiers in Covington Co. Alabama Cemeteries.

I have searched the available cemeteries on the internet for both Covington and Sandy Ridge Lowndes Co. Alabama area. I have not been able to locate him. My belief is that he is more likely to have been buried in the Sawyer Cemetery, near his wife and children; since he died while living at home. Unless, they were living in Covington, then the wife and children moved to Sandy Ridge area. The explanation for why there is no tombstone is puzzling(?)

NOTE OF INTEREST: There IS NO RECORD OF ANY BRIGHTWELLS LIVING IN PIKE CO.AL. BEFORE THE CW. and it WAS SOME TIME AFTER THE CW BEFORE A BRIGHTWELL FAMILY MOVED IN TO PIKE CO. AL. There are NO SLAVE RECORDS ON ANY BRIGHTWELLS in Pike Co. Al.

More About LEN REYNOLDS BRIGHTWELL:
Burial: Died at his home in Covington Co.

Notes for ELIZABETH CAROLINE PARKER:

CAROLINE BRIGHTWELL

ID: I267
Name: Elizabeth Caroline Parker
Sex: F
Birth: ABT 1827 in GA
Note: 1860 census
Note: 1850 census: Name: Elizabeth Brightwell Age: 22 Estimated Birth Year: 1827 Birth Place: Georgia Gender: Female Home in 1850 (City,County,State): Box Ankle, Stewart, Georgia Page: 63 Roll: M432_82 Caroline Elizabeth Parker Brightwell (wife of L.R. Brightwell)was daughter of Daniel C. Parker and Mary Mitchell.(see 1850 census of Stewart co. Ga.)& Butler co. al. census 1860.--Widow Caroline Brightwell & children on 1866 census of Covington co. al. & Crenshaw co. al. Census 1870. 1860 census: Name: E C Brightwell Age in 1860: 30 Birthplace: Georgia Home in 1860: Precinct 15, Butler, Alabama Gender: Female Value of real estate: View image Post Office: Leon and Rainsville Roll: M653_3 Page: 7 Year: 1860 1870 census: BRIGHTWELL, CAROLINE (1870 U.S. Census) ALABAMA , CRENSHAW, RUTLEDGE P O Age: 42, Female, Race: WHITE, Born: GA Series: M593 Roll: 12 Page: 107 1870 Crenshaw Co. Census Records, Township-Eleven Family #4: Bright, Caroline.....42.....wf.....GA Sarah........20.....wf.....GA Martha.......19.....wf.....GA Mary.........17.....wf.....AL Missouri.....15.....wf.....AL Matilda......13.....wf.....AL Albert.......11.....wm.....AL James........08.....wm.....AL
Change Date: 18 SEP 2004

Father: Daniel C. Parker b: ABT 1805 in SC
Mother: Mary Mitchell

Our L. Reynolds Brightwell married Caroline Parker in Stewart Co. Ga. Sept. 13, 1846. (Box Ankel Dist. now Richland ga.)Since she got married in Stewart Co., Georgia it is a probability that the PARKER family members will be found in Stewart Co., Georgia. When Len Reynold Brightwell and Caroline Parker were first married they were living in the home of Daniel C. Parker and family on the 1850 census of Stewart Co., Ga. Daniel C. Parker age 50; his wife - Mary age 38; their son-John age 15 years and then Elizabeth Caroline age 22 and her husband Reynolds age 25 are listed too. There is a 10 year difference in the ages of Caroline and John. Daniel C. Parker served the County as Coroner of Stewart Co., Georgia from January 18, 1834 through January 13, 1836.

In the Census of 1860 of Butler Co. Alabama; Reynolds Brightwell is found living next door to William Brightwell and Daniel C. Parker is living down the road next door to Mary Mitchell (his mother-in-law).

Caroline Brightwell is shown head of household in 1866 Census of Covington County, Alabama census. The William Brightwell listed in Covington Co., Ala. is believed to be Len Reynold Brightwell's brother. William went back to Georgia and settled in the Colquitt Co. area (near Rodney Brightwell) and is buried in Georgia, in the 1870 Census. William Brightwell was in the Home guard during the civil War in Covington Co., Alabama before moving to Georgia.

Len Reynolds Brightwell had died by the time this census of 1866 was done; and Caroline is listed a Head of Household with her children; shown as widow.
    She was widowed age 52 yrs living in Sandy Ridge, Lowndes Co. Alabama, shown keeping house. It shows her as a Widow in the Pension Files for her husband and she received the pension the rest of her life. It shows her family from Stewart Co., Ga. Her state of birth was discrepancy,, Georgia or S. Carolina listed. Familysearch.com

    In her later years, widowed, she is found in Census records with her youngest son, James H. Brightwell still living at home.

Caroline is shown as a Widow in the 1866 Census of Covington Co., AL and Crenshaw Alabama Census of 1870.

L. (Len) Reynolds Brightwell b. 1825 Barnwell S.C. Son of William 1 Brightwell and Sarah Windsor (See will of Anderson Windsor, Barnwell SC.)-L.Reynolds Brightwell died May 1863 in Covington Co. al as result of the Civil War.Co c Ala. 37th.

Caroline Elizabeth Parker Brightwell (wife of L.R. Brightwell)was daughter of Daniel C. Parker and Mary Mitchell.(see 1850 census of Stewart co. Ga.)& Butler co. al. census 1860.--Widow Caroline Brightwell & children on 1866 census of Covington co. al. & Crenshaw co. al. Census 1870.

ID: I266
Name: L. (Len) Reynolds Brightwell
Sex: M
Birth: 1825 in Barnwell, SC
Death: MAY 1863 in Covington Co., AL
Note: 1850 US Census: Brightwell, Reynolds (links to incorrect image) State: Georgia Year: 1850 County: Stewart Roll: M432_82 Township: Box Ankle District Page: 63 Image: 128 1860 census: BRIGHTWELL, L R (1860 U.S. Census) ALABAMA , BUTLER, 15-PCT Age: 33, Male, Race: WHITE, Series: M653 Roll: 3 Page: 7 Household: L R Brightwell Precinct 15, Butler, AL 33 1826 Male E C Brightwell Precinct 15, Butler, AL 30 1829 Georgia Female S J Brightwell Precinct 15, Butler, AL 11 1848 Female M A Brightwell Precinct 15, Butler, AL 9 1850 Female M E Brightwell Precinct 15, Butler, AL 7 1852 Alabama Female M E Brightwell Precinct 15, Butler, AL 5 1854 Female M C Brightwell Precinct 15, Butler, AL 3 1856 Female H A Brightwell Precinct 15, Butler, AL 1 1858 Male died as result of the Civil War. Co c Ala. 37th. Brightwell, Len Reynolds (sic Burnel) Private Company C Age at Enlistment: 38 Enlisted 31 March 1862 at Leon AL for a period of three years; Appears on Muster Roll of Company C dated 13 May 1862 at Auburn AL; Believed WIA in unknown action and died of his wounds at home while in service; Died 20 May 1863 and claim for deceased soldier filed 27 May 1863 by Caroline Brightwell, widow, at Covington AL (speed by which claim was filed supports belief that he was home at time of death); Appears on Pay Roll dated 31 Oct 1863 at Montgomery AL with notation "Died in Covington County, Alabama" (during the pay period); He was son of William Brightwell and Sara Windsor Brightwell of Barnwell SC; Wife/widow Caroline E. Parker Brightwell was daughter of Daniel C. Parker and Mary Mitchell; Included in report of Covington Rifles, SCV Camp #1586 of Andalusia, Alabama entitled "Known Gravesites of Confederate Soldiers and Sailors Buried in Covington County, Alabama" as one of "... buried on the battlefields or believed to be buried in unmarked graves in Covington County" with this entry: "Brightwell, L. Reynolds. Died in service 20 May 1863. Co. C, 37th Alabama Infantry. Believed to have died at home while on furlough. Wife Caroline."; Record in AL Archives for "Burnel Brightwell" contains identical information and is clearly a misread of "Reynolds" for "Burnel" by an unknown copyist
Change Date: 16 SEP 2004

Father: William Brightwell
Mother: Sarah Windsor

Marriage 1 Elizabeth Caroline Parker b: ABT 1827 in GA
Children
 Sarah Jane Brightwell b: 30 AUG 1849 in Stewart Co., GA
 Martha A. Brightwell b: ABT 1850
 Mary E. Brightwell b: ABT 1853
 Missouri E. Brightwell b: MAY 1854 in AL
 Matilda C. Brightwell b: ABT 1857
 Hilery Albert Brightwell b: ABT 1859
 James H. Brightwell b: 1861 in Butler Co., AL

More About ELIZABETH CAROLINE PARKER:
Burial: Sawyer Cemetery, Sandy Ridge, Alabama
Census: 1900, 73 yrs old in home of son James H. Brightwell in 1900 Cen Alabama/Crenshaw Co.

More About LEN BRIGHTWELL and ELIZABETH PARKER:
Marriage: 13 Sep 1846, Md Stewart Co., Ga. Box Ankel Dist/Now Richland Co. Ga.

Children of LEN BRIGHTWELL and ELIZABETH PARKER are:

35.   i.   SARAH JANE⁶ BRIGHTWELL, b. 30 Aug 1849, [tombstone shows 8/31/1849]born Crenshaw, Ala; d. Moved w/fam to Stewart Co. Ga. [Cherry Lake area].

    ii.   MARTHA A. BRIGHTWELL, b. 1851; m. D. S. ELLIS, 1874, Marriage Crenshaw Co. Alabama.

> Notes for MARTHA A. BRIGHTWELL:
> Martha BRIGHTWELL
> BIRTH: 10 JUN 1795 [S6] [S66]
> DEATH: 16 MAY 1868, Prince Edward Co. Virginia [S6] [S66]
> Family 1: Henry Y. JENKINS
> MARRIAGE: 15 JAN 1818
> Mary E. JENKINS
> Sarah Ann JENKINS
> James JENKINS
> Henry B. JENKINS
> Martha F.(Patsy) JENKINS
> Abraham (Louis) JENKINS
> Jane W. JENKINS
> Benjamin JENKINS
>
> More About D. ELLIS and MARTHA BRIGHTWELL:
> Marriage: 1874, Marriage Crenshaw Co. Alabama

    iii.   MARY ELIZABETH BRIGHTWELL, b. 1853.

36.   iv.   MISSOURI ELIZABETH BRIGHTWELL, b. May 1854, born Alabama/F/age 25 Farm Laborer in Sandy Ridge,Lowdes Co. AL; d. Born in Alabama.

    v.   MATILDA C. "CALLIE" BRIGHTWELL, b. 1857; m. POUNCEY.

37.   vi.   HILLARY 'HILEY' [BURT] ALBERTUS BRIGHTWELL, b. 1859, Born Ala single in 1880 Census/male/white Farming; d. Liv in Montgomery AL,Crenshaw Co. AL 1910.

38.   vii.   JAMES "JIMMIE" HILERY (SR) BRIGHTWELL, b. 18 Jul 1861, Butler Co. Ala.18 yrs old/1880 Cen. Sandy Ridge, Lowndes Co.,Ala.; d. 09 Sep 1938, Crenshaw Co., Alabama/Magnolia Cemetery.

Generation No. 6

23. JULIA ANN⁶ BRIGHTWELL (*BARNETT U.⁵, CHARLES (SR)⁴, REYNOLDS³, REYNOLDS OR RANDALL², THE BRIGHTWELL FAMILY¹ HISTORY*) was born 1813, and died Aft. 1880. She married MERCER BRIGHTWELL 15 Dec 1834 in Marriage Prince Edward Co. Virginia, son of WILLIAM BRIGHTWELL and NANCY BRIGHTWELL. He was born 1813 in Prince Edward Co. VA.

Notes for MERCER BRIGHTWELL:
JULIA ANN BRIGHTWELL (JUDITH W.7, REUBAN BAKER6, JOHN5, JOHN4, JOHN3, JOHN2, JOHN1) was born 1813, and died Aft. 1880. She married MERCER BRIGHTWELL 15 Dec 1834 in Prince Edward County, Virginia, son of WILLIAM BRIGHTWELL. He was born Abt. 1813 in Prince Edward County, Virginia.

Children of JULIA BRIGHTWELL and MERCER BRIGHTWELL are:

    i. MARCELLA V. BRIGHTWELL, b. 1838.
    ii. LUCY A. BRIGHTWELL, b. 1842.
    iii. ZACHARIAD TAYLOR BRIGHTWELL, b. 1847.
    iv. WILLIAM B. BRIGHTWELL, b. 1851.
    v. MARTHA JANE BRIGHTWELL, b. 26 Nov 1853.

More About MERCER BRIGHTWELL and JULIA BRIGHTWELL:
Marriage: 15 Dec 1834, Marriage Prince Edward Co. Virginia

Children of JULIA BRIGHTWELL and MERCER BRIGHTWELL are:
  i.   MARCELLA V.[7] BRIGHTWELL, b. 1838, Prince Ed. Co. Virginia.
  ii. LUCY A. BRIGHTWELL, b. 1842, Prince Ed. Co Virginia.
  iii. ZACHARIAH TAYLOR BRIGHTWELL, b. 1847, Prince Ed. Co Virginia.
  iv. WILLIAM B. BRIGHTWELL, b. 1851, Prince Ed. Co Virginia.
  v.   MARTHA JANE BRIGHTWELL, b. 26 Nov 1853, Prince Ed. Co Virginia.

24. ELIZA JANE[6] BRIGHTWELL *(BARNETT U.[5], CHARLES (SR)[4], REYNOLDS[3], REYNOLDS OR RANDALL[2], THE BRIGHTWELL FAMILY[1] HISTORY)* was born 13 Oct 1816 in Buckingham CO. Virginia, and died 1888. She married JOSEPH H. GLENN in Married. He was born Abt. 1821 in Prince Edward Co. Virginia.

Notes for ELIZA JANE BRIGHTWELL:

More About JOSEPH GLENN and ELIZA BRIGHTWELL:
Marriage: Married

Children of ELIZA BRIGHTWELL and JOSEPH GLENN are:
  i.   PATTY B.[7] GLENN, b. 1845.
  ii. JUDY A. GLENN, b. 1847.

25. MERCER[6] BRIGHTWELL *(WILLIAM B. (JR)[5], CHARLES (SR)[4], REYNOLDS[3], REYNOLDS OR RANDALL[2], THE BRIGHTWELL FAMILY[1] HISTORY)* was born 1813 in Prince Edward Co. VA. He married JULIA ANN BRIGHTWELL 15 Dec 1834 in Marriage Prince Edward Co. Virginia, daughter of BARNETT BRIGHTWELL and JUDITH BOATWRIGHT. She was born 1813, and died Aft. 1880.

Notes for MERCER BRIGHTWELL:
JULIA ANN BRIGHTWELL (JUDITH W.7, REUBAN BAKER6, JOHN5, JOHN4, JOHN3, JOHN2, JOHN1) was born 1813, and died Aft. 1880. She married MERCER BRIGHTWELL 15 Dec 1834 in Prince Edward County, Virginia, son of WILLIAM BRIGHTWELL. He was born Abt. 1813 in Prince Edward County, Virginia.

Children of JULIA BRIGHTWELL and MERCER BRIGHTWELL are:

  i.   MARCELLA V. BRIGHTWELL, b. 1838.
  ii. LUCY A. BRIGHTWELL, b. 1842.
  iii. ZACHARIAD TAYLOR BRIGHTWELL, b. 1847.
  iv. WILLIAM B. BRIGHTWELL, b. 1851.
  v.   MARTHA JANE BRIGHTWELL, b. 26 Nov 1853.

More About MERCER BRIGHTWELL and JULIA BRIGHTWELL:
Marriage: 15 Dec 1834, Marriage Prince Edward Co. Virginia

Children are listed above under (23) Julia Ann Brightwell.

26. WILLIAM B.[6] BRIGHTWELL *(JOHN M.[5], BARNETT (SR)[4], REYNOLDS[3], REYNOLDS OR RANDALL[2], THE BRIGHTWELL FAMILY[1] HISTORY)* was born 1818 in born in Virginia Oglethorpe Co. Georgia, and died in 1860 census shows 42 yrs VA.. He married ELIZABETH CLOTILDA WILKINS, daughter of MATT WILKINS and MARTHA W.. She was born 1818 in born GA.

Notes for WILLIAM B. BRIGHTWELL:
Brightwell, John M 45 GA
, Elizabeth 45 GA

, Naomi 22 GA
, George 21 GA
, Joe 20 GA
, James 18 Ga
, Emily 15 GA
, John 14 GA
, Sarah 12 Ga
, Ella 8 GA
, Evie 5 GA
, Mamie 3 GA
NOTE: son of John Brightwell & Frances H Glenn, married Elizabeth Patrick (b.1825-living 1900)

I noticed that in Ogelthorpe Ga the person who was the assistant Marshall who signed the census sheets at the top is William B. Brightwell.

ID: I2806
Name: William B. BRIGHTWELL
Sex: M
Will: Montgomery, AL
Note: Left 17 slaves who took the Brightwell name confusing reacher even more they took the same first names.
Birth: ABT 1815 in SC
Event: Moved to another state ABT 1875 Montgomery, AL
Birth: 18 OCT 1817 in Va.
Death: 11 JUL 1892
Burial: 1892 Wm B Brightwell family Cem., Oglethrope Co., GA
Note: Keith Moody-E-Mail- 13 Dec. 1999
Event: Built fertillizer Mill 1874 Maxeys, Oglethrope Co., GA
Event: Lived in ABT 1837 Maxeys, Oglethrope Co., GA
Event: Admin. of Will of 13 AUG 1853 Augustine Slaughter, Greene Co., GA
Note: Augustine Slaughter, late of Alabama..."
Event: Legal notice 13 AUG 1853 Greensboro Herald
Event: Legal notice 8 OCT 1853 Greensboro Herald
Note: Estate sale of A. Slaughter.
Event: Legal notice 19 NOV 1853 Greensboro Herald
Note: Estae sale of A.Slaughter
Event: Subscription to Banner 17 MAR 1855 Greene Co., GA
Event: Legal notice 17 MAR 1855 Greensboro Herald
Event: Estate of Burdett Finch 15 DEC 1855 Greene Co., GA
Event: Legal notice 15 DEC 1855 Greensboro Herald
Event: Legal notice 10 NOV 1870 Greensboro Herald
Note: 285 acres...levied on as property of SSNickelson, to satisfy executions...in favor of W.H.Brimberry and
W.B.Brightwell..."
RELA: Natural
RELA: Natural
Note:

William B. Brightwell was the first member of the Brightwell family to settle in Maxeys Georgia and was one of the
first settlers on the land that originally belonged to Jesse Maxey.
During the gold boom of the 1870s William invested heavily in themines in Oglethorpe Co. but not enough gold
was found to justify the money invested.

The Story of Oglethorpe County by Lena Smith Wise(Mastser's Thesis for MA in Practical Education-

1953)
pub by the Historic Oglethorpe County, Inc. 1980

Father: John BRIGHTWELL b: ABT 1784 in Prince Edward Co., Virginia
Mother: Frances H. GLENN b: ABT 1790 in Va.

Marriage 1 Elizabeth Clotilda BELL b: 16 NOV 1817

Married: 15 OCT 1839 in Clarke Co., Ga.
Note: Keith Moody-E-Mail- 13 Dec. 1999
Event: None

Children

1. Jasper Harrison BRIGHTWELL b: 7 DEC 1840
2. Augustine Thomas BRIGHTWELL b: 15 APR 1843
3. Martha W. BRIGHTWELL b: 1845
4. Anna E. BRIGHTWELL b: 1847
5. Eveline B. BRIGHTWELL b: JAN 1850
6. William W. BRIGHTWELL b: NOV 1853 in GA.
7. Sarah Evie BRIGHTWELL b: 1 DEC 1855

Children of WILLIAM BRIGHTWELL and ELIZABETH WILKINS are:
  i.   AUGUSTUS T.[7] BRIGHTWELL, b. 1843, born in Georgia; m. HELEN MEDORA FLEMING; b. 1851, born in GA..
  ii.   JASPER H. BRIGHTWELL, b. 1841, born Ga.
  iii.   EVA B. BRIGHTWELL, b. 1850.
  iv.   WILLIAM W. BRIGHTWELL, b. 1854.

27. JOHN[6] BRIGHTWELL (*JOHN M.*[5], *BARNETT (SR)*[4], *REYNOLDS*[3], *REYNOLDS OR RANDALL*[2], *THE BRIGHTWELL FAMILY*[1] *HISTORY)* was born 1825 in READ his notes, and died in 36 yrs old 1870 Ga Census. He married ELIZABETH PATRICK. She was born 1825.

Notes for JOHN BRIGHTWELL:
Brightwell, John M 45 GA
, Elizabeth 45 GA
, Naomi 22 GA
, George 21 GA
, Joe 20 GA
, James 18 Ga
, Emily 15 GA
, John 14 GA
, Sarah 12 Ga
, Ella 8 GA
, Evie 5 GA
, Mamie 3 GA
NOTE: son of John Brightwell & Frances H Glenn, married Elizabeth Patrick (b.1825-living 1900)

Children of JOHN BRIGHTWELL and ELIZABETH PATRICK are:
  i.   GEORGE[7] BRIGHTWELL, b. 1849.
  ii.   JOSIAH "JOE" BRIGHTWELL, b. 1850.

iii. JAMES BRIGHTWELL, b. 1852.
iv. EMILY BRIGHTWELL, b. 1855.
v. JOHN BRIGHTWELL, b. 1856.
vi. SARAH BRIGHTWELL, b. 1858.
vii. ELLA BRIGHTWELL, b. 1868.
viii. EVIE BRIGHTWELL, b. 1865.
ix. MAMIE BRIGHTWELL, b. 1867.
x. NAOMI BRIGHTWELL, b. 1845.

28. GEORGE[6] BRIGHTWELL *(WILLIAM BARNETT[5], SAMUEL[4], REYNOLDS[3], REYNOLDS OR RANDALL[2], THE BRIGHTWELL FAMILY[1] HISTORY)* was born 1839 in born in GA. in other records he is called "Charles"???, and died in Was George middle name or census error????. He married MARGARET. She was born 1843.

Children of GEORGE BRIGHTWELL and MARGARET are:
    i. WILLIAM[7] BRIGHTWELL, b. 1863.
    ii. REUBIN BRIGHTWELL, b. 1866.

29. JOHN A.[6] MITCHELL *(NANCY[5] BRIGHTWELL, WILLIAM[4], REYNOLDS[3], REYNOLDS OR RANDALL[2], THE BRIGHTWELL FAMILY[1] HISTORY)* was born 1835 in Liv 1850.

Children of JOHN A. MITCHELL are:
    i. WILLIAM HENRY[7] MITCHEL.
    ii. JOHN MITCHELL.

30. WILLIAM[6] BRIGHTWELL *(JOHN JACKSON[5], WILLIAM[4], REYNOLDS[3], REYNOLDS OR RANDALL[2], THE BRIGHTWELL FAMILY[1] HISTORY)* was born 1842 in born in Georgia. Read ALL HIS NOTES. of Terrell Co. Ga., and died in Census 1860-1870 Webster Co. Ga.; 1880 Terrell Co. Ga.. He married MARY J. ELIZABETH WINSON in Married Terrrell Co. Ga.. She was born 1844 in Her name on James T. Brightwell's Death Certificate..

Notes for WILLIAM BRIGHTWELL:
Children of William Brightwell (1832-1881) & Mary _____ (b.18__-living 1880); grandchildren of John Jackson Brightwell & Sarah (Winzer?)
Census: 1860-1870 Webster Co GA; 1880 Terrell Co GA

1)Sarah E Brightwell (b.Dec 1855GA-living 1910 Mitchell Co GA--dead by 1925) md 1878 Terrell Co GA to Eugene D Bolton (b.Jan 1856-living 1910)--No children.
2)John L Brightwell (b.Jan 1860-living 1900 Terrell Co GA--dead by 1925)) md 1886 Terrell Co GA to Elizabeth "Lizzie" Brightwell (b.1864-d.pre.1900), dau of William Brightwell (1815-1884)
3)James T Brightwell (b.1865GA-d.1925FL) md 14 Dec 1890 Terrell Co GA to Lela Stokes. Buried Moultrie, Colquitt Co GA
4)W L Alac Brightwell (b.abt.1867-living 1880)
5)Susie F Brightwell (b.Sep 1871-living 1925 Terrell Co GA) md 1885 Terrell Co GA to John F Leverette (b.Sep 1859-liv 1900)
6)George W Brightwell (b.abt.1874-living 1925 Atlanta GA)
7)Richard Edward Brightwell (b.1877-living 1925 Atlanta GA) md 28 May 1899 Terrell Co GA to Ellen Clements (b.1876-living 1910)
8)Eugene Linwood Brightwell (b.1880GA-d.1944 Hillsborough Co FL) md Dora Lastinger (b.18__-d.1980FL)

More About WILLIAM BRIGHTWELL and MARY WINSON:
Marriage: Married Terrrell Co. Ga.

Children of WILLIAM BRIGHTWELL and MARY WINSON are:

i. SARAH A. E.[7] BRIGHTWELL, b. Dec 1855, Born GA. liv 1910 Mitchell Co. Ga.; d. dead by 1925; m. EUGENE D. BOLTON, 1878, Married Terrell Co. Ga. NO CHILDREN.; b. Jan 1856, Liv in 1910.

More About EUGENE BOLTON and SARAH BRIGHTWELL:
Marriage: 1878, Married Terrell Co. Ga. NO CHILDREN.

ii. JOHNNY L. BRIGHTWELL, b. Jan 1860, Liv in 1900 Census son of William Brightwell (1832); d. Married his first cousin. dead by 1925; m. ELIZABETH "LIZZIE" BRIGHTWELL, 1886, Married Terrell Co Ga. lst Cousin,; b. 1864; d. Bet. 1887 - 1900.

More About JOHNNY BRIGHTWELL and ELIZABETH BRIGHTWELL:
Marriage: 1886, Married Terrell Co Ga. lst Cousin,

iii. JAMES T. BRIGHTWELL, b. 25 Mar 1866, Born GA. liv 1910 Mitchell Co. Ga. Farmer; d. 20 Aug 1925, Hillsboro Co. Fla. Buried Moultire Colquitt Co. Ga.; m. LELA STOKES, 14 Dec 1890, Terrell Co. Ga. Wife signed husb. death certificate..

More About JAMES T. BRIGHTWELL:
Burial: Moultrie Georgia cemetery. died suddenly Bright's Disease

More About JAMES BRIGHTWELL and LELA STOKES:
Marriage: 14 Dec 1890, Terrell Co. Ga. Wife signed husb. death certificate.

iv. W. L. ALAC BRIGHTWELL, b. 1865, Liv in 1880 census; d. 1870 Ga. census states him as 3 years old..
v. SUSIE F. BRIGHTWELL, b. Sep 1871, Liv in 1925 Terrell Co. Ga. Census; m. JOHN F. LEVERETTE, 1885, Terrell Co. Ga.; b. Sep 1859, Liv in 1900.

More About JOHN LEVERETTE and SUSIE BRIGHTWELL:
Marriage: 1885, Terrell Co. Ga.

vi. GEORGE W. BRIGHTWELL, b. Abt. 1874, Liv in 1925 Atlanta Georgia Fulton Co.; m. ORA ELLA VICKERS, 19 Nov 1901, Married Mitchell Co. Georgia.; b. of Colquitt County, Georgia.

More About GEORGE BRIGHTWELL and ORA VICKERS:
Marriage: 19 Nov 1901, Married Mitchell Co. Georgia.

vii. RICHARD EDWARD BRIGHTWELL, b. 1877, Liv in 1925 Atlanta Fulto Co. Georgia; m. ELLEN CLEMENTS, 28 May 1899, Terrell Co. Ga.; b. 1876, Liv in 1910.

More About RICHARD BRIGHTWELL and ELLEN CLEMENTS:
Marriage: 28 May 1899, Terrell Co. Ga.

viii. EUGENE LINWOOD BRIGHTWELL, b. 1880, Born in Georgia; d. 1944, Died Hillsborough Co. Florida; m. DORA LASTINGER; b. Born 18__(?); d. 1980, Died in Florida..

39. ix. WILLIE CLYNTON BRIGHTWELL, b. 09 Apr 1900, Death Cert shows his age, birth, death. "FatherJames Brightwell"; d. 27 Dec 1958, Osceola Co. Kissimmee, FLA, 58 yrs "Add. Boggy Creek Rd.".

31. MARY MISSOURI[6] BRIGHTWELL *(JOHN JACKSON[5], WILLIAM[4], REYNOLDS[3], REYNOLDS OR RANDALL[2], THE BRIGHTWELL FAMILY[1] HISTORY)* was born 1846 in Liv in 1860 Census.. She married J. FRANCIS MCCLENDON 1853 in Stewart Co. Ga.. He was born 1842 in Liv in 1860 Census.

More About J. MCCLENDON and MARY BRIGHTWELL:
Marriage: 1853, Stewart Co. Ga.

Child of MARY BRIGHTWELL and J. MCCLENDON is:
40. i. FALBY[7] MCCLENDON.

32. ANDREW JACKSON[6] BRIGHTWELL *(JOHN JACKSON[5], WILLIAM[4], REYNOLDS[3], REYNOLDS OR RANDALL[2],*

THE BRIGHTWELL FAMILY[1] HISTORY) was born 1848 in born Georgia/Andrew found on Orphans List., and died 1924 in 22 yrs ld in 1870 Census Georgia.. He married (1) BARBARA ANN. She was born 1848 in Living in 1920 Census.. He married (2) CYNTHIA PATMAN. She was born in his 1st wife..

Notes for ANDREW JACKSON BRIGHTWELL:
p.414
Brightwell, William 28 GA
, Mary J 30 GA
, Sarah 15 GA
, Johnny 10 GA
, James 4 GA
, W L 3 GA
NOTE: William Brightwell (1832-1881), son of John Jackson Brightwell & Sarah (Winzer?)

Children of ANDREW BRIGHTWELL and BARBARA ANN are:
  i. WILLIAM JACKSON[7] BRIGHTWELL, b. 1870, of Blakly Georgia.; d. 1948, 6 months old in 1870 census of Georgia.; m. EMMA JORDAN.
  ii. ELENTUDE BRIGHTWELL, b. 1869, born in Georgia; d. 1 year old in 1870 Census.

Child of ANDREW BRIGHTWELL and CYNTHIA PATMAN is:
  iii. MARY[7] BRIGHTWELL, b. 1837, born GA; m. WILLIAM PATMAN, Married.

        More About WILLIAM PATMAN and MARY BRIGHTWELL:
        Marriage: Married

33. MARY J.[6] BRIGHTWELL *(WILLIAM THOMAS[5], WILLIAM[4], REYNOLDS[3], REYNOLDS OR RANDALL[2], THE BRIGHTWELL FAMILY[1] HISTORY)* was born 1849 in born S. Carolina shown age 48 in 1870 Ga Census, and died in Liv in 1880 census -unmarried as of 1880.

More About MARY J. BRIGHTWELL:
Burial: Webster Co. Georgia

Child of MARY J. BRIGHTWELL is:
  i. JOHN F.[7] BRIGHTWELL, b. 1849, Webster Co. Ga..

34. WILLIAM H.[6] BRIGHTWELL *(WILLIAM THOMAS[5], WILLIAM[4], REYNOLDS[3], REYNOLDS OR RANDALL[2], THE BRIGHTWELL FAMILY[1] HISTORY)* was born 1856 in Liv in 1886 Census- Born Mississippi, and died in 1880 Census of Precinct 4, Bell, Texas. He married NANNIE CAIN 14 Sep 1886 in Married Terrell Co. Ga.. She was born 1858 in Born in Alabama.

More About WILLIAM BRIGHTWELL and NANNIE CAIN:
Marriage: 14 Sep 1886, Married Terrell Co. Ga.

Child of WILLIAM BRIGHTWELL and NANNIE CAIN is:
  i. FANNEY[7] BRIGHTWELL, b. 1878.

35. SARAH JANE[6] BRIGHTWELL *(LEN REYNOLDS[5], WILLIAM[4], REYNOLDS[3], REYNOLDS OR RANDALL[2], THE BRIGHTWELL FAMILY[1] HISTORY)* was born 30 Aug 1849 in [tombstone shows 8/31/1849]born Crenshaw, Ala, and died in Moved w/fam to Stewart Co. Ga. [Cherry Lake area]. She married JOHN WESLEY KISER 25 Nov 1875 in Crenshaw Co. Alabama. He was born 30 Sep 1853 in Crenshaw Co. Ala, and died 10 Mar 1937 in Madison Co. FL/Pine Grove Cemetery.

Notes for SARAH JANE BRIGHTWELL:
hSara Jane Brightwell 1st. Child of L.R. and Caroline Parker Brightwell can be found on 1850 Census of Stewart Co. Ga.age 1 yr. of age. Most likely Sara Jane Brightwell was born in Stewart Co. Ga., as her Parents were married there.

ID: I12
Name: Sarah Jane Brightwell
Sex: F
Birth: 30 AUG 1849 in Stewart Co., GA
Note: tombstone shows 8-31-1849
Death: 18 JUN 1923 in Madison, Madison Co., FL
Burial: Pine Grove Cemetery, Madison Co., FL
Note: 1880 census: Name: Sarah KISOR Age: 30 Estimated birth year: <1850> Birthplace: Alabama Relation: Wife Home in 1880: Madison, Madison, Florida Occupation: Keeping House Marital status: Married Race: White Gender: Female Head of household: John KISOR Father's birthplace: AL Mother's birthplace: AL 1900 census lists her as 50 yr old wife of John Kiser, Macedonia, Madison Co., FL 1910 census lists her as 60 yr old wife of John Kiser Florida MADISON Co., CHERRY LAKE Series: T624 Roll: 164 Page: 220 1920 census lists her as 70 yr old wife of John W. Kiser.
Change Date: 22 APR 2004

Father: L. (Len) Reynolds Brightwell b: 1825 in Barnwell, SC
Mother: Elizabeth Caroline Parker

Marriage 1 John Wesley Kiser b: 30 SEP 1853 in Crenshaw Co., AL
Married: 25 NOV 1875 in Crenshaw Co., AL
Children
 Andrew Bevley Kiser b: 9 SEP 1876 in FL
 Leola Kiser b: ABT 1879 in FL
 John Edward Kiser b: 6 APR 1883
 Mamie R. Kiser b: JUN 1887 in FL
 Eugene Pasco Kiser Sr. b: 10 SEP 1890 in Madison, Madison Co., FL

More About SARAH JANE BRIGHTWELL:
Burial: 18 Jun 1923, Madison Co; FL Pine Grove Cemetery

Notes for JOHN WESLEY KISER:
ID: I11
Name: John Wesley Kiser
Sex: M
Birth: 30 SEP 1853 in Crenshaw Co., AL
Death: 10 MAR 1937 in Madison, Madison Co., FL
Burial: Pine Grove Cemetery, Madison Co., FL
Note: Dad remembers that he had a mustache and liked to eat corn bread, beans and pot liquor. He ran a grist mill @ Chair Lake, FL. 1880 census: Name: John KISOR Age: 26 Estimated birth year: <1854> Birthplace: Alabama Relation: Self Home in 1880: Madison, Madison, Florida Occupation: Farm Laborer Marital status: Married Race: White Gender: Male Head of household: John KISOR Father's birthplace: AL Mother's birthplace: AL 1900 census lists him in Macedonia, Madison Co., FL 1910 census: JOHN W 57 M W AL FL MADISON CHERRY LAKE 1920 Census: Kiser, John W Age: 65 Year: 1920 Birthplace: Alabama Roll: T625_225 Race: White Page: 12A State: Florida ED: 111 County: Madison Image: 540 Township: Pinetta 1930 census: Kiser, W Age: 75 Year: 1930 Birthplace: Alabama Roll: T626_324 Race: White Page: 1A State: Florida ED: 12 County: Madison Image: 0542 Township: Pinetta Relationship: Head Florida Death Index, 1937 Name: John Westley Kiser Place of Death: Madison Gender: M Race: W Volume: 752 Certificate: 6354 Death Date: 1937
Change Date: 22 APR 2004

Father: William Kiser b: in AL
Mother: Nancy Yon b: in AL

Marriage 1 Sarah Jane Brightwell b: 30 AUG 1849 in Stewart Co., GA
Married: 25 NOV 1875 in Crenshaw Co., AL
Children
 Andrew Bevley Kiser b: 9 SEP 1876 in FL
 Leola Kiser b: ABT 1879 in FL
 John Edward Kiser b: 6 APR 1883
 Mamie R. Kiser b: JUN 1887 in FL
 Eugene Pasco Kiser Sr. b: 10 SEP 1890 in Madison, Madison Co., FL

More About JOHN KISER and SARAH BRIGHTWELL:
Marriage: 25 Nov 1875, Crenshaw Co. Alabama

Children of SARAH BRIGHTWELL and JOHN KISER are:
        i.   ANDREW BEVLEY[7] KISER, b. 09 Sep 1876, born Florida.
        ii.   LEOLA KISER, b. Abt. 1879, bn FL.
        iii. JOHN EDWARD KISER, b. 06 Apr 1883.
        iv. MAMIE R. KISER, b. Jun 1887.
41.   v.   EUGENE PASCO (SR) KISER, b. 10 Sep 1890, born Madison,Madison Co. FL; d. 23 Jul 1937, Pine Grove Cem Madison Florida.

36. MISSOURI ELIZABETH[6] BRIGHTWELL *(LEN REYNOLDS[5], WILLIAM[4], REYNOLDS[3], REYNOLDS OR RANDALL[2], THE BRIGHTWELL FAMILY[1] HISTORY)* was born May 1854 in born Alabama/F/age 25 Farm Laborer in Sandy Ridge,Lowdes Co. AL, and died in Born in Alabama. She married JOHN J. BETTERTON 01 Dec 1881 in Lowndes Co. Alabama, son of EPHRAIM BETTERTON and MARTHA BRIGHTWELL. He was born Oct 1853 in Born in Rose Hill, Covington, Alabama, and died in Alabama Covington Co..

Notes for MISSOURI ELIZABETH BRIGHTWELL:
ID: I527
Name: Missouri E. Brightwell
Sex: F
Birth: MAY 1854 in AL
Note: 1860 census: Name: M E Brightwell Age in 1860: 5 Home in 1860: Precinct 15, Butler, Alabama Gender: Female Value of real estate: View image Post Office: Leon and Rainsville Roll: M653_3 Page: 7 Year: 1860 Head of Household: L R Brightwell ---------------- 1870 census: Name: Missouri Brightwell Age in 1870: 15 Estimated Birth Year: 1854 Birthplace: Alabama Home in 1870: Township 11, Crenshaw, Alabama Race: White Gender: Female Value of real estate: View Image Post Office: Rutledge Roll: M593_12 Page: 107 Image: 210 Year: 1870 --------------- 1880 census: Name: Mipouri BRIGHTWELL Age: 25 Estimated birth year: <1855> Birthplace: Alabama Occupation: Farm Laborer Relationship to head-of-household: Daughter Home in 1880: Sandy Ridge, Lowndes, Alabama Marital status: Single Race: White Gender: Female Father's birthplace: GA Mother's name: Caroline BRIGHTWELL Mother's birthplace: SC Image Source: Year: 1880; Census Place: Sandy Ridge, Lowndes, Alabama; Roll: T9_21; Family History Film: 1254021; Page: 310C; Enumeration District: 113; Image: 0121.
Change Date: 18 JUL 2005

Father: L. (Len) Reynolds Brightwell b: 1825 in Barnwell, Barnwell Co., SC
Mother: Elizabeth Caroline Parker b: ABT 1827 in GA

Marriage 1 John J. Betterton b: OCT 1853 in Rose Hill, Covington Co., AL
Married: 1 DEC 1881 in Lowndes Co., AL
Children
 Lee Betterton b: FEB 1884 in Lowndes Co., AL
 James Betterton b: OCT 1885 in AL

More About JOHN BETTERTON and MISSOURI BRIGHTWELL:
Marriage: 01 Dec 1881, Lowndes Co. Alabama

Children of MISSOURI BRIGHTWELL and JOHN BETTERTON are:
42.   i.   LEE[7] BETTERTON, b. Feb 1884, Born in Alabama; d. 29 Aug 1963, died in Alabama.
       ii. JAMES 'JIM' BETTERTON, b. Oct 1885, Born in Alabama.

37. HILLARY 'HILEY' [BURT] ALBERTUS[6] BRIGHTWELL *(LEN REYNOLDS[5], WILLIAM[4], REYNOLDS[3], REYNOLDS OR RANDALL[2], THE BRIGHTWELL FAMILY[1] HISTORY)* was born 1859 in Born Ala single in 1880 Census/male/white Farming, and died in Liv in Montgomery AL,Crenshaw Co. AL 1910. He married SALLY (SARAH) BEDGOOD 28 Sep 1882 in Crenshaw Co. Alabama, daughter of SAMUEL BEDGOOD and SOPHRONIA NIX. She was born Apr 1860, and died in both Buried at Providence Cemetery-No headstones..

Notes for HILLARY 'HILEY' [BURT] ALBERTUS BRIGHTWELL:
1870 Crenshaw Co. Census Records, Township-Eleven Family #4:
Bright, Caroline.....42.....wf.....GA
Sarah........20.....wf.....GA
Martha.......19.....wf.....GA
Mary.........17.....wf.....AL
Missouri.....15.....wf.....AL
Matilda......13.....wf.....AL
Albert.......11.....wm.....AL
James........08.....wm.....AL

_____

1890 Tax List of Crenshaw County, Alabama
Beat 1...James Brightwell
Beat 1...Burt (Albert?) Brightwell
The land was in Beat 1 but the exact details
were not given, you might find them on BLM.

_____

Crenshaw County Alabama Marriage, Vol. 1
Pg 55:
Brightwell, M.A...m. D.S. Ellis.....18 Oct 1874 bk B pg 208

" M.C...m. W.L. Pouncey...17 Jan 1874 bk B pg 141

" M.E...m. W.L. Pouncey...16 Dec 1874 bk B pg 136
" Sarah Jane...m. John W.Kiser...04 Nov 1875 bk B pg 174
Pg 5:
Brightwell, H.A..m. Sallie Bedgood..28 Sep 1882 bk C pg 36

_____

There is mention of a Sheriff Theodore Brightwell in Washington Co. AL in the book, "The History of Alabama"
by Pickens. The time period would be Feb 18, 1807. It was in connection with Aaron Burr.

HILLARY ALBERTUS BRIGHTWELL.Last known to live south of Montgomery AL. in CRENSHAW CO. AL. YR.1910. wife SALLIE. children CLEVELAND,ETHEL, CLIFTON and JANE.

Hilery Albert BRIGHTWELL
" ID: I266
" Name: L. (Len) Reynolds Brightwell
" Sex: M

" Birth: 1825 in Barnwell, SC
" Death: MAY 1863 in Covington Co., AL
" Note: 1850 US Census: Brightwell, Reynolds (links to incorrect image) State: Georgia Year: 1850
County: Stewart Roll: M432_82 Township: Box Ankle District Page: 63 Image: 128 died as result of the
Civil War.Co c Ala. 37th.

ID: I515
Name: Hilery or Hillary Albert Brightwell
Sex: M
Birth: ABT 1859
Note: 1860 census: Name: H A Brightwell Age in 1860: 1 Home in 1860: Precinct 15, Butler, Alabama
Gender: Male Value of real estate: View image Post Office: Leon and Rainsville Roll: M653_3 Page: 7
Year: 1860 Head of Household: L R Brightwell ------------------- 1880 census: Name: Hilery A.
BRIGHTWELL Age: 21 Estimated birth year: <1859> Birthplace: Alabama Occupation: Farming
Relationship to head-of-household: Son Home in 1880: Sandy Ridge, Lowndes, Alabama Marital status:
Single Race: White Gender: Male Father's birthplace: GA Mother's name: Caroline BRIGHTWELL
Mother's birthplace: SC Image Source: Year: 1880; Census Place: Sandy Ridge, Lowndes, Alabama; Roll:
T9_21; Family History Film: 1254021; Page: 310C; Enumeration District: 113; Image: 0121. ----------------
1900 census: BRIGHTWELL, HILLARY A (1900 U.S. Census) ALABAMA , CRENSHAW, SURLES
Age: 41, Male, Race: WHITE, Born: AL Series: T623 Roll: 11 Page: 8
Change Date: 6 APR 2006

Father: L. (Len) Reynolds Brightwell b: 1825 in Barnwell, Barnwell Co., SC
Mother: Elizabeth Caroline Parker b: ABT 1827 in GA

Marriage 1 Sally or Sallie or Sarah Bedgood b: APR 1860 in AL
Married: 28 SEP 1882 in Crenshaw Co., AL
Note: Crenshaw County Alabama Marriage, Vol. 1 Pg 55: Brightwell, M.A...m. D.S. Ellis.....18 Oct 1874
bk B pg 208 " M.C...m. W.L. Pouncey...17 Jan 1874 bk B pg 141 " M.E...m. W.L. Pouncey...16 Dec 1874
bk B pg 136 " Sarah Jane...m. John W.Kiser...04 Nov 1875 bk B pg 174 Pg 5: Brightwell, H.A..m. Sallie
Bedgood..28 Sep 1882 bk C pg 36
Children
 James Cleveland Brightwell b: 19 SEP 1884 in AL
 Ethel Brightwell b: DEC 1886 in AL
 Clifton Brightwell b: JAN 1888 in AL
 Ione Brightwell b: JUL 1891 in AL

More About HILLARY BRIGHTWELL and SALLY BEDGOOD:
Marriage: 28 Sep 1882, Crenshaw Co. Alabama

Children of HILLARY BRIGHTWELL and SALLY BEDGOOD are:
        i.   JAMES CLEVELAND "BRO. DOC"[7] BRIGHTWELL, b. 19 Sep 1884, born in Alabama.
43.   ii. MARY ETHEL BRIGHTWELL, b. Dec 1886, born in Alabama; d. 99 yrs death [Big Sister]Buried in
              Cem.bet Henderson-Troy, ALA..
44.   iii. CLIFTON F. BRIGHTWELL, b. Jan 1888, born in Alabama.
       iv. JANE BRIGHTWELL, b. Bet. 1888 - 1891, born Alabama.
45.   v. LILLIAN IONE "BIG MOMMA" BRIGHTWELL, b. Jul 1891, born in Alabama; d. 21 Feb 1964,
              Providence Cem. Ch./Glenwood,Ala..

38. JAMES "JIMMIE" HILERY (SR)[6] BRIGHTWELL *(LEN REYNOLDS[5], WILLIAM[4], REYNOLDS[3], REYNOLDS OR
RANDALL[2], THE BRIGHTWELL FAMILY[1] HISTORY)* was born 18 Jul 1861 in Butler Co. Ala.18 yrs
old/1880 Cen. Sandy Ridge, Lowndes Co.,Ala., and died 09 Sep 1938 in Crenshaw Co., Alabama/Magnolia
Cemetery. He married (1) MARY E. "LIZZIE" STEPHENS BRAZZELL in Marriage. She died in Buried
w/husb. Magnolia Bapt Ch. Cem. Ala.. He married (2) MARY ELIZABETH (MOLLIE) BEDGOOD 21 Jan 1885
in Lowndes Co., Alabama, daughter of SAMUEL BEDGOOD and SOPHRONIA NIX. She was born 19 Apr

1861 in Lowndes Co. Alabama, and died 04 Oct 1914 in Died-Cancer in Womb./Sawyer Cem.Ala..

Notes for JAMES "JIMMIE" HILERY (SR) BRIGHTWELL:
1870 Census Alabama:
JAMES H. Brightwell of Crenshaw County, Alabama.
He first appears in a 1870 Census in Alabama in Crenshaw Co. Alabama. He is shown as 8 yrs old in the family of his mother-Caroline Brightwell who is listed as head of household at 42 years of age.

1900 Census Alabama:
James H. Brightwell is now shown as Head of Household at age 39 yrs. living in the Crenshaw - Surles Area of Alabama. It also shows that his mother: Caroline born 1827-age 73 years is living in his home. The children listed in 1900 are: James July 1890; Arthur Feb 1892; Robert E. Nov. 1893; Ira July 1897 son; and Ila July 1897 Daug.
James's daughter Sarah was not living in his home anymore-she died 1889.
Charles M. Brightwell was not living in the home anymore.-he died 1889.
Estelle Brightwell was not born until after the 1900 census so she would not have been on the record.
Leroy Brightwell would also not have been on the record.

Magnolia Baptist Church History 1907:
In 1907 a small group of Baptist people were meeting at Fomble school house. On Aug. 16,1908, the following members met and agreed to build a church: J.W.Taylor, J.H.BRIGHTWELL, Sr., J.H. Brightwell, Jr., N.E. Brightwell, Arthur Brightwell, Lee Betterton, Sisters Annie Taylor, Mary Brightwell, Martha Betterton (James Sr. sister), Mattie Edwards, Velma Beck, Addie Taylor, Georgia Taylor. JAMES H. BRIGHTWELL's name on deed. You can find the deed at the Crenshaw County Alabama court House Luverne Alabama.You can find the History of the Church at the Greenville Alabama Lib. In research room. I think there may be a copy at the Luverne Lib. It is beleived that two of James H. Brightwell Sr. sons married two Rhodes. James H. Brightwell Jr. married Anna Bell Rhodes and R.E. Brightwell married Lucy Mae Rhodes. It is said that a Methodist Church was there before Magnolia Bapt. Church

Brightwell, Moseleyy & Rhodes, in the book, "Cemeteries Crenshaw County Alabama", by Joyce Morgan English:
Brightwell:
1. A Brightwell with no name given in the Tatum lot
2. J.H. b. Jul 18 1861 d. Sep 09 1938
3. James H. b. Jul 27 1890 d. Dec 07 1972
4. Lucy R. b. Nov 09 1899 d. Aug 07 1981
5. Mary A.H. b. May 08 105 d. No date
6. Moscoe? b. Oct 05 1932 d. Aug 01 1960 AL Sgt US Army
7. R.E. b. Nov 05 1894 d. Nov 17 1838
8. W. James b. Nov 11 1923 d. Oct 04 1951
9. Wallace Lester b. Nov 07 1924 d. Aug 23 1982 Sgt US Army WW II

Moseley:
1. Albert No dates Co. B. 63rd Alabama Inf CSA
2. Lizzie(Sexton) b. Nov 01 1880 d. Nov 23 1961
3. Mattie M. b. Apr 03 1845 d. Mar 27 1903
4. Twin b. Mar 07 1912 d. Mar 10 1912
5. " " " " " " " "
6. William P. b. Jul 23 1913 d. Jul 28 1915
7. William Robert b. May 28 1875 d. Aug 19 1950

Rhodes:
01. Benjamin F. b. May 16 1923 d. Mar 12 1989
02. Emma b. Mar 01 1916 d. Apr 09 1916
03. Ernest b. Apr 13 1892 d. Aug 13 1893
04. Felix b. Aug 16 1901 d. Mar 20 1988

05. G.A. b. Jun 27 1871 d. Aug 17 1968
06. Gladys b. Mar 09 1917 d. Feb 12 1918
07. Horace Woodrow b. Apr 24 1912 d. Nov 26 1979
08. Jesse Albert b. Oct 09 1890 d. Apr 11 1986
09. Joey Dewayne b. Jul 18 1978 d. Oct 31 1978
10. Lucille b. Mar 15 1915 d. May 03 1915
11. Margaret Ann b. Jan 07 1980 d. Mar 03 1980
12. Margaret Jean b. Aug 05 1927 d. Aug 30 1971
13. Mattie B. b. Jul 18 1905 d. Dec 28 1946
14. McAdo b. Feb 04 1920 d. Jan 12 1924
15. Rosco b. Jan 23 1894 d. May 21 1897
16. Ruby [Henley] b. Oct 31 1909 d. unknown [w/o Horace Woodrow Rhodes]
17. Sallie Alene [Baker] b. Jun 08 1909 d. unknown
18. W.J. b. b. Aug 20 1856 d. Dec 29 1830
19. William A. b. Apr 22 1932 d. Jan 30 1986 h/o Jane Manse Rhodes m. Dec 01 1951

Magnolia Cemetery is located 1/2 mile South of the Montgomery County line in Crenshaw Co. on Hwy 97 North. There seems to be more young children's deaths in the Rhodes family than you commonly find in any one family.
I wonder if there might have been a flu epidemic at that time.
ANSWER: by: Bonnie Betterton . I grew up in the country as we called it . Knowing some of the Rhodes family . There was a lot of them and if I am thinking correctly it may have been polio at that time. not sure those .. for all the younger deaths
     The ones I new where Jane Rhodes (Mother) (she could not walk had polio as a child) Mary Gail Rhodes (daughter) Sandy Rhodes (daughter) Marth Jane Rhodes (daughter).

The BRIGHTWELL family first settled in Butler County, Alabama.

On Familysearch.com James H. Brightwell was born in the year 1862 in Alabama. It shows his age as 18 years in the 1880 Census living in Sandy Ridge, Lowndes Co., Alabama and that he was a Farm Laborer, White, Male. It shows that his father was born in Georgia but didn't list who he was. He stated that his mother was Caroline Brightwell and that she was born in South Carolina; however there appears to be a question about this, because on the page of her information, it shows her born in Georgia (?) a discrepancy. It shows her keeping house; and it shows her living in the same household as James H. Brightwell and that she was a widow.
     James H. Brightwell's brother was listed as Hiley A. Brightwell White Male, 21 years old born in Alabama, Farming. Single at the time of the census. His sister is listed as Mipouri Brightwell, dau. Female age 25 born in Ala, Farm Laborer. And she was single in this 1880 Census, Sandy Ridge, Lowndes Co., Alabama.

1910 Census of Alabama:
James H. Brightwell was 48 years old, male, white born Alabama. Living in Crenshaw Co. Alabama in Surles Area. James wife's name was listed as Mary E. age 48 yrs. The children listed wre:
     Jimmie Brightwell son, age 19 born 1881
     Arthur Brightwell son, age 17 born 1893
     Robert E. Brightwell son, age 15 born 1895
     Ila Brightwell Daughter, age 11 born 1899
     Elumie E. Brightwell, Daugh age 7 yrs. born 1903
     Leroy Brightwell, son age 5 years born 1905
Note: some of these birth dates years are errors of the census taker as cemetery and birth records are different in some of the children's cases.

In 1920 Census of ALABMA:

James name is shown as "Jimmie" married to Lizzie at the time. He was 60 yrs old in that census. Lizzie-wife was 38 yrs. His children by first marriage that still lived at home was Arthur S-28 yrs.; Estelle Daugh- 18; Leroy son age 16; Anna D. daugh age 10. Lizzie's children wre Hilery - son 3 yrs.; William A. 2 yrs.son and John son 3 months.

SAWYER CEMETERY, Sandy Ridge, Alabama
Brightwell, Charles M. son of J. H. and M. E. Brightwell; he was born 2-8-1886 and died 6-26-1889.
Brightwell, Ira, born 7-21-1897 died 10-4-1914
Brightwell, Mary E. (wife of James H. Brightwell) born April 19, 1861, died October 4, 1914
Brightwell, Saraha born Oct. 31, 1888 and died Sept. 12, 1889

ID: I531
Name: James H. Brightwell
Sex: M
Birth: 1861 in Butler Co., AL
Death: SEP 1938 in Crenshaw Co., AL
Note: 1870 census: Name: James Brightwell Age in 1870: 8 Estimated Birth Year: 1861 Birthplace: Alabama Home in 1870: Township 11, Crenshaw, Alabama Race: White Gender: Male Value of real estate: View Image Post Office: Rutledge Roll: M593_12 Page: 107 Image: 210 Year: 1870 ----------------
1880 census: Name: James H. BRIGHTWELL Age: 18 Estimated birth year: <1862> Birthplace: Alabama Occupation: Farm Laborer Relationship to head-of-household: Son Home in 1880: Sandy Ridge, Lowndes, Alabama Marital status: NA Race: White Gender: Male Father's birthplace: GA Mother's name: Caroline BRIGHTWELL Mother's birthplace: SC Image Source: Year: 1880; Census Place: Sandy Ridge, Lowndes, Alabama; Roll: T9_21; Family History Film: 1254021; Page: 310C; Enumeration District: 113; Image: 0121. ------------------1900 United States Federal Census Record: Name: James H Brightwell Home in 1900: Surles, Crenshaw, Alabama Age: 38 Estimated birth year: abt 1862 Birthplace: Alabama Race: White Relationship to head-of-house: Head Occupation: Farmer ----------------- Alabama Deaths, 1908-59 Record: Name: James H Brightwell Death Date: Sep 1938 Death County: Crenshaw Volume: 40 Certificate: 19819 Roll: 3
Change Date: 6 APR 2006

Father: L. (Len) Reynolds Brightwell b: 1825 in Barnwell, Barnwell Co., SC
Mother: Elizabeth Caroline Parker b: ABT 1827 in GA

Marriage 1 Mary b: 19 APR 1861 in AL
Children
 Charles M. Brightwell b: 8 FEB 1886 in AL
 Sarah or Sarahe Brightwell b: 31 OCT 1888 in AL
 James Hillery Brightwell b: 27 JUL 1890 in AL
 Arthur Brightwell b: FEB 1892 in AL
 Robert E. Brightwell b: NOV 1893 in AL
 Ira Brightwell b: JUL 1897 in AL
 Ila Brightwell b: JUL 1897 in AL

Marriage 2 Lizzie b: ABT 1882 in AL
Children
 Hilry or Hilery A. Brightwell b: ABT 1917 in AL
 William D. Brightwell b: ABT 1919 in AL
 Living Brightwell

More About JAMES "JIMMIE" HILERY (SR) BRIGHTWELL:
Rersidence: 1880, Sandy Ridge Lowndes Co ALABAMA
Residence: 1910, Surles Crenshaw Co. Alabama

More About JAMES BRIGHTWELL and MARY BRAZZELL:
Marriage: Marriage

Notes for MARY ELIZABETH (MOLLIE) BEDGOOD:
BEDGOOD FAMILY:

Mary (Mollie) Bedgood married James H. Brightwell 21st. Jan. 1885 in Lowndes Co.Al. James H. and Mollie Brightwell lived most of their married life in north Crenshaw Co.Al. near Montgomery and lowndes Co. line.

Here are the bedgoods. [Information provided by Martha Brightwell]
 Samuel died in CW and Saphronia married Wiley Wren.

Saphronia Elizabeth NIX sister to Edward NIX wife of Samuel Bedgood and Wiley Wren. Saphronia's two daughters married brightwells . Mollie (Mary Elizabeth) bedgood married James H. brightwell and Sally (sarah) Bedgood married Hillery Albert Brightwell in Alabama. Edward Nix was born in 1817 Oglethorpe County, Ga. Married Jane Perry , daughter of John Perry on Dec,24, 1839. Jane Perry was born 30 oct.1820, Wake co. NC.Jane died 4 jan.1901 Oaky Streak, Butler co. Alabama and is buried Oaky Streak Methodist Church Cemetary in southeast section of Butler Co.Alabam. (south of Greenville AL. near Crenshaw and Cuvington county line.

More About MARY ELIZABETH (MOLLIE) BEDGOOD:
Burial: Buried at Sawyer Cemetery, Sandy Ridge, Alabama

More About JAMES BRIGHTWELL and MARY BEDGOOD:
Marriage: 21 Jan 1885, Lowndes Co., Alabama

Children of JAMES BRIGHTWELL and MARY BRAZZELL are:
     i. HILERY A.[7] BRIGHTWELL, b. 1917, born Alabama/3 yrs old in 1920 Cen AL; m. FRANCIS WEBB.
     ii. WILLIAM DAVID "JUICE" BRIGHTWELL, b. 1918, born Alabama/2 yrs on 1920 Cen AL; m. MS. JORDAN.
46.   iii. JOHN JOSEPH BRIGHTWELL, b. 1920, 5 months in 1920 Cens./born Alabama - living.

Children of JAMES BRIGHTWELL and MARY BEDGOOD are:
     iv. SARAH[7] BRIGHTWELL, b. 31 Oct 1888, born Alabama; d. 12 Sep 1889, Sandy Ridge Alabama Lowndes Co..

        Notes for SARAH BRIGHTWELL:
        ID: I856
        Name: Sarah or Sarahe Brightwell
        Sex: F
        Birth: 31 OCT 1888 in AL
        Death: 12 SEP 1889
        Burial: Sawyer Cemetery, Sandy Ridge, Lowndes Co., AL
        Change Date: 6 APR 2006

        Father: James H. Brightwell b: 1861 in Butler Co., AL
        Mother: Mary b: 19 APR 1861 in AL

        More About SARAH BRIGHTWELL:
        Burial: Sawyer Cemtery, Sandy Ridge, Lowndes Co.

47.   v. CHARLES M. BRIGHTWELL, b. 08 Feb 1889, Born Crenshaw Ala./31 yrs in 1920 Cen. Crenshaw AL; d. 26 Jun 1889, Sandy Ridge, Lowndes Co. Ala..
     vi. JAMES HILERY JR. BRIGHTWELL, b. 27 Jul 1890, Sandy Ridge Alabama Lowndes Co.; d. Dec 1972,

Alabama; m. ANNA OR "ANNIE" BELL RHODES; b. Abt. 1897, born Alabama.

Notes for JAMES HILERY JR. BRIGHTWELL:
ID: I850
Name: James Hillery Brightwell
Sex: M
Birth: 27 JUL 1890 in AL
Death: DEC 1972 in AL
Note: 1900 United States Federal Census Record : Name: James Brightwell Home in 1900: Surles, Crenshaw, Alabama Age: 9 Estimated birth year: abt 1891 Birthplace: Alabama Race: White Relationship to head-of-house: Son ---------------- World War I Draft Registration Cards, 1917-1918 Record: Name: James Hillary Brightwell City: Not Stated County: Crenshaw State: Alabama Birthplace: Alabama;United States of America Birth Date: 27 Jul 1890 Race: Caucasian Roll: 1509375 DraftBoard: 0 -------------- Social Security Death Index Record: Name: James Brightwell SSN: 424-36-2345 Last Residence: 36108 Montgomery, Montgomery, Alabama, United States of America Born: 27 Jul 1890 Died: Dec 1972 State (Year) SSN issued: Alabama (Before 1951)
Change Date: 6 APR 2006

Father: James H. Brightwell b: 1861 in Butler Co., AL
Mother: Mary b: 19 APR 1861 in AL

Marriage 1 Annie B. b: ABT 1897 in AL
Children
 Living Brightwell
 Living Brightwell
 Living Brightwell
 Living Brightwell

More About JAMES HILERY JR. BRIGHTWELL:
Adoption: Farmer

     vii.   WILLIAM ARTHUR BRIGHTWELL, b. Feb 1892, born Alabama/1920 Cen. by himself 38 yrs; d. Sandy Ridge Cem/Lowndes Co. ALA.; m. THELMA SMITH.

Notes for WILLIAM ARTHUR BRIGHTWELL:
ID: I851
Name: Arthur Brightwell
Sex: M
Birth: FEB 1892 in AL
Note: 1900 United States Federal Census Record: Name: Arthur Brightwell Home in 1900: Surles, Crenshaw, Alabama Age: 8 Estimated birth year: abt 1892 Birthplace: Alabama Race: White Relationship to head-of-house: Son
Change Date: 6 APR 2006

Father: James H. Brightwell b: 1861 in Butler Co., AL
Mother: Mary b: 19 APR 1861 in AL

48.   viii.   ROBERT E. BRIGHTWELL, b. Nov 1894, Alabama/1900 Cen AL shows 6 yrs..
     ix.   ILA (TWIN) BRIGHTWELL, b. 21 Jul 1897, born Al/1900 cen shows 2 yrs..
     x.   IRA (TWIN) BRIGHTWELL, b. 21 Jul 1897, born Ala/1900 cen shows 2 yrs.; d. 04 Oct 1914, Sandy Ridge, Lowndes Co. AL/died YellowJacketStings.

Notes for IRA (TWIN) BRIGHTWELL:
ID: I853
Name: Ira Brightwell
Sex: M
Birth: JUL 1897 in AL
Death: 22 JAN 1908
Burial: Sawyer Cemetery, Sandy Ridge, Lowndes Co., AL

Note: 1900 United States Federal Census Record: Name: Ira Brightwell Home in 1900: Surles, Crenshaw, Alabama Age: 2 Estimated birth year: abt 1898 Birthplace: Alabama Race: White Relationship to head-of-house: Son
Change Date: 6 APR 2006

Father: James H. Brightwell b: 1861 in Butler Co., AL
Mother: Mary b: 19 APR 1861 in AL

More About IRA (TWIN) BRIGHTWELL:
Burial: Sawyer Cemetery, Sandy Ridge, Alabama

        xi.   ESTELLE BRIGHTWELL, b. 1902, Alabama/shwn 18 yrs in 1920 cen ALA; m. MR. HALL.
49.   xii.   LEROY BRIGHTWELL, b. 25 Mar 1908, Born Crenshaw Co. Ala./1910 cens. shows him 5 yrs. old- yr. 1905 (???); d. 07 Apr 1955, Laverne, Crenshaw Co., Ala.Death Cert. # 6797.
      xiii.   _CRAY(?) BRIGHTWELL, b. 1904, Son shwn 16 yrs old in 1920 Cen. AL.
      xiv.   ANNA BRIGHTWELL, b. 1910, Daugh shown as 10 yrs in 1920 Census ALA..

Generation No. 7

39. WILLIE CLYNTON[7] BRIGHTWELL *(WILLIAM[6], JOHN JACKSON[5], WILLIAM[4], REYNOLDS[3], REYNOLDS OR RANDALL[2], THE BRIGHTWELL FAMILY[1] HISTORY)* was born 09 Apr 1900 in Death Cert shows his age, birth, death. "FatherJames Brightwell", and died 27 Dec 1958 in Osceola Co. Kissimmee, FLA, 58 yrs "Add. Boggy Creek Rd.". He married FLORENCE WORSHAM 14 Jan 1919 in Married..

More About WILLIE CLYNTON BRIGHTWELL:
Burial: Auto Accident/HEart Damage Bur. Moultrie Georgia.

More About WILLIE BRIGHTWELL and FLORENCE WORSHAM:
Marriage: 14 Jan 1919, Married.

Children of WILLIE BRIGHTWELL and FLORENCE WORSHAM are:
      i.   EADY ( )[8] BRIGHTWELL, b. 19 Nov 1921.
      ii.   JAMES CLYNTON BRIGHTWELL, b. 18 Oct 1919.
      iii.   CHARLIE EDWARD BRIGHTWELL, b. 17 Jun 1923.
      iv.   COY CECILBRIGHTWELL, b. 30 Dec 1924.
      v.   J. B. BRIGHTWELL, b. 26 Nov 1926.

40. FALBY[7] MCCLENDON *(MARY MISSOURI[6] BRIGHTWELL, JOHN JACKSON[5], WILLIAM[4], REYNOLDS[3], REYNOLDS OR RANDALL[2], THE BRIGHTWELL FAMILY[1] HISTORY)* She married PINKNEY SLATON.

Child of FALBY MCCLENDON and PINKNEY SLATON is:
      i.   CAROL[8] SLATON, b. 1863.

41. EUGENE PASCO (SR)[7] KISER *(SARAH JANE[6] BRIGHTWELL, LEN REYNOLDS[5], WILLIAM[4], REYNOLDS[3], REYNOLDS OR RANDALL[2], THE BRIGHTWELL FAMILY[1] HISTORY)* was born 10 Sep 1890 in born Madison,Madison Co. FL, and died 23 Jul 1937 in Pine Grove Cem Madison Florida. He married NEVA JOHNSON 24 Oct 1909 in Married Madison Co. Fl/Divorced 1911. She was born in of Madison Co. Florida.

Notes for EUGENE PASCO (SR) KISER:
ID: I6
Name: Eugene Pasco Kiser Sr.
Sex: M
Birth: 10 SEP 1890 in Madison, Madison Co., FL

Death: 23 JUL 1937 in Madison, Madison Co., FL
Burial: Pine Grove Cemetery, Madison Co., FL
Note: Tombstone shows date of birth as 8/10/1890, also had written note found in Eugene Pasco Jr's personal effects after his death. I orig had the date as 9-24-1890 but do not know where I got the info. Florida Death Index, 1937 Name: Eugene Pasco Kiser Place of Death: Madison Gender: M Race: W Volume: 766 Certificate: 13295 Death Date: 1937 WWI draft number was 1118 1920 census: Kiser, Pasco Age: 29 Year: 1920 Birthplace: Florida Roll: T625_225 Race: White Page: 11A State: Florida ED: 111 County: Madison Image: 538 Township: Pinetta 1930 census: Hiser, Sasco E (s/b Kiser, Pasco E.) Age: 38 Year: 1930 Birthplace: Florida Roll: T626_324 Race: White Page: 3B State: Florida ED: 15 County: Madison Image: 0606 Township: Macedonia Relationship: Head
Change Date: 22 APR 2004

Father: John Wesley Kiser b: 30 SEP 1853 in Crenshaw Co., AL
Mother: Sarah Jane Brightwell b: 30 AUG 1849 in Stewart Co., GA

Marriage 1 Neva Johnson
Married: BEF 1911
Divorced: 20 SEP 1911 in Madison Co., FL
Note: Madison Co. Divorce Records Book & Page C666
Note: Chancery Book "C" MADISON COUNTY DIVORCE RECORDS: C 666 Kiser, Pasco Kiser, Neva 20 Sep 1911

Marriage 2 Annie Mae Barclay b: 12 OCT 1895 in Greenville, Madison Co., FL
Married: 1 MAR 1914 in Madison Co., FL
Children
 Eugene Pasco Kiser Jr. b: 19 NOV 1917 in Madison, Madison Co., FL
 Howard Barnard Kiser b: 3 MAR 1919 in Madison Co., FL
 Lela Mae Kiser b: 4 MAY 1921 in Pasco Co., FL
 Colon Angrish Kiser b: 1 APR 1923
 Living Kiser
 Doris Virginia Kiser b: 25 MAR 1926 in Fort Meade, Polk Co., FL
 Eugene Lindsey Kiser b: 20 JUN 1927 in Fort Meade, Polk Co., FL
 Living Kiser
 Harmon (Buddy) Kiser b: 4 JUL 1931 in Madison Co., FL
 Allard Lamar Kiser b: 11 FEB 1935 in Madison, Madison Co., FL

More About EUGENE PASCO (SR) KISER:
Burial: 15 May 2002, Acadia Memorial Park, Seattle, KingCo. WA.

More About EUGENE KISER and NEVA JOHNSON:
Marriage: 24 Oct 1909, Married Madison Co. Fl/Divorced 1911

Child of EUGENE KISER and NEVA JOHNSON is:
    i.   EUGENE PASCO JR.[8] KISER, d. 06 May 2002, Smith Co. Texas.

42. LEE[7] BETTERTON (*MISSOURI ELIZABETH[6] BRIGHTWELL, LEN REYNOLDS[5], WILLIAM[4], REYNOLDS[3], REYNOLDS OR RANDALL[2], THE BRIGHTWELL FAMILY[1] HISTORY*) was born Feb 1884 in Born in Alabama, and died 29 Aug 1963 in died in Alabama. He married PARALEE CATHINE "KITTIE" HALL 01 Dec 1912 in Lowndes Co. Alabama. She was born 17 Aug 1890 in born Alabama, and died 26 Feb 1935 in died Alabama.

More About LEE BETTERTON and PARALEE HALL:
Marriage: 01 Dec 1912, Lowndes Co. Alabama

Children of LEE BETTERTON and PARALEE HALL are:
50.   i.   CLARA MAE[8] BETTERTON, b. 01 May 1914, born Alabama.
      ii. JIMMIE LEE BETTERTON, b. 03 Jun 1919, in Alabama; d. Nov 1972, Letohatchee, Alabama.

43. MARY ETHEL[7] BRIGHTWELL *(HILLARY 'HILEY' [BURT] ALBERTUS[6], LEN REYNOLDS[5], WILLIAM[4], REYNOLDS[3], REYNOLDS OR RANDALL[2], THE BRIGHTWELL FAMILY[1] HISTORY)* was born Dec 1886 in born in Alabama, and died in 99 yrs death [Big Sister]Buried in Cem.bet Henderson-Troy, ALA.. She married WALTERS.

Notes for MARY ETHEL BRIGHTWELL:
ID: I858
Name: Ethel Brightwell
Sex: F
Birth: DEC 1886 in AL
Note: 1900 United States Federal Census Record: Name: Ethel Brightwell Home in 1900: Surles, Crenshaw, Alabama Age: 13 Estimated birth year: abt 1887 Birthplace: Alabama Race: White Relationship to head-of-house: Daughter
Change Date: 6 APR 2006

Father: Hilery or Hillary Albert Brightwell b: ABT 1859
Mother: Sally or Sallie or Sarah Bedgood b: APR 1860 in AL

Marriage 1 Walters
Children
 Rebecca Walters b: ABT 1913 in AL
 James Walters b: ABT 1915 in AL

Children of MARY BRIGHTWELL and WALTERS are:
    i.   REBECCA[8] WALTERS, b. 1913, born Alabama.
    ii. JAMES WALTERS, b. 1915, born Alabama.

44. CLIFTON F.[7] BRIGHTWELL *(HILLARY 'HILEY' [BURT] ALBERTUS[6], LEN REYNOLDS[5], WILLIAM[4], REYNOLDS[3], REYNOLDS OR RANDALL[2], THE BRIGHTWELL FAMILY[1] HISTORY)* was born Jan 1888 in born in Alabama. He married MARY E. HOUGH 22 Dec 1907 in Married Glenwood, ALA., daughter of THAD HOUGH.

More About CLIFTON BRIGHTWELL and MARY HOUGH:
Marriage: 22 Dec 1907, Married Glenwood, ALA.

Children of CLIFTON BRIGHTWELL and MARY HOUGH are:
    i.   JULIAN[8] BRIGHTWELL.
    ii. MARY BRIGHTWELL.
   iii. FANNIE BRIGHTWELL.
   iv. WILLIE BRIGHTWELL.

45. LILLIAN IONE "BIG MOMMA"[7] BRIGHTWELL *(HILLARY 'HILEY' [BURT] ALBERTUS[6], LEN REYNOLDS[5], WILLIAM[4], REYNOLDS[3], REYNOLDS OR RANDALL[2], THE BRIGHTWELL FAMILY[1] HISTORY)* was born Jul 1891 in born in Alabama, and died 21 Feb 1964 in Providence Cem. Ch./Glenwood,Ala.. She married NEWTON WARREN KING 21 Feb 1908 in Marriage, son of LEWIS KING and MARY STOVALL. He died in Providence Cem. Ch./Glenwood,Ala..

More About NEWTON KING and LILLIAN BRIGHTWELL:
Marriage: 21 Feb 1908, Marriage

Children of LILLIAN BRIGHTWELL and NEWTON KING are:

51. i. VONCILE[8] KING, b. 25 Jan 1916; d. Buried Providence Cem/Providence Alabama.
     ii. JAMES LEE KING, b. 23 Aug 1909.
     iii. ETHEL NELL KING, b. 08 Aug 1911; d. 03 Sep 1925.
     iv. ROBERT NEHEMIAH KING, b. 20 Jan 1914.
     v. FREDDIE MAE KING, b. 16 Apr 1918; d. 07 Mar 1946.
     vi. HILARY NEWTON KING, b. 11 Aug 1919.
     vii. DOROTHY ANNETTE KING, b. 30 Jan 1922.
     viii. ANNIE GRANT KING, b. 21 Apr 1923; d. 24 May 1975.
     ix. L. LEON KING, b. 06 Sep 1931; d. 14 Feb 1975.

46. JOHN JOSEPH[7] BRIGHTWELL *(JAMES "JIMMIE" HILERY (SR)[6], LEN REYNOLDS[5], WILLIAM[4], REYNOLDS[3], REYNOLDS OR RANDALL[2], THE BRIGHTWELL FAMILY[1] HISTORY)* was born 1920 in 5 months in 1920 Cens./born Alabama - living. He married CODINE "COOT" WALKER. She was born in RH Positive Blood.

Child of JOHN BRIGHTWELL and CODINE WALKER is:
     i. 2 CHILDREN UNMARKED GRAVES NEXT TO[8] PARENTS, d. Mag. Bat. Ch Cemetery.

47. CHARLES M.[7] BRIGHTWELL *(JAMES "JIMMIE" HILERY (SR)[6], LEN REYNOLDS[5], WILLIAM[4], REYNOLDS[3], REYNOLDS OR RANDALL[2], THE BRIGHTWELL FAMILY[1] HISTORY)* was born 08 Feb 1889 in Born Crenshaw Ala./31 yrs in 1920 Cen. Crenshaw AL, and died 26 Jun 1889 in Sandy Ridge, Lowndes Co. Ala.. He married MARY E. in Married Crenshaw AL New Providence Area. She was born 1877 in Born Crenshaw Ala./43 yrs in 1920 cen AL.

Notes for CHARLES M. BRIGHTWELL:
ID: I855
Name: Charles M. Brightwell
Sex: M
Birth: 8 FEB 1886 in AL
Death: 26 JUN 1889
Burial: Sawyer Cemetery, Sandy Ridge, Lowndes Co., AL
Note: Cemetery transcription: BRIGHTWELL, Charles M., son of J. H. and M. E. Brightwell, 2-8-1886, d. 6-26-1889
Change Date: 6 APR 2006

Father: James H. Brightwell b: 1861 in Butler Co., AL
Mother: Mary b: 19 APR 1861 in AL

More About CHARLES M. BRIGHTWELL:
Burial: Sawyer Cemetery, Sandy Ridge, Alabama

More About CHARLES BRIGHTWELL and MARY E.:
Marriage: Married Crenshaw AL New Providence Area

Children of CHARLES BRIGHTWELL and MARY E. are:
     i. MARY L.[8] BRIGHTWELL, b. 1909, Born Crenshaw Ala..
     ii. JULIAN F. BRIGHTWELL, b. 1911, Born Crenshaw Ala..
     iii. FRANCIS F. BRIGHTWELL, b. 1911, Born Crenshaw Ala..
     iv. WILMA IRENE BRIGHTWELL, b. 1920, 2 months old in 1920 Cen. Crenshaw AL..

48. ROBERT E.[7] BRIGHTWELL *(JAMES "JIMMIE" HILERY (SR)[6], LEN REYNOLDS[5], WILLIAM[4], REYNOLDS[3], REYNOLDS OR RANDALL[2], THE BRIGHTWELL FAMILY[1] HISTORY)* was born Nov 1894 in Alabama/1900 Cen AL shows 6 yrs.. He married LIZZIE "LUCY" MAE RHODES in Montgomery Co AL area Married. She was born 1900 in 20 yrs in 1920 Cen Ala..

Notes for ROBERT E. BRIGHTWELL:
ID: I852
Name: Robert E. Brightwell
Sex: M
Birth: NOV 1893 in AL
Note: 1900 United States Federal Census Record: Name: Robert E Brightwell Home in 1900: Surles,
Crenshaw, Alabama Age: 6 Estimated birth year: abt 1894 Birthplace: Alabama Race: White Relationship
to head-of-house: Son
Change Date: 6 APR 2006

Father: James H. Brightwell b: 1861 in Butler Co., AL
Mother: Mary b: 19 APR 1861 in AL

More About ROBERT BRIGHTWELL and LIZZIE RHODES:
Marriage: Montgomery Co AL area Married

Children of ROBERT BRIGHTWELL and LIZZIE RHODES are:
     i. GEORGIA M.[8] BRIGHTWELL, b. 1917, Daugh/3 yrs old in 1920 cen AL.
    ii. CHARLEY O. BRIGHTWELL, b. 1920, 3 months old in 1920 Cen. Alabama..

49. LEROY[7] BRIGHTWELL (*JAMES "JIMMIE" HILERY (SR)[6], LEN REYNOLDS[5], WILLIAM[4], REYNOLDS[3], REYNOLDS OR RANDALL[2], THE BRIGHTWELL FAMILY[1] HISTORY*) was born 25 Mar 1908 in Born Crenshaw Co. Ala./1910 cens. shows him 5 yrs. old- yr. 1905 (???), and died 07 Apr 1955 in Laverne, Crenshaw Co., Ala.Death Cert. # 6797[1]. He married (1) EVA LUCILLE PERDUE in Married at the home of her parents., daughter of WILLIAM PERDUE and IDA STAGGERS. She was born 21 Apr 1915 in Eva was married once before this marriage.[2], and died Jun 1981 in SS# 416-66-7927-Montgomery, Ala./Mag. Bapt Ch Cemetery w/husband Leroy.. He married (2) ONEAL BEASLEY in His first wife of part Indian Descendent., daughter of WILLIE BEASLEY and VERNIE PARRETT.

Notes for LEROY BRIGHTWELL:

Leroy Brightwell's first marriage was to a part Native Indian American.

  Leroy BRIGHTWELL
   Birth Date: 25 Mar 1908
   Death Date: Aug 1984
   Social Security Number: 217-10-0806
   State or Territory Where Number Was Issued: Maryland

  Death Residence Localities
   ZIP Code: 21701
   Localities: Frederick, Frederick, Maryland
  Harmony Grove, Frederick, Maryland
  Hood College, Frederick, Maryland
  Hopeland, Frederick, Maryland
  Lewistown, Frederick, Maryland
  Lime Kiln, Frederick, Maryland
  Oak Acres, Frederick, Maryland
  Pine Cliff, Frederick, Maryland
  Tulip Hill, Frederick, Maryland

Children: Eva Purdue was married before she married Leroy and had two step-children. Then marrying Leroy, she had twelve more children of their own.

Leroy Brightwell
Age: 24
Estimated birth year: 1905
Birthplace: Alabama
Relation to Head-of-house: Head
Race: White
Home in 1930: Luverne, Crenshaw, Alabama
Year: 1930; Census Place: Luverne, Crenshaw, Alabama; Roll: T626_11; Page: 4B; Enumeration District: 19; Image: 0424.

Troy is located in Pik County, Alabama. a bit of important informatin. There IS NO RECORD OF ANY BRIGHTWELLS LIVING IN PIKE CO.AL. BEFORE THE Civil War and it WAS SOME TIME AFTER THE CW
BEFORE A BRIGHTWELL FAMILY MOVED IN TO PIKE CO. AL. There are NO SLAVE RECORDS ON ANY BRIGHTWELLS in Pike Co. Al.

Brightwell's that married in Pike County. Alabama
Brightwell E. E. married Gertrude Hurley 4-4-1895
Brightwell G.F. married Hilda M. Rhodes 2-27-1898
Brightwell J. F. married S. E. Darby 5-1-1879

At Family Reunion in Anadulsia Alabama August 19 & 20th, 2005; the following Children of James H. Brightwell and wife Mary Elizabeth "Mollie" were present:
Huey Brightwell; Bruce Brightwell; Ted Brightwell; Robert Brightwell; Ed Brightwell, Horace Brightwell; Betty Brightwell and Bobby Brightwell

    More About LEROY BRIGHTWELL:
Burial: Buried Magnolia Baptist Church Cem. Crenshaw, Ala.
Death Information: 17 Apr 1955, 51 years old at death.

Notes for EVA LUCILLE PERDUE:
FamilySearch™ U.S. Social Security Death Index
30 September 2000
Select record to download - Maximum: 50

 Eva BRIGHTWELL
  Birth Date: 21 Apr 1915
  Death Date: Jun 1981
  Social Security Number: 416-66-7927
  State or Territory Where Number Was Issued: Alabama

 Death Residence Localities
  ZIP Code: 36107
  Localities: Montgomery, Montgomery, Alabama

A Daniel Perdue is buried at Little Sandy Ridge Cemetery as follows in Alabama:
PERDUE, Dasnel B., son of J. L. & J. E. PERDUE, January 17, 1880, April 13, 1883
PERDUE, Samuel Elijah, son of John J. & Mary M. PERDUE, aged 11 years, 10 months, , October 4, 1853, mother was Mary M. Gingles PERDUE

PERDUE, J. J., age 17 years, , October 30, 1862

PERDUE, Infant of G. W. & M. F. PERDUE

PERDUE, Alice Adonia, daughter of J. M. & L. F. PERDUE, March 24, 1871, June 29, 1895

PERDUE, Estelle, 1879-1879

PERDUE, Eugenia, 1877-1879

PERDUE, David Greely, 'Buddy', 1872-1909

PERDUE, George Taylor, 1839-1915

PERDUE, Jesse Davis, 1875-1879

PERDUE, Julia Reeves, 1848-1932

PERDUE, Lydia R., 1870-1874

PERDUE, Robert, son of J. H. and Jane Perdue, 7-31-1850, 1-8-1861

PERDUE, Alice T., 1866-1956, double stone with Jacob C.

PERDUE, Clara A. Stone, 1864-1942, wife of Issac

PERDUE, infant of J. C. and A. T. Perdue, born and died 1-11-1894

PERDUE, Issac, 1859-1925

PERDUE, Jacob C., 1860-1915

PERDUE, James Leonard, son of T. and N. Perdue, 6-31-1870, d. 11-2-1898

PERDUE, Rev. John B., 4-5-1788, 9-26-1860

PERDUE, Nancy, 1835-1915, wife of Thomas Perdue

PERDUE, Nancy E., youngest dau. of G. T. and Anna Perdue, 9-15-1854, 11-15-1861

PERDUE, Thomas, Jr., son of Thomas and Nancy Perdue, 10-23-1873, 9-25-1896

PERDUE, Thomas, 1833-1899

PERDUE, Thomas I., 2-1-1908, 9-24-1962

PERDUE, William S., son of Thomas and Nancy Perdue, 12-26-1870, 12-16-1889

More About EVA LUCILLE PERDUE:
Burial: Buried Magnolia Baptist Church, Crenshaw, Ala.

More About LEROY BRIGHTWELL and EVA PERDUE:
Marriage: Married at the home of her parents.

More About LEROY BRIGHTWELL and ONEAL BEASLEY:
Marriage: His first wife of part Indian Descendent.

Children of LEROY BRIGHTWELL and EVA PERDUE are:

52.	i.	BOBBY RAY[8] BRIGHTWELL.
53.	ii.	HORACE GREGORY BRIGHTWELL, b. Lives in Semmes/Mobile Alabama
54.	iii.	HUEY LANE BRIGHTWELL, b. Live in Highland Home, Alabama
55.	iv.	JAMES EDWARD "ED" BRIGHTWELL, b/Brantley Alabama.
56.	v.	MARGARET "PEGGY" IRENE BRIGHTWELL, d. 2003, Deceased.
	vi.	MARY LOUISE BRIGHTWELL, d. Died at 6 mths of Whooping Cough.
57.	vii.	ROBERT WAYNE BRIGHTWELL.
	viii.	JAMES WILLIAM "MOSCOE" [SGT. BRIGHTWELL, b. Abt. 1930, Born Vernledge/Crenshaw Co. Alabama; d. Buried/Magnolia Bapt. Ch. Cemetery; m. VIRGINIA PETTY, Married/Divorced.

Notes for JAMES WILLIAM "MOSCOE" [SGT. BRIGHTWELL:
James was the FIRST child of his parents. He grew up and joined the ARMY then served in Germany. He was born in Crenshaw Co. Alabama.

After coming home from the service; he worked in the logging business. He passed away in bed at Brantley, Alabama. There were reports of a truck accident the day before. The insurance company paid money to his mother Eva Purdue Brightwell. She used the money to purchase the home of her father Fletcher [Future} Perdue in Crenshaw Creek, Alabama near Ivy Creek.

Moscoe was the name he was referred by; and he was married only once to Virginia Petty but later they divorced. It is believed that he had a son named James William Brightwell but not known for sure. At the time of James death they were divorced. He is buried at Magnolia Baptist Church Cemetery in Crenshaw Cem. Alabama

More About JAMES BRIGHTWELL and VIRGINIA PETTY:
Marriage: Married/Divorced

    ix.   THURMAN "TED" BRIGHTWELL, b. 26 May 1942; m. SUE ANN ALDRIDGE, 16 Jan 1970,.; b. 11 Aug 1943, Decatur , Ala..

        More About THURMAN BRIGHTWELL and SUE ALDRIDGE:
        Marriage: 16 Jan 1970,

58.   x.   BRUCE "JIMMY" BRIGHTWELL, b. 21 Jul 1944, Brantley, Ala./now Fredericksburg, Virginia; d.
59.   xi.   BETTY JOYCE BRIGHTWELL, b. 22 Sep 1948, Alabama.

Children of LEROY BRIGHTWELL and ONEAL BEASLEY are:
60.   xii.   NELLIE GRAY (NELL)[8] BRIGHTWELL, d. Buried Magnolia Bat Ch. Cem..
61.   xiii.   ANNIE MAE "ANN" BRIGHTWELL, d. Buried in Missippi w/Haskel Jones Family..

Generation No. 8

50. CLARA MAE[8] BETTERTON *(LEE[7], MISSOURI ELIZABETH[6] BRIGHTWELL, LEN REYNOLDS[5], WILLIAM[4], REYNOLDS[3], REYNOLDS OR RANDALL[2], THE BRIGHTWELL FAMILY[1] HISTORY)* was born 01 May 1914 in born Alabama. She married CODY FRANK (JR) NOBLE 02 Oct 1909 in Married In Alabama. He died 04 Jun 1998 in died in Lapine, Alabama.

More About CODY NOBLE and CLARA BETTERTON:
Marriage: 02 Oct 1909, Married In Alabama

Child of CLARA BETTERTON and CODY NOBLE is:
    i.   CODY FRANK (JR)[9] NOBLE, b. 23 Nov 1946, Born in Alabama; d. 09 Feb 2002, in Pb Alabama; m. SINGLETON.

51. VONCILE[8] KING *(LILLIAN IONE "BIG MOMMA"[7] BRIGHTWELL, HILLARY 'HILEY' [BURT] ALBERTUS[6], LEN REYNOLDS[5], WILLIAM[4], REYNOLDS[3], REYNOLDS OR RANDALL[2], THE BRIGHTWELL FAMILY[1] HISTORY)* was born 25 Jan 1916, and died in Buried Providence Cem/Providence Alabama. She married CLIFF HOLMES. He died in Buried Providence Cemetery/Glenwood Alabama.

Children of VONCILE KING and CLIFF HOLMES are:
    i.   HENRY MILTON[9] HOLMES, b. 23 Nov 1941, 334/335-6039/P.O.Box 54-Rutledge,Alabama 36071.
    ii.   REBA HOLMES, b. 07 Oct 1935.
    iii.   VERDIE MAE HOLMES, b. 19 Jul 1939.
    iv.   WINDHAM NEWTON HOLMES, b. 10 Oct 1946.
    v.   JANICE MARIE HOLMES, b. 09 Aug 1950.
    vi.   HANNIS HOLMES, b. Bet. 1013 - 1953.

52. BOBBY RAY[8] BRIGHTWELL *(LEROY[7], JAMES "JIMMIE" HILERY (SR)[6], LEN REYNOLDS[5], WILLIAM[4], REYNOLDS[3], REYNOLDS OR RANDALL[2], THE BRIGHTWELL FAMILY[1] HISTORY)* He married MARTHA FRAZIER in Married.

More About BOBBY BRIGHTWELL and MARTHA FRAZIER:
Marriage: Married

Children of BOBBY BRIGHTWELL and MARTHA FRAZIER are:
    i.   MACHELLE[9] BRIGHTWELL.
    ii.   MICHAEL BRIGHTWELL.

53. HORACE GREGORY[8] BRIGHTWELL *(LEROY[7], JAMES "JIMMIE" HILERY (SR)[6], LEN REYNOLDS[5], WILLIAM[4], REYNOLDS[3], REYNOLDS OR RANDALL[2], THE BRIGHTWELL FAMILY[1] HISTORY)* was born in Lives in Semmes/Mobile Alabama. He married BONNIE TILLMAN, daughter of TILLMAN. She was born in Of Mobile Ala. sister to Sheriff of Mobile, ALA..

Children of HORACE BRIGHTWELL and BONNIE TILLMAN are:
  i.   KAREN[9] BRIGHTWELL.
  ii. HORACE GREGORY BRIGHTWELL, b. 1952.

54. HUEY LANE[8] BRIGHTWELL *(LEROY[7], JAMES "JIMMIE" HILERY (SR)[6], LEN REYNOLDS[5], WILLIAM[4], REYNOLDS[3], REYNOLDS OR RANDALL[2], THE BRIGHTWELL FAMILY[1] HISTORY)* was born in Live in Highland Home, Alabama. He married (1) MARTHA LAMARLES CARROLL in Her 2nd marriage (Griffin-lst). He married (2) JENNIFER KOUCH in Married no children..

More About HUEY BRIGHTWELL and MARTHA CARROLL:
Marriage: Her 2nd marriage (Griffin-lst)

More About HUEY BRIGHTWELL and JENNIFER KOUCH:
Marriage: Married no children.

Children of HUEY BRIGHTWELL and MARTHA CARROLL are:
  i.   LUCILLE[9] BRIGHTWELL, b. Bur. Mag. Bapt Ch Cem; d. Died young-peneumonia..
  ii. LOUISE BRIGHTWELL, b. Burt Mag Bapt Ch Cem.; d. Died young-Diptheria..

55. JAMES EDWARD "ED"[8] BRIGHTWELL *(LEROY[7], JAMES "JIMMIE" HILERY (SR)[6], LEN REYNOLDS[5], WILLIAM[4], REYNOLDS[3], REYNOLDS OR RANDALL[2], THE BRIGHTWELL FAMILY[1] HISTORY)* was born in Brantley Alabama. He married MARTHA PATRICIA CLARK in Married/Anadalusia Alabama. She was born in Of Montgomery Alabama.
More About JAMES BRIGHTWELL and MARTHA CLARK:
Marriage: Married/Anadalusia Alabama

Children of JAMES BRIGHTWELL and MARTHA CLARK are:
  i.   JAMES EDWARD "EDDIE" JR.[9] BRIGHTWELL, ; m. PATRICIA MARIE THOMAS, 31 Mar 1982, Salamar, FLA /high school sweetheart.

       More About JAMES BRIGHTWELL and PATRICIA THOMAS:
       Marriage: 31 Mar 1982, Salamar, FLA /high school sweetheart

  ii. SANDRA PATRICIA BRIGHTWELL.
  iii. VICKI BELINDA BRIGHTWELL, m. STEVE ZETTERLUND; b. 60 Miranda Rd./Warrior, Ala. 941/61-9171.
  iv. DONNA JO BRIGHTWELL.
  v.   CURTIS LYNN BRIGHTWELL, b. 03 Apr 1963, Tuscaloosa Alabama; d. Nov 1996, Magnolia Bapt. Church Cem/Alabama; m. NEVER MARRIED, NO CHILDREN..

       Notes for CURTIS LYNN BRIGHTWELL:
       Curtis was the fifth child of his parents; his father was manager of Pake-McKeen Sporting Goods Store in downtown Tuscaloosa, Alabama. Curtis was a wonderful person. Most everyone liked him and loved him. He was called "movie star" by some when he was young. Curtis never married and has no children.
            Curtis was one of the best foreign car mechanics that ever lived. He could take a jaquar car apart then put it back together again and it would run like new.
            Curtis was a true lover of the animal kingdom. He had two or more cats and several dogs in his home most of the time whether it was at Palm Beach, Florida South Beach, Florida or Alabama. He loved to hunt and fish. He was at one time the captain of a charter fishing boat. One story that is told

by Curtis's brother in law, Steve Zetterlund of Punta Gorda, Florida, is how one day Curtis was passing by some people fishing. They had been fishing all day and had not caught any fish. Curtis went over to them, took a knife and jumped into the water. He came out with several large fish and handed them to the people and went on his way. Another story is about when Curtis was very young living in Dothan, Alabama. There was a pet show, Curtis picked up a stray black and white cat and took it to the show. The next day on the front page of the Dothan Eagle Newspaper there was a picture of him smiling, holding the cat.

Curtis played football, baseball (pitcher), kick boxing, and was a black belt in karate. Curtis was a believer in the Bible and had great faith in its teachings.

Curtis attended school in Dothan, Alabama and Fort Walton Beach, Florida. At the time of his accidental death, Curtis was living in South Beach, Florida. He is buried at Magnolia Baptist Church where most of his ancestors are buried in Alabama. [written by Donna Brightwell, brother to Curtis.]

    vi.   MARTHA ELIZABETH.

56. MARGARET "PEGGY" IRENE[8] BRIGHTWELL *(LEROY[7], JAMES "JIMMIE" HILERY (SR)[6], LEN REYNOLDS[5], WILLIAM[4], REYNOLDS[3], REYNOLDS OR RANDALL[2], THE BRIGHTWELL FAMILY[1] HISTORY)* died 2003 in Deceased. She married ROY MCGEHEE in Married.

More About ROY MCGEHEE and MARGARET BRIGHTWELL:
Marriage: Married

Children of MARGARET BRIGHTWELL and ROY MCGEHEE are:
    i.   LYNN[9] BRIGHTWELL.
    ii.   STEVE BRIGHTWELL.

57. ROBERT WAYNE[8] BRIGHTWELL *(LEROY[7], JAMES "JIMMIE" HILERY (SR)[6], LEN REYNOLDS[5], WILLIAM[4], REYNOLDS[3], REYNOLDS OR RANDALL[2], THE BRIGHTWELL FAMILY[1] HISTORY)* He married (1) GLADYS BILLIE BLIZZARD in Married. He married (2) ROBBIE BOLT.

More About ROBERT BRIGHTWELL and GLADYS BLIZZARD:
Marriage: Married

Child of ROBERT BRIGHTWELL and GLADYS BLIZZARD is:
    i.   ROBERT WAYNE JR.[9] BRIGHTWELL.

58. BRUCE "JIMMY"[8] BRIGHTWELL *(LEROY[7], JAMES "JIMMIE" HILERY (SR)[6], LEN REYNOLDS[5], WILLIAM[4], REYNOLDS[3], REYNOLDS OR RANDALL[2], THE BRIGHTWELL FAMILY[1] HISTORY)* was born 21 Jul 1944 in Brantley, Ala./now Fredericksburg, Virginia,. He married (1) BARBARA JEAN GRIFFIN in Chesapeake, Virginia. She was born 03 Feb 1952. He married (2) PATRICIA ANN WILKINSON 02 May 1964 in Arlington, First Presb. Church, Virginia, daughter of NORMAN WILKINSON and MIRIAM GIBBS. She was born 02 May 1942 in Salisbury, MD/resides in DE-Seaford-Millsboro-Georgetown.

Notes for BRUCE "JIMMY" BRIGHTWELL:
Notes on BRUCE BRIGHTWELL of Fredericksburg, Virginia.

Bruce grew up his final years at the Alabama Baptist Home for Children in Troy, or Brantley, Alabama. Crenshaw County. He was taken there because Eva was ill and unable to take care of him. Bruce was only age 19 - when he married Pat when she was 22 years old. Married her on her birthday. They were married nine years. Bruce Brightwell has remarried to Barbara Griffin and has more children.
Bruce and Barbara they live in Fredericksburg, Virginia.

Bruce Brightwell was a Warrant Officer in Marine Corp. of the United States. He served his country in the Vietnam War. His son Norman Russell Brightwell was born 1968 - during the Vietnam War Period.

More About BRUCE "JIMMY" BRIGHTWELL:
Burial: Marine Corp. Soldier/Warrant Officer Vietnam War Veteran.
Illness: Survived Diptheria as a young child.

More About BRUCE BRIGHTWELL and BARBARA GRIFFIN:
Marriage: Chesapeake, Virginia

More About BRUCE BRIGHTWELL and PATRICIA WILKINSON:
Marriage: 02 May 1964, Arlington, First Presb. Church, Virginia

Children of BRUCE BRIGHTWELL and BARBARA GRIFFIN are:
      i.   ANNA ELIZABETH "BETH"[9] BRIGHTWELL, b. 16 Mar 1980 of Cheasapeake VA.; m. CHUCK PASTORAL.
62.   ii. BENJAMIN BRUCE BRIGHTWELL, b. 10 Mar 1984, Thomasville/Grady Co. GA.
     iii. BLAKE THOMAS BRIGHTWELL, b. 02 Mar 1966, Thomasville, Ga./Grady Co. Ga..

Children of BRUCE BRIGHTWELL and PATRICIA WILKINSON are:
     iv. KEVIN JAMES NORMAN[9] BRIGHTWELL, b. 04 Feb 1965, Bethesada Naval Base, Virginia.
63.   v. NORMAN RUSSELL BRIGHTWELL, b. 04 Jul 1968, PGH Medical Center, Salisbury, Maryland; d. Named after g-father/Norman Russell Wilkinson on his mother's side of family..

59. BETTY JOYCE[8] BRIGHTWELL (*LEROY[7], JAMES "JIMMIE" HILERY (SR)[6], LEN REYNOLDS[5], WILLIAM[4], REYNOLDS[3], REYNOLDS OR RANDALL[2], THE BRIGHTWELL FAMILY[1] HISTORY*) was born 22 Sep 1948 in Alabama. She married PAUL (JR) BOATWRIGHT in Married. He was born 09 Mar 1942, and died 2004 in Deceased.

More About PAUL BOATWRIGHT and BETTY BRIGHTWELL:
Marriage: Married

Child of BETTY BRIGHTWELL and PAUL BOATWRIGHT is:
64.   i. ALICIA DANIELLE[9] BOATWRIGHT.

60. NELLIE GRAY (NELL)[8] BRIGHTWELL (*LEROY[7], JAMES "JIMMIE" HILERY (SR)[6], LEN REYNOLDS[5], WILLIAM[4], REYNOLDS[3], REYNOLDS OR RANDALL[2], THE BRIGHTWELL FAMILY[1] HISTORY*) died in Buried Magnolia Bat Ch. Cem.. She married EARNEST EAGERTON in Married.

More About EARNEST EAGERTON and NELLIE BRIGHTWELL:
Marriage: Married

Children of NELLIE BRIGHTWELL and EARNEST EAGERTON are:
     i. JANICE[9] EAGERTON, d. Died young-car acc. Troy, ALA>.
     ii. RANDY EAGERTON.

61. ANNIE MAE "ANN"[8] BRIGHTWELL (*LEROY[7], JAMES "JIMMIE" HILERY (SR)[6], LEN REYNOLDS[5], WILLIAM[4], REYNOLDS[3], REYNOLDS OR RANDALL[2], THE BRIGHTWELL FAMILY[1] HISTORY*) died in Buried in Missippi w/Haskel Jones Family.. She married HASKEL JONES in Married.

More About HASKEL JONES and ANNIE BRIGHTWELL:
Marriage: Married

Children of ANNIE BRIGHTWELL and HASKEL JONES are:
     i. LINDA[9] JONES.

    ii.   CAROLYN JONES.
   iii.   HILDA JONES.
   iv.   PORCHA JONES.
    v.   HUEY HASKEL JONES.

Generation No. 9

62. BENJAMIN BRUCE[9] BRIGHTWELL (*BRUCE "JIMMY"[8], LEROY[7], JAMES "JIMMIE" HILERY (SR)[6], LEN REYNOLDS[5], WILLIAM[4], REYNOLDS[3], REYNOLDS OR RANDALL[2], THE BRIGHTWELL FAMILY[1] HISTORY)* was born 10 Mar 1984 in Thomasville/Grady Co. GA. He married KYSHA TAYLOR.

Child of BENJAMIN BRIGHTWELL and KYSHA TAYLOR is:
    i.   DIONDRE[10] "STEP-SON".

63. NORMAN RUSSELL[9] BRIGHTWELL (*BRUCE "JIMMY"[8], LEROY[7], JAMES "JIMMIE" HILERY (SR)[6], LEN REYNOLDS[5], WILLIAM[4], REYNOLDS[3], REYNOLDS OR RANDALL[2], THE BRIGHTWELL FAMILY[1] HISTORY)* was born 04 Jul 1968 in PGH Medical Center, Salisbury, Maryland, and died in Named after g-father/Norman Russell Wilkinson. He met (1) LANETTE BROWN in Met, June 17, 2002 Engaged March 2003, daughter of J. BROWN and THELMA BRYANT. She was born 14 May 1953 in Pavo/Brooks Co., GA.[re Birth Cert.]1/8 Cherokee Indian Blood. He met (2) HOLLI KAY FEATHERS 18 Aug 1995 in Sussex County, Georgetown, Delaware. She was born in of Frankfort, Delaware.

More About NORMAN BRIGHTWELL and LANETTE BROWN:
Other-Begin: Met, June 17, 2002 Engaged March 2003

More About NORMAN BRIGHTWELL and HOLLI FEATHERS:
Other-Begin: 18 Aug 1995, Sussex County, Georgetown, Delaware

Children of NORMAN BRIGHTWELL and HOLLI FEATHERS are:
    i.   CHRISTIAN RUSSELL[10] BRIGHTWELL, b. 28 Jan 1997, Born Frankfort, Delaware.
   ii.   KYLER NICHOLAS-NORMAN BRIGHTWELL, b. 13 Apr 1998, Born Frankfort, Delaware.

64. ALICIA DANIELLE[9] BOATWRIGHT (*BETTY JOYCE[8] BRIGHTWELL, LEROY[7], JAMES "JIMMIE" HILERY (SR)[6], LEN REYNOLDS[5], WILLIAM[4], REYNOLDS[3], REYNOLDS OR RANDALL[2], THE BRIGHTWELL FAMILY[1] HISTORY)*

Child of ALICIA DANIELLE BOATWRIGHT is:
    i.   DALTON PAUL[10] BOATWRIGHT, b. 08 Jul 1993.

Descendants of THE BEDGOOD FAMILY HISTORY

Generation No. 1

1. THE BEDGOOD FAMILY[1] HISTORY was born in READ THE NOTES..

Notes for THE BEDGOOD FAMILY HISTORY:
ABOUT BEDGOOD surname:
BEDGOOD is one of the hundreds of surnames that the Melungeons inter-married, mixed.

The Melungeons are most likely the descendants of the late 16th century Portuguese and Turks stranded on the Carolina shores when the settlement of Santa Elena, South Carolina was abandoned by the Spanish. They later intermarried with the Powhatan, Pamunkey, Chickahominy and Catawba Indians.

After being abandoned in the outlying Spanish forts, they settled in the Appalachians and further intermarried with the Chreokees and much later with the northern European settlers; primarily the Scotch-Irish, becoming part of the American Melting Pot.

The word Melungeon is both Portuguese, meaning "white person" and Turkish, meaning "cursed soul."

Certain surnames are associated with this highly interesting group of people. Beware, however,that many people bearing these surnames, even if they come from the Appalachian area, are NOT connected to the Melungeons. The surnames are to be used as an indicator of possible Melungeon ancestry. Also, note that many Melungeon women "out-married," carrying the heritage with them, but not the names. Not having one of these names does not mean that the family was not of Melungeon descent.

So, keep this in mind when researching the BEDGOOD family history in the United States. Family photos are good indicators of Melungeon Heritage.

A Alabama Submission:
Bedgood
  submitted by:Carla Bedgood<bedgood@aol.com> 7-7-2003
Father
306 James Bedgoed (should be Bedgood).
b about 1788 in NC,
Mother
Pheraby
born about 1788 in NC

Child 1.
John Bedgood
b 1826 GA
d. 5-18-1890 in Butler Co., AL
m. Mary P. Roach
b 4-22-1830 Duke's Mill, Butler Co. (Now Crenshaw) AL
d 6-4-1916 Covington Co., AL
m 2-7-1854 Butler Co., AL

Child 2
Mary Ann Bedgood
b.about 1829 in AL

Child 3
Jane Bedgood

b about 1833 in AL

Sources: 1850 census and family records

Butler Co. Alabama Cemetery Records of some BEDGOOD family members:
Bedgood   A.Z.   Maye Cemetery
Bedgood   Alice   Fort Dale Cemetery

Child of THE BEDGOOD FAMILY HISTORY is:
2.   i.   JOHN[2] BEDGOOD, b. Abt. 1730, Revolutionary Soldier; d. Abt. 1832, Riddleville, Washington Co. GA
                  at age 112..

Generation No. 2

2. JOHN[2] BEDGOOD *(THE BEDGOOD FAMILY[1] HISTORY)* was born Abt. 1730 in Revolutionary Soldier,
and died Abt. 1832 in Riddleville, Washington Co. GA at age 112.. He married (1) MARY GLOVER Bef.
1770 in He Married first wife at age 40.. She was born in First Wife/two children.. He married (2) MARY
WHITE Bef. 1775 in Married 2nd Wife at age 45.

Notes for JOHN BEDGOOD:

    Washington County Georgia, was created from Creek and Cherokee land cessions, and was the first in
the nation to be named for President George Washington. Its first settlers were Revolutionary War veterans,
who were given land grants for their service to the country.

    This [Washington] county was established [25 February] in 1784. It then included all the territory from
the Cherokee Corner, north, extending from the Ogeechee to the Oconee, south to Liberty County. In 1786
a portion of it was added to Greene; in 1793, a part to Hancock; in 1807, a part to Baldwin; in 1811, a part
to Laurens; and in 1812 and 1826, more to Baldwin.

John Bedgood R.S. received land in 1827 Washington Co. Ga. as well as Samuel Bedgood.

1820 Census Washington Co. Georgia:
133B 13 Bedgood   Alexander   pg0126a.txt
136B 29 Bedgood   John   pg0126a.txt
136B 8   Bedgood   John, Jr.   pg0126a.txt
137A 4   Bedgood   Richard   pg0137a.txt
136B 9   Bedgood   Samuel   pg0126a.txt

1830 Census Washington Co. Ga.:
Bedgood   John   pg0252a.txt 255A/B   9
Bedgood   Richard   pg0265a.txt 269A/B 23
Bedgood   Samuel   pg0265a.txt 269A/B 19

More About JOHN BEDGOOD and MARY GLOVER:
Marriage: Bef. 1770, He Married first wife at age 40.

More About JOHN BEDGOOD and MARY WHITE:
Marriage: Bef. 1775, Married 2nd Wife at age 45

Children of JOHN BEDGOOD and MARY GLOVER are:

3.   i.   JOHN JR.[3] BEDGOOD, b. 1775.
      ii.   JULIA BEDGOOD.
      iii. PRISCILLA JANE BEDGOOD, b. 1864.

Children of JOHN BEDGOOD and MARY WHITE are:

4.   iv. SAMUEL FRANKLIN (SR)[3] BEDGOOD, b. Abt. 1780, Born in Georgia; d. 13 Nov 1850, He was 70 yrs old Riddlevlle, Washington Co. Ga..
      v.   JANE BEDGOOD, m. GLOVER.
      vi. RICHARD BEDGOOD, m. ELIZABETH WHITFIELD.
      vii. ELI BEDGOOD, m. POWELL.
      viii. HOLLIE BEDGOOD, m. HAWTHORNE.
      ix. SALLIE BEDGOOD, b. 1815.

Generation No. 3

3. JOHN JR.[3] BEDGOOD *(JOHN[2], THE BEDGOOD FAMILY[1] HISTORY)* was born 1775. He married MARY.

Children of JOHN BEDGOOD and MARY are:

5.   i.   NANCY[4] BEDGOOD, b. 1822.
6.   ii.   GUILFORD BEDGOOD, b. 1822.
      iii. MARY BEDGOOD, b. 1827.

4. SAMUEL FRANKLIN (SR)[3] BEDGOOD *(JOHN[2], THE BEDGOOD FAMILY[1] HISTORY)* was born Abt. 1780 in Born in Georgia, and died 13 Nov 1850 in He was 70 yrs old Riddlevlle, Washington Co. Ga.. He married MARY ROGERS Abt. 1808 in He Married at 28 yrs of age..

Notes for SAMUEL FRANKLIN (SR) BEDGOOD:

1870 Census of Crenshaw Co. Ala.13 BEDGOOD   Samuel   25 wm GA
    "   Amanda   24 wf AL
    "   Osrella   1 wf AL

Alabama BUTLER County Land Grant Federal
Bedgood   Richmond   Butler 16E 9N 21 1843

Montgomery County Alabama 1870 Census lists the following BEDGOOD family:
BEDFORD A?izy Male White 56 NJ Blacksmith
Susan Fem White 50 NJ Housekeeper
Edwin Male White 24 AL
Anna Fem White 15 AL

More About SAMUEL BEDGOOD and MARY ROGERS:
Marriage: Abt. 1808, He Married at 28 yrs of age.

Children of SAMUEL BEDGOOD and MARY ROGERS are:

7.   i.   SAMUEL FRANKLIN (JR)[4] BEDGOOD, b. 27 Sep 1831, Russell, Ala.Postmaster/Pigeon Creek, Butler Co. Ala.; d. 1862, Died during the Civil War..
8.   ii.   JAMES MADISON BEDGOOD, b. 13 Mar 1814, born Riddleville, Washington Co. Ga.; d. Bef. 1870, He was 55 yrs old..
9.   iii. JOHN RICHARD BEDGOOD, b. 1810, Riddleville, Washington Co. Georgia; d. 23 Aug 1888, Died at age 78 yrs..
10.   iv. CYRUS BEDGOOD, b. 20 Aug 1815, bornin Riddleville, Washington County, Ga.; d. 07 Apr 1879,

Died at age 63 years.

11.   v.   ELI BEDGOOD, b. 08 Oct 1818, Riddleville, Washington Co. Ga.; d. 25 Nov 1885, Died Washington Co. Ga. at age 67.

  vi.   ELIZABETH BEDGOOD, b. 1820.

  vii.   JANE BEDGOOD, b. 1825, born in Riddleville, Washington Co. Ga.; m. (1) CALVIN VANN, 10 Apr 1845, Married Wasington Co. Ga. She was 20 yrs old; m. (2) ROBERT SUMMER, 13 Sep 1849, Married Him at age 24 yrs. old..

More About CALVIN VANN and JANE BEDGOOD:
Marriage: 10 Apr 1845, Married Wasington Co. Ga. She was 20 yrs old

More About ROBERT SUMMER and JANE BEDGOOD:
Marriage: 13 Sep 1849, Married Him at age 24 yrs. old.

12.   viii.   JORDAN BEDGOOD, b. 10 May 1834, Riddleville, Washington Co. Ga./CSA Civil War Soldier; d. 1914, Died 79 yrs./Pension Shws Parolled Petersburg,VA 1865.

13.   ix.   MARY BEDGOOD, b. 1836, born Riddleville, Washington Co. Ga.; d. Children bornin Georgia..

  x.   MARTHA BEDGOOD, b. 1839, born in Riddleville, Washington Co. Ga.; d. 1850, Died at age 11 years old..

Generation No. 4

5. NANCY[4] BEDGOOD *(JOHN JR.[3], JOHN[2], THE BEDGOOD FAMILY[1] HISTORY)* was born 1822. She married JESSE GLOVER.

Children of NANCY BEDGOOD and JESSE GLOVER are:
  i.   SARAH[5] BEDGOOD, b. 1840.
  ii.   RICHARD BEDGOOD, b. 1842.
  iii.   ELIAS BEDGOOD, b. 1845.
  iv.   WILLIAM BEDGOOD, b. 1847.

6. GUILFORD[4] BEDGOOD *(JOHN JR.[3], JOHN[2], THE BEDGOOD FAMILY[1] HISTORY)* was born 1822. He married LUCINDA.

Children of GUILFORD BEDGOOD and LUCINDA are:
  i.   JOHN A.[5] BEDGOOD, b. Aft. 05 Nov 1850.
  ii.   JOHNATHAN J. BEDGOOD, b. Abt. 1851.
  iii.   LINY E. BEDGOOD, b. 1856.
  iv.   JAMES W. BEDGOOD, b. Abt. 1859.

7. SAMUEL FRANKLIN (JR)[4] BEDGOOD *(SAMUEL FRANKLIN (SR)[3], JOHN[2], THE BEDGOOD FAMILY[1] HISTORY)* was born 27 Sep 1831 in Russell, Ala.Postmaster/Pigeon Creek, Butler Co. Ala., and died 1862 in Died during the Civil War.. He married SOPHRONIA ELIZABETH NIX 31 Aug 1856 in Butler Co. Alabma Marriage Record, daughter of ELIJAH NIX and MARTHA EDWARDS. She was born 12 Jun 1837 in born Russell Co. Alabama She remarried after his death..

Notes for SAMUEL FRANKLIN (JR) BEDGOOD:
BEDGOOD FAMILY RESEARCH AND NOTES:

Samuel Franklin Bedgood Jr. was born on September 27, 1831 in Riddleville, Washington County, Georgia. Samuel Franklin died about 1862 and he was 30 years old. He died in the Civil War.

    He was Postmaster at Pigeon Creek. Pigeon Creek was a community in Butler County a few miles north of Oakey Streak. The Spaniards named the road from Andalusia to Greenville Alabama the Montezuma Road, but the natives always called it the Pigeon Creek Road or the Oakey Streak Road. The Pigeon Creek Post Office was Established in 1856. It was discontinued on October 9, 1866 and was re-established July 6, 1868. It discontinued three years later, but re-established in 1873.

oN aUGUST 28, 1856 WHEN sAMUEL fRANKLIN WAS 24, HE MARRIED sAPHRONIA eLIZABETH nIX, DAUGHTER OF eLIJAH nIX AND mARTHA eDWARDS. [More research is being done to find the marriage record].

Marriage Record: _____ McCAMACK to John L. BEDGOOD 6 SEP 1880 Escambia Co., AL

SOME BEDGOOD FAMILY RESEARCH:

BEDGOOD, ROACH, and SEALE families of Greenville, Butler County, Alabama. My grandfather was Louis Kendrick BEDGOOD (1899 - 1963). His parents were William Henry BEDGOOD (1861 - 1937) and Daisy Mae SEALE (1881 - 1954). William Henry BEDGOOD's parents were John BEDGOOD (1822/1828 in Georgia - 1890) and Mary P. ROACH (1830 - 1916). Daisy Mae SEALE's parents were Henry Oliver SEALE (1839 - 1913) and Mary Susan Huson HENDERSON (1843 - 1915).

Cemetery Record Butler Co. Alabama THE MAY CEMETERY DIRECTIONS: Traveling south on Interstate 65 from Greenville, go 16 miles and take the Starlington/Georgiana exit 144 and travel west on State Hwy. 106 for 6.5 miles. Pass Jct. 17, and continue to travel on Hwy 106 and turn left (south) at Highway 15. Go 2.5 miles pass Long Creek Baptist Church on the left and the old Long Creek Baptist Church on the right. Shortly thereafter on the left is an unpaved red dirt road. Bordered on each side of the road are pine trees that tower like guards along this diagonal road. The road is narrow which eventually exits onto a clearing which is the cemetery. There are no signs stating this is the May Cemetery.

4. A.Z. Bedgood born 26 Mar 1817, died 14 Oct 1948.

More About SAMUEL BEDGOOD and SOPHRONIA NIX:
Marriage: 31 Aug 1856, Butler Co. Alabma Marriage Record

Children of SAMUEL BEDGOOD and SOPHRONIA NIX are:
14. i. MARY ELIZABETH (MOLLIE)[5] BEDGOOD, b. 19 Apr 1861, Lowndes Co. Alabama; d. 04 Oct 1914, Died-Cancer in Womb./Sawyer Cem.Ala..
15. ii. SALLY (SARAH) BEDGOOD, b. Apr 1860; d. both Buried at Providence Cemetery-No headstones..
     iii. MISSOURI BEDGOOD.

8. JAMES MADISON[4] BEDGOOD (SAMUEL FRANKLIN (SR)[3], JOHN[2], THE BEDGOOD FAMILY[1] HISTORY) was born 13 Mar 1814 in born Riddleville, Washington Co. Ga., and died Bef. 1870 in He was 55 yrs old.. He married MATILDA CUNNINGHAM 08 Jul 1842 in Married Washington Co. Ga.. She was born 1826 in born in S. Carolina, and died 1911 in Died age 86.

Notes for JAMES MADISON BEDGOOD:
1860 Covington, Alabama p 421 - under James M. Bedgood
    James M. Bedgood, age 46 born in S. Carolina
    Matilda age 34 bornin S. Carolina
    Samuel J. age 16 born in Georgia
    Mary Ann Bedgood age 12 months
    William M. Bedgood age 9 months
    Jesse age 8 months
    Martha T. age 6 months
    Martha E. age 3 months born in Alabama
    Jefferson age 9 months born in Alabama

1870 Covington, Alabama page 484
    Bedgood, Matilda age 44 Ga ??? [this is wrong]
    William Bedgood age 18 born in Alabama
    Franklin Bedgood age 16 born in Alabama
    Martha J. age 15 born in Alabama
    Mary Elizabeth age 12 born in Alabama

1910 Franklin Tex under Jessie F. Bedgood

More About MATILDA CUNNINGHAM:
Burial: Mt. Providence Cemetery, Vernon Texas

More About JAMES BEDGOOD and MATILDA CUNNINGHAM:
Marriage: 08 Jul 1842, Married Washington Co. Ga.

Children of JAMES BEDGOOD and MATILDA CUNNINGHAM are:
    i.   SAMUEL JASPER[5] BEDGOOD, b. 1844; d. 1908.
    ii.   MARYANN W. BEDGOOD, b. 1845.
    iii. WILLIAM MADISON BEDGOOD, b. 1850.
    iv.   JESSE FRANKLIN BEDGOOD, b. 1852; d. 1935.
    v.   MARTHA JANE BEDGOOD, b. 23 Sep 1854, Born in Alabama.
    vi.   MATILDA ELIZABETH BEDGOOD, b. 1857; d. 1935.
    vii. JEFFERSON RICHMOND, b. 1859; d. 1925.
    viii. JOHN T. BEDGOOD, b. 24 Sep 1847, Born in Georgia.
    ix.   ANDREW CALVIN BEDGOOD, b. 1862; d. 1928.

9. JOHN RICHARD[4] BEDGOOD *(SAMUEL FRANKLIN (SR)[3], JOHN[2], THE BEDGOOD FAMILY[1] HISTORY)* was born 1810 in Riddleville, Washington Co. Georgia, and died 23 Aug 1888 in Died at age 78 yrs.. He married RHONDA in Married.

More About JOHN BEDGOOD and RHONDA:
Marriage: Married

Child of JOHN BEDGOOD and RHONDA is:
    i.   JAMES WILLIAM[5] BEDGOOD, b. 1842.

10. CYRUS[4] BEDGOOD *(SAMUEL FRANKLIN (SR)[3], JOHN[2], THE BEDGOOD FAMILY[1] HISTORY)* was born 20 Aug 1815 in bornin Riddleville, Washington County, Ga., and died 07 Apr 1879 in Died at age 63 years. He married (1) CHARLOTTE M. VICKERS 19 Dec 1839 in He married Wasington Co. Ga. at age 24.   He married (2) ELIZA CRAWFORD 18 May 1844 in Married; his second wife..

More About CYRUS BEDGOOD and CHARLOTTE VICKERS:
Marriage: 19 Dec 1839, He married Wasington Co. Ga. at age 24

More About CYRUS BEDGOOD and ELIZA CRAWFORD:
Marriage: 18 May 1844, Married; his second wife.

Children of CYRUS BEDGOOD and CHARLOTTE VICKERS are:
    i.   WILLIAM HENRY HARRISON[5] BEDGOOD, b. 05 Oct 1840, Born in Georgia/CSA Priv. Co. F. 14th Reg. Ga Infantry; d. 20 May 1864, Ocean Pond, Florida and he was 23 years old..

          Notes for WILLIAM HENRY HARRISON BEDGOOD:
          William Henry Harrison Bedgood; Died during the Civil War. He enlisted as a Private Co. F. 14th Reg. GA Infantry July 11, 1861. He transferred to Co. A, 28th Reg. Ga Infantry and was appointed Musician. He was killed at Ocean Pond, Florida on 2-20-1864 [Roster of GA Soldier Vol 3, page

361].

More About WILLIAM HENRY HARRISON BEDGOOD:
Burial: Died as a Civil War Soldier

   ii.   JOHN ANDREW BEDGOOD, b. 22 Feb 1843, bornin Georgia./Priv. Civil War CSA; d. 27 Jun 1862, Killed at Cold Harbor at age 19 years..

More About JOHN ANDREW BEDGOOD:
Burial: Enltd as Priv. 4/22/1861

Children of CYRUS BEDGOOD and ELIZA CRAWFORD are:
   iii.   JAMES ALLEN[5] BEDGOOD, b. 1845.
   iv.   JASON THOMAS BEDGOOD, b. 1847; d. 1882.
   v.   MARY ANN SAMANTHA BEDGOOD, b. 1849; d. 1930.
   vi.   GREEN MARTIN BEDGOOD, b. 02 Jun 1854; d. 12 Sep 1854, Only lived four months..
   vii.   CHARLES MILTON BEDGOOD, b. 1855; d. 1928.
   viii.   SARAH ANN ELIZABETH "SALLIE" BEDGOOD, b. 1859; d. 1944.

11. ELI[4] BEDGOOD *(SAMUEL FRANKLIN (SR)[3], JOHN[2], THE BEDGOOD FAMILY[1] HISTORY)* was born 08 Oct 1818 in Riddleville, Washington Co. Ga., and died 25 Nov 1885 in Died Washington Co. Ga. at age 67.

Children of ELI BEDGOOD are:
   i.   M. J.[5] BEDGOOD, b. 1858, Born in Alabama.
   ii.   S. E. BEDGOOD, b. 1860, Alabama.

12. JORDAN[4] BEDGOOD *(SAMUEL FRANKLIN (SR)[3], JOHN[2], THE BEDGOOD FAMILY[1] HISTORY)* was born 10 May 1834 in Riddleville, Washington Co. Ga./CSA Civil War Soldier, and died 1914 in Died 79 yrs./Pension Shws Parolled Petersburg,VA 1865. He married MARY ANN PRICE 18 Oct 1855 in He Married at age 21 yrs..

More About JORDAN BEDGOOD:
Burial: Priv. 5/1/1862/Wounded Gettsburg,PA 7/2/1863.

More About JORDAN BEDGOOD and MARY PRICE:
Marriage: 18 Oct 1855, He Married at age 21 yrs.

Children of JORDAN BEDGOOD and MARY PRICE are:
   i.   ELIZABETH[5] BEDGOOD, b. 1856, born in GA.
   ii.   MARY ANN BEDGOOD, b. 1857, bornin GA.
   iii.   HARRIET BEDGOOD, b. 1858, born in GA.
   iv.   JOHN BEDGOOD, b. 1867.
   v.   WILLIAM H. BEDGOOD, b. 1868.
   vi.   JULIANN BEDGOOD, b. 1871.
   vii.   ROBERT JAMES BEDGOOD, b. 1873.
   viii.   JOHN F. BEDGOOD, b. 1876.
   ix.   ANNIE F. BEDGOOD, b. 1879.

13. MARY[4] BEDGOOD *(SAMUEL FRANKLIN (SR)[3], JOHN[2], THE BEDGOOD FAMILY[1] HISTORY)* was born 1836 in born Riddleville, Washington Co. Ga., and died in Children bornin Georgia.. She married WILEY SMALLPEACE 15 Aug 1854 in She married at age 18 yrs. Emanuel Co. Georgia.

More About WILEY SMALLPEACE and MARY BEDGOOD:
Marriage: 15 Aug 1854, She married at age 18 yrs. Emanuel Co. Georgia

Children of MARY BEDGOOD and WILEY SMALLPEACE are:
- i. SARAH[5] SMALLPEACE, b. 1856.
- ii. WILEY SMALLPIECE, b. 1858.
- iii. MARTHA SMALLPEACE, b. 1860.
- iv. JORDAN SMALLPEACE, b. 1862.

Generation No. 5

14. MARY ELIZABETH (MOLLIE)[5] BEDGOOD *(SAMUEL FRANKLIN (JR)[4], SAMUEL FRANKLIN (SR)[3], JOHN[2], THE BEDGOOD FAMILY[1] HISTORY)* was born 19 Apr 1861 in Lowndes Co. Alabama, and died 04 Oct 1914 in Died-Cancer in Womb./Sawyer Cem.Ala.. She married JAMES "JIMMIE" HILERY (SR) BRIGHTWELL 21 Jan 1885 in Lowndes Co., Alabama, son of LEN BRIGHTWELL and ELIZABETH PARKER. He was born 18 Jul 1861 in Butler Co. Ala.18 yrs old/1880 Cen. Sandy Ridge, Lowndes Co.,Ala., and died 09 Sep 1938 in Crenshaw Co., Alabama/Magnolia Cemetery.

Notes for MARY ELIZABETH (MOLLIE) BEDGOOD:
BEDGOOD FAMILY:

Mary (Mollie) Bedgood married James H. Brightwell 21st. Jan. 1885 in Lowndes Co.Al. James H. and Mollie Brightwell lived most of their married life in north Crenshaw Co.Al. near Montgomery and lowndes Co. line.

Here are the bedgoods. [Information provided by Martha Brightwell]
Samuel died in CW and Saphronia married Wiley Wren.

Saphronia Elizabeth NIX sister to Edward NIX wife of Samuel Bedgood and Wiley Wren. Saphronia's two daughters married brightwells . Mollie (Mary Elizabeth) bedgood married James H. brightwell and Sally (sarah) Bedgood married Hillery Albert Brightwell in Alabama. Edward Nix was born in 1817 Oglethorpe County, Ga. Married Jane Perry , daughter of John Perry on Dec,24, 1839. Jane Perry was born 30 oct.1820, Wake co. NC.Jane died 4 jan.1901 Oaky Streak, Butler co. Alabama and is buried Oaky Streak Methodist Church Cemetary in southeast section of Butler Co.Alabam. (south of Greenville AL. near Crenshaw and Cuvington county line.

More About MARY ELIZABETH (MOLLIE) BEDGOOD:
Burial: Buried at Sawyer Cemetery, Sandy Ridge, Alabama

Notes for JAMES "JIMMIE" HILERY (SR) BRIGHTWELL:
1870 Census Alabama:
JAMES H. Brightwell of Crenshaw County, Alabama.
He first appears in a 1870 Census in Alabama in Crenshaw Co. Alabama. He is shown as 8 yrs old in the family of his mother-Caroline Brightwell who is listed as head of household at 42 years of age.

1900 Census Alabama:
James H. Brightwell is now shown as Head of Household at age 39 yrs. living in the Crenshaw - Surles Area of Alabama. It also shows that his mother: Caroline born 1827-age 73 years is living in his home. The children listed in 1900 are: James July 1890; Arthur Feb 1892; Robert E. Nov. 1893; Ira July 1897 son; and Ila July 1897 Daug.
James's daughter Sarah was not living in his home anymore-she died 1889.
Charles M. Brightwell was not living in the home anymore.-he died 1889.
Estelle Brightwell was not born until after the 1900 census so she would not have been on the record.
Leroy Brightwell would also not have been on the record.

Magnolia Baptist Church History 1907:

In 1907 a small group of Baptist people were meeting at Fomble school house. On Aug. 16,1908, the following members met and agreed to build a church: J.W.Taylor, J.H.BRIGHTWELL, Sr., J.H. Brightwell, Jr., N.E. Brightwell, Arthur Brightwell, Lee Betterton, Sisters Annie Taylor, Mary Brightwell, Martha Betterton (James Sr. sister), Mattie Edwards, Velma Beck, Addie Taylor, Georgia Taylor. JAMES H. BRIGHTWELL's name on deed. You can find the deed at the Crenshaw County Alabama court House Luverne Alabama.You can find the History of the Church at the Greenville Alabama Lib. In research room. I think there may be a copy at the Luverne Lib. It is beleived that two of James H. Brightwell Sr. sons married two Rhodes. James H. Brightwell Jr. married Anna Bell Rhodes and R.E. Brightwell married Lucy Mae Rhodes. It is said that a Methodist Church was there before Magnolia Bapt. Church

Brightwell, Moseleyy & Rhodes, in the book, "Cemeteries Crenshaw County Alabama", by Joyce Morgan English:
Brightwell:
1. A Brightwell with no name given in the Tatum lot
2. J.H. b. Jul 18 1861 d. Sep 09 1938
3. James H. b. Jul 27 1890 d. Dec 07 1972
4. Lucy R. b. Nov 09 1899 d. Aug 07 1981
5. Mary A.H. b. May 08 105 d. No date
6. Moscoe? b. Oct 05 1932 d. Aug 01 1960 AL Sgt US Army
7. R.E. b. Nov 05 1894 d. Nov 17 1838
8. W. James b. Nov 11 1923 d. Oct 04 1951
9. Wallace Lester b. Nov 07 1924 d. Aug 23 1982 Sgt US Army WW II

Moseley:
1. Albert No dates Co. B. 63rd Alabama Inf CSA
2. Lizzie(Sexton) b. Nov 01 1880 d. Nov 23 1961
3. Mattie M. b. Apr 03 1845 d. Mar 27 1903
4. Twin b. Mar 07 1912 d. Mar 10 1912
5. " " " " " " " " "
6. William P. b. Jul 23 1913 d. Jul 28 1915
7. William Robert b. May 28 1875 d. Aug 19 1950

Rhodes:
01. Benjamin F. b. May 16 1923 d. Mar 12 1989
02. Emma b. Mar 01 1916 d. Apr 09 1916
03. Ernest b. Apr 13 1892 d. Aug 13 1893
04. Felix b. Aug 16 1901 d. Mar 20 1988
05. G.A. b. Jun 27 1871 d. Aug 17 1968
06. Gladys b. Mar 09 1917 d. Feb 12 1918
07. Horace Woodrow b. Apr 24 1912 d. Nov 26 1979
08. Jesse Albert b. Oct 09 1890 d. Apr 11 1986
09. Joey Dewayne b. Jul 18 1978 d. Oct 31 1978
10. Lucille b. Mar 15 1915 d. May 03 1915
11. Margaret Ann b. Jan 07 1980 d. Mar 03 1980
12. Margaret Jean b. Aug 05 1927 d. Aug 30 1971
13. Mattie B. b. Jul 18 1905 d. Dec 28 1946
14. McAdo b. Feb 04 1920 d. Jan 12 1924
15. Rosco b. Jan 23 1894 d. May 21 1897
16. Ruby [Henley] b. Oct 31 1909 d. unknown [w/o Horace Woodrow Rhodes]
17. Sallie Alene [Baker] b. Jun 08 1909 d. unknown
18. W.J. b. b. Aug 20 1856 d. Dec 29 1830
19. William A. b. Apr 22 1932 d. Jan 30 1986 h/o Jane Manse Rhodes m. Dec 01 1951

Magnolia Cemetery is located 1/2 mile South of the Montgomery County line in Crenshaw Co. on Hwy 97 North. There seems to be more young children's deaths in the Rhodes family than you commonly find in any one family.

I wonder if there might have been a flu epidemic at that time.
ANSWER: by: Bonnie Betterton . I grew up in the country as we called it . Knowing some of the Rhodes family . There was a lot of them and if I am thinking correctly it may have been polio at that time. not sure those .. for all the younger deaths

The ones I new where Jane Rhodes (Mother) (she could not walk had polio as a child) Mary Gail Rhodes (daughter) Sandy Rhodes (daughter) Marth Jane Rhodes (daughter).
More About JAMES "JIMMIE" HILERY (SR) BRIGHTWELL:
Rersidence: 1880, Sandy Ridge Lowndes Co ALABAMA
Residence: 1910, Surles Crenshaw Co. Alabama

More About JAMES BRIGHTWELL and MARY BEDGOOD:
Marriage: 21 Jan 1885, Lowndes Co., Alabama

Children of MARY BEDGOOD and JAMES BRIGHTWELL are:
     i. SARAH[6] BRIGHTWELL, b. 31 Oct 1888, born Alabama; d. 12 Sep 1889, Sandy Ridge Alabama Lowndes Co..

Notes for SARAH BRIGHTWELL:
ID: I856
Name: Sarah or Sarahe Brightwell
Sex: F
Birth: 31 OCT 1888 in AL
Death: 12 SEP 1889
Burial: Sawyer Cemetery, Sandy Ridge, Lowndes Co., AL
Change Date: 6 APR 2006

Father: James H. Brightwell b: 1861 in Butler Co., AL
Mother: Mary b: 19 APR 1861 in AL

More About SARAH BRIGHTWELL:
Burial: Sawyer Cemtery, Sandy Ridge, Lowndes Co.

Descendants of THE PARKER FAMILY HISTORY

Generation No. 1

1. THE PARKER FAMILY[1] HISTORY

Notes for THE PARKER FAMILY HISTORY:
1. Martha Ann Bush married Samuel Parker, October 25, 1866, in Butler Co. AL. Samuel was the son of the   Rev. Noah Parker and Catherine Eddins. He was born February 27, 1842 and died May 19, 1926. Samuel and Martha are buried at Brushy Creek Cemetery outside Chapman, Butler Co AL. Samuel served in the Civil War with his father and brothers in the 15th Confederate Calvary, Co E from Milton Florida. Samuel married 2nd Mrs Alice Payne, March 25, 1914.

Obit-Greenville Library-Surname file 6-2-1926
Sam Parker, Confederate Veteran, Passes Away
   Sam Parker, a member of Jas. H. Dunklin Camp U.C.V., died at his home a few miles from Chapman on the 19th of May. He had been confined to his home for some months. He was a little passed 83 years of age and was always an attendant upon the Camp meetings until his health failed him. Mr Parker is survived by his widow, four children, a step daughter and many grand children.
   Sam Parker was a good soldier and citizen. Engaged in farming all of his life and though age had come upon him, until a year ago was active in his calling. He has gone to be with his comrades on the other shore.

Children of Martha and Samuel:
   11. Ada J   b. Mar 18, 1869   d. Jan 14, 1900
    m. Aaron Kemp
    b. Brushy Creek Cemetery
   12. Susan   b. abt 1870   d. bef 1880
  +13. James R   b. Mar 20, 1873   d. Aug 14, 1929
  +14. George W   b. abt 1875   d.
  +15. Pearl Ada   b. Aug 1875   d. Jan 17, 1972
   16. Emma   b. Nov 23, 1880   d. 1962
    m. William L Henderson
  +17. John   b. Oct 1882

Child of THE PARKER FAMILY HISTORY is:
2.   i.   PETER[2] PARKER, b. N. Carolina before moving to S. Carolina; then to Alabama..

Generation No. 2

2. PETER[2] PARKER *(THE PARKER FAMILY[1] HISTORY)* was born in N. Carolina before moving to S. Carolina; then to Alabama.. He married SARAH BARNES.

Notes for PETER PARKER:

The Charles, 1616 Voyages are listed at ship name on Ship List
1616 The Charles, from London, arrived at Virginia

Ship and Passenger Information:
Passengers from the Port of London on the Charles to Virginia:
Parker, William . . . . . -- Age 20 in Virginia Muster, February 7, 1624/5

Jamestown Virginia Lists:
1624 ELIZABETH CITY CO.   VA P626 PARKER   , William

Parker, Samuel, (nunc.) Colonial Wills, Maryland
-- Nov., 1660; 10th Oct., 1661. To William Hurds and John Douglas, personalty. Wife, (unnamed) residuary legatee. Test: Robt. Slye, Edward Naufaun. 1. 151.
Parker, Edward, St. Inigoes Manor, St. Mary's Co., 3rd Jan., 1669; 29th Jan., 1669. To father-in-law, Nicholas Young, "Fresh Pond Neck." To mother of testator, plantation at Cedar Point, Charles Co. To brother Samuel, 800 A. "Parker's Delight,"; Baltimore Co. To sister Eliza: and Catholic Church, personalty. Test: Nicholas Solby, Richard Ridgell, Wm. Gifford. 1. 367. Colonial Wills, Maryland
Parker, Edward, St. Inigoes Manor, St. Mary's Co., 3rd Jan., 1669; 29th Jan., 1669. To father-in-law Nicholas Young, "Fresh Pond Neck." To mother of testator, plantation at Cedar Point, Charles Co. To brothers Samuel and Edward, 800 A, "Parker's Land,"; Baltimore Co. To sister Eliza: and Roman Catholic Church, personalty. In event of death of 2 brothers afsd. under age, sd. sister Eliza: to inherit land. Exs.: Father-in-law Nicholas Young and kinsman Wm. Bretton. Test: Nicholas Solby, Richard Ridgell, Wm. Gifford. 1. 367.
Colonial WILLS, Maryland

From Census records found thus far; the PARKER family is found back in North Carolina as early as the 1800's up to around 1848. The PARKER family is found migrating down into South Carlina and some children are born in S. Carolina; then the family migrated tthrough Georgia and some children were born in that State. Finally, the family settled in Covington Co. Alabama as seen in the 1860 Census Records reflecting three or more PARKER families living there at the same time.

There was the family of JAMES PARKER, born ca 1780, migrated to Houston County, Georgia, from North Carolina prior to the 1830 Federal Census in which he is recorded as head of household . James was the son of John and Mary Weeks Parker of Edgecombe and Cumberland County, North Carolina.
In Edgecombe County, records can be found a marriage bond for John Parker and Mary Weeks. The date on this document is not clear but appears to be September 27, 1760 or 1764. Mary Weeks was the daughter of James and Sarah Moore Weeks. John Parker is believed to be the "John Parker" who was one of the 39 signers of the "Liberty Point Declaration of Independence", which was signed by North Carolina patriots on June 20, 1775. A Bible record for John and Mary Weeks Parker can be found in the book, Bible Records of Early Edgecombe, by Williams and Griffin. It records the names of the children of John and Mary Weeks Parker as:

Weeks Parker, 1768-1844
Margaret Parker
Theophilus Parker, 1775-1849
Martha Parker
Mary Weeks Parker
Sarah Parker b. 1777
John Parker
James Parker m. _____ Murray and moved to Tenn.
Archibald Parker

The James Parker found in this Bible record and with the notation, "married _____ Murray and moved to Tenn " is believed to be the same James Parker found in 1830 Census in Houston County, Georgia. It is unclear as to what time James may have spent in Tennessee if indeed the Bible notation is correct. Also it is thought that James married twice both times in North Carolina, the first marriage ca 1800 and the second ca 1810. It is sad that the names of these wives are unknown. The only name that has been recalled by some

Parker descendants is "Granny Teets" which was a name of affection probably for the second Mrs. Parker. It is also interesting to note that James Parker's only daughter was named Jane and so was one of his son's (Theophilus) daughters, Nancy Jane. Could it be that one of these wives's could have been named Jane?

The children of James Parker were:

Theophilus L. Parker Born ca 1800, North Carolina
Died ca 1851, Georgia
Mary Jane Parker Born ca 1814, North Carolina
Died ca 1897, Georgia
James Parker, Jr. Born ca 1820, North Carolina
Died ca 1862, Georgia
William Parker Born ca 1822, North Carolina
Died ca 1872, Georgia
Carey Weeks Parker Born Dec. 22, 1824, North Carolina
Died July 19, 1884, Georgia
Archibald Andrew Parker Born Dec. 17, 1832, North Carolina
Died Nov. 29, 1873, Georgia

Theophilus L. Parker first married Roxy Ann Daughtry on March 8, 1847 in Houston County, Georgia. Roxy Ann was the daughter of Bryant and Nancy Neel Daughtry of Houston County. Before Theophilus's death about 1851 in Pulaski County, Georgia, he and Roxy Ann had at least two children, both daughters: Sarah Clifford Parker and Nancy Jane Parker. After Theophilus's death, Roxy Ann married again to James Elbert Holley and they had a daughter, Georgia Elizabeth Holley who later married a nephew of Theophilus Parker, Benjamin Franklin Parker. Theophilus is believed to be buried in an unmarked grave at the Parker Family Cemetery.

Mary Jane Parker was the only known daughter of James Parker. She married Alford Lawson Hudson on April 30, 1837 in Houston County, Georgia. Alford was born ca. 1814 can died at about age 40 ca 1854. He is probably buried in an unmarked grave at the Parker Family Cemetery. After Alford's death Jane Parker Hudson moved her family to Columbus, Muscogee County, Georgia, where she died at about the age of 83, ca 1897. The children of Alford and Mary Jane Parker Hudson were: James Hudson, William Hudson, Matthew Hudson, Hamilton Hudson, Mary Hudson, Weeks Hudson.

JAMES PARKER JR. was a farmer on land purchased with his brothers in Houston County which consisted of 580 acres at the current location of the intersection of Lake Joy Road and Langston Road between Perry and Warner Robins, Georgia. It is believed that he never married. He died ca 1862 and is buried in an unmarked grave in the Parker Family Cemetery.

William Parker married Rebecca Jane Peddy on August 27, 1857 in Houston County, Georgia and was a farmer on land purchased with his brothers. Rebecca Jane was born on June 16, 1837 and was the daughter of John Peddy. She was also the sister of William's brother Arch's wife, Mary Ann. William died ca 1872 at about age 50 leaving Rebecca with five minor children: William A. Parker, Shaulten P. Parker, Mary Rebecca Jane Parker, Josephine Parker and Arasbus Parker. There was a sixth child, Eliza A. Parker, who was the first born; however there is no record of Eliza after 1870. William is buried at the Parker Family Cemetery in a grave marked by a stone honoring his service in the South's struggle for independence. Rebecca died September 20, 1886; her grave at the same cemetery is unmarked.

Carey Weeks Parker (my ggg-grandfather) was born in North Carolina and married Nancy Elizabeth Ivey daughter of Myrick Ivey and his wife Lucinda. Weeks and Nancy were married on his birthday, December 22, 1846. They resided on a farm adjoining that of his brothers and had ten known children: Benjamin Franklin, George Washington, Francis Marion, Lucinda Ann, Sarah Frances, Louis Hill, Laura Emma, Joseph Weeks, Sylvester V. and James Myrick. Weeks Parker was a Confederate veteran and his grave in the Parker Family Cemetery is marked with a military marker bearing the "Southern Cross of Honor". Nancy is also buried there and though her grave is marked the information on the poured stone is barely visible.

Archibald Andrew Parker the youngest of the sons of James Parker was also born in North Carolina. On June 8, 1851 he married Mary Ann Elizabeth Peddy, born October 30, 1830 and the daughter of John Peddy and his wife. Farming on land purchased with his brothers, Arch and Mary Ann made their home also along what was then known as Tharpe's Mill Rd. but is today known as Lake Joy Rd. Arch died at age 41 on November 29, 1873 of pneumonia as reported in the Houston Home Journal and Mary Ann died only a month later, December 20, 1873 at age 43. Mary's death came only 17 days after giving birth to the couple's last child. Their deaths left the following orphaned children: James Madison, John Thomas, Walter T. Colquitt, Mary Emma, Charles Edwin, Archibald Parker, Jr. and Anna Elizabeth. Archibald Parker is buried in the Parker Family Cemetery with a marker honoring his Confederate service. Also buried there is Mary but her grave is not marked.

Three of James Parker's sons joined an artillery battalion, the Southern Rights Battery, formed in Houston County in March of 1862, to defend against the Yankee aggressors. A history of the Southern Rights Battery also known as Havis's Battery can be found elsewhere on this site. This history is dedicated to the Parker brothers, William, Arch and Weeks and also to Benjamin Franklin Parker, son of Weeks Parker, who at age 14 joined the Southern Rights Battery as a replacement for his father who had been discharged due to illness. Ben Parker was my gg-grandfather.

Additional information and a more detailed history of this family can be found in William A. Mills' publication, The James Parker Family of Georgia, 1780-1930.

UPSON COUNTY, GEORGIA:
PARKER FAMILY CEMETERY
Location:
Barnesville Road (State 36 north)out of Thomaston Courthouse Square
5.2 miles on the left side of road.

Parker, Lucy
?1766 - Nov 11, 1845
(79 years old)

Parker, Daniel
?1756 - Aug 14, 1844
(age 88)
Revolutionary Soldier
(father-in-law of Miles Meadows)

1840 Census
PARKER, Daniel
(free white persons pg 50a)
Males
1 age 20-30
1 age 80-90
Females
1 age 20-30
1 age 70-80
(slaves pg 50b)
Males
1 age 10-24
2 age 24-36
2 age 36-55
1 age 55-100
females

3 under age 10
1 age 10-24
1 age 36-55
(occupation)
6 persons in agriculture

Feb 4, 1845 Deed
Wm Trice and Jeptha Walker, Ex ot Daniel Parker, Sr
to R.M. Collier lot in 10th District.

Aug 9, 1837 Daniel Parker, Sr to his daugher, lucy Parker lot in 10Dis

Dec 4, 1832 Wm B. Hester to Daniel Parker, Sr lot in 10th Dis

Will of Daniel Parker Sr.
Wife: Lucy Parker
Children: Mary Hudman, Nancy Meadows, Faytha Dark, Stephen Parker, Daniel Parker, Jr. Phileman
Parker, Sherwood Parker, Lucy Parker, Thomas Parker, and Susannah Meadows.
Wit: Chas P. Hansford, Jonathan Colquitt, Allen Ware

Daniel Parker's Claim, Age 73
Entered service as private in Horse Company at
Chatham Court House, NC, September 15, 1780 under
Capt Mark patterson attached to Col Thos Taylor's
Reg. Remained so two months and afterwards served as
private in Horse Company of William Griffin attached
to Col Ramsey's Reg and remained three months for
which term he enlisted and then received a
discharge. Was a resident at time of Chatham Co, NC.
That he entered first term for three months but in
consequence of furnishing a horse he was only
required to serve two months.
Certified by Zach H. Gordon, Aug 30, 1832
M.R. Meadows

Revolutionary Soldier PARKER, ELISHA. "Departed this life in Morgan County, Ala., on the 21st ult.,
ELISHA PARKER, in the 97th year of his age, a native of Connecticut, and a soldier of the Revolution. He
was greatly esteemed and respected by all who knew him." The Democrat, Huntsville, May 6, 1846.

Revolutionary Soldier
PARKER, WILLIAM, age not given, a resident of Madison County; private, 4th Regular U.S. Infantry;
enrolled on September 6, 1820, payment to date from March 11, 1819; annual allowance, $96; sums
received to date of publication of list, $1,437.90; Acts Military establishment.-- Revolutionary Pension
Roll, in Vol. xiv, Sen. Doc. 514, 23rd Cong., 1st sess., 1833-34.

1850 LUMPKIN CO. Georgia CENSUS FEDERAL

64A	7	Parker	Benjamin	20	SC	pg0059B.txt
93A	4	Parker	Drury	1	GA	pg0090B.txt
64A	8	Parker	Elizabeth	19	GA	pg0059B.txt
65B	2	Parker	Juliann	16	GA	pg0059B.txt
65A	42	Parker	Margaret	37	Unknown	pg0059B.txt
107B	25	Parker	Milly	23	SC	pg0099B.txt
103B	11	Parker	Polly	50	GA	pg0099B.txt
65A	41	Parker	William	49	NC	pg0059B.txt
103B	13	Parker	William	13	GA	pg0099B.txt

1840 CENSUS of LUMPKIN Co. Georgia Federal

Parker, Barnett	255a	CAPT. DAVIS'	GMD 935
Parker, Daniel	276a	CAPT. TURNER'S	GMD 836
Parker, Polly	274a	CAPT. WALKER'S	GMD 900
Parker, William	262a	CAPT. BARRETT'S	GMD 916

1860 Covington Co. Alabama Census
307/307 Benjamin PARKER 60 m shoe maker   236 NC

Winney	47 f		GA
Mary	17 f		AL
James	16 m		
Alexander	12 m		
Winford	3 f		
William	4/12 m		

538/538 William PARKER 40 m farmer   10 SC

Epsy	35 f	
George L.	14 m	GA
Samuel	12 m	SC
Mary Jane	7 f	GA
Darli C.	9 m	
Ellen	4 f	
Martha	2 f	AL
Florida	5/12 f	

801/801 James PARKER   50 m farmer   800 1813 GA

Elizabeth	50 f		NC
Gabriel	18 m	farm laborer	AL
Lucretia	16 f		
James B.	14 m		

CENSUS of ALABAMA - Montgomery County, ALA 1860 CENSUS

29	697	651	Parker	Elizebeth	33	F			AL	
30	697	651	Parker	Thomas	16	M			AL	X
31	697	651	Parker	Warreen	1	M			AL	
32	697	651	Parker	****	26	F			GA	

REMARKS: Unreadable letters. Might be Jane.

33	698	652	Parker	D. H.	24	M	X	Merchant	500	GA
34	698	652	Parker	Sarah	23	F			GA	
35	698	652	Parker	Mary	4	F			AL	
36	698	652	Parker	Henry	2	M			AL	

FOUND HENRY CO. Alabama:

6	107	109	Parker	Henry	39	M	Farmer	SC	
7	107	109	Parker	Elizabeth	34	F		SC	
8	107	109	Parker	Rebecca	17	F		SC	
9	107	109	Parker	Miles	15	M		SC	
10	107	109	Parker	Jessee	13	M		SC	X

REMARKS: Col. 11 = 6

11	107	109	Parker	Adaline	11	F		SC	
12	107	109	Parker	Terildy	9	F		AL	
13	107	109	Parker	James M.	8	M		AL	
14	107	109	Parker	William Riley	7	M		AL	

15 107 109 Parker   William   4   M   AL

Marriage Record: Martha J. PARKER, b. Ga. 1832 married John W. LEFLORE 1859 in Butler County, AL.

New Prespect Methodist Church Cemetery RecordsButler Co. Alabama:
PARKER
norman parker jan 5, 1920 - dec 6, 1998
sybel parker may 3, 1923
george dewey parker jan 2, 1899 - aug 21, 1978
nettie (majors) parker jan 31, 1902 - sep 14, 1994
jimmy L. parker feb 19, 1955 - nov 14, 1989
margie S. oct 13, 1947
dewey L (TOP) parker sep 27, 1927 - aug 5, 1974
   Union Babtist Church   Butler Co. Alabama
James R. Parker 3/20/1873 - 8/14/1929
Sallie Mae Parker 9/16/1873 - 1/3/1950
Fannie M. (Parker) Pitts 1894 - 1953

Children of PETER PARKER and SARAH BARNES are:
3.   i.   BENJAMIN[3] PARKER, b. 1800, Born N. Carolina/60 in 1860 Ala./Covington Co. Census Shoemaker born N. Carolina.
4.   ii.   JAMES PARKER, b. 1810, Born in Georgia 50 yrs old CovingtonCo. Alabama Census 1860; d. Farmer.
5.   iii.   WILLIAM PARKER, b. 1820, Parker Fam. found moving to Ala.around 1858. from S. Carolina; d. Born S. Carolina; Died Alabama.

Generation No. 3

3. BENJAMIN[3] PARKER *(PETER[2], THE PARKER FAMILY[1] HISTORY)* was born 1800 in Born N. Carolina/60 in 1860 Ala./Covington Co. Census Shoemaker born N. Carolina. He married WINNEY in Married. She was born 1813 in Born in Georgia. 47 yrs old in 1860 Census Covington Co. Ala..

Notes for BENJAMIN PARKER:
Butler Co. Alabama Burials of PARKER FAMILY:

Parker		Elizabeth Cemetery
Parker	Alice Grant	Antioch East Cemetery
Parker	Alonzo	Macedonia Cemetery
Parker	Annie Odom	Pleasant Hill (offsite link)
Parker	Avery C.	Macedonia Cemetery
Parker	Bessie	Pleasant Hill (offsite link)
Parker	Clara C.	Antioch East Cemetery
Parker	D. T.	Pleasant Hill (offsite link)
Parker	Dewey L. Top	New Prospect Methodist
Parker	Dollie L.	Macedonia Cemetery
Parker	Dotiline	Pleasant Hill (offsite link)
Parker	Eddie Lee	Pleasant Hill (offsite link)
Parker	Emma G.	Moriah Cemetery
Parker	Eugenia	Pleasant Hill (offsite link)
Parker	George Dewey	New Prospect Methodist
Parker	George E.	Pleasant Hill (offsite link)
Parker	Grace	Moriah Cemetery
Parker	Hilary Herbert	Moriah Cemetery

Parker	Howard C.	Antioch East Cemetery
Parker	Inez B.	Pleasant Hill (offsite link)
Parker	Issac S.	Pleasant Hill (offsite link)
Parker	J. T.	Pleasant Hill (offsite link)
Parker	J. T., Mrs.	Pleasant Hill (offsite link)
Parker	James B.	Pleasant Hill (offsite link)
Parker	James B.	Pleasant Hill (offsite link)
Parker	James C.	Pleasant Hill (offsite link)
Parker	James D.	Moriah Cemetery
Parker	James R	Union Church, Part I
Parker	Jimmy L.	New Prospect Methodist
Parker	Joe V.	Pleasant Hill (offsite link)
Parker	Katie Mae	Pleasant Hill (offsite link)
Parker	Laborn Granderson	Pleasant Hill (offsite link)
Parker	Lonnie	Pleasant Hill (offsite link)
Parker	Lucille Bush	Antioch East Cemetery
Parker	M. A.	Antioch East Cemetery
Parker	M. Mae	Pleasant Hill (offsite link)
Parker	Margie S.	New Prospect Methodist
Parker	Mollie	Pleasant Hill (offsite link)
Parker	Myron K	Pleasant Hill (offsite link)
Parker	Nettie Majors	New Prospect Methodist
Parker	Norman	New Prospect Methodist
Parker	Paris	Union Church, Part I
Parker	Phillip T.	Macedonia Cemetery
Parker	Prudence	Pleasant Hill (offsite link)
Parker	Sallie Mae	Union Church, Part I
Parker	Sudie G.	Pleasant Hill (offsite link)
Parker	Sybel	New Prospect Methodist
Parker	Vina Jane	Elizabeth Cemetery
Parker	W.A.	Macedonia Cemetery
Parker	William Edgar	Pleasant Hill (offsite link)
Parker	William W.	Pleasant Hill (offsite link)
Parker	Wilson R.	Pleasant Hill (offsite link)

Marriage RECORDS FOUND: Eliza MONTGOMERY married Philemon PARKER on 3 Feb. 1828 in Jefferson Co., AL by Jesse Turner, J.P. <martha@arc.net>

Miss Emma MORRISON to W. S. PARKER 30th December 1897. E.A. Phillips, Judge of Probate. Clay County, Alabama. Copy of actual marriage license. <JHEND64@aol.com>

B.G. PARKER married Emily HARBISON on 9/7/1899, Cullman Co., AL. <beulah@airnet.net>
* John PARKER to Mary HIGGIGNS 23 Aug 1835 Limestone Co, AL by Samuel LENTZ, JP <Mfolkner@aol.com> * Joseph T. PARKER to Martha HIGGINS 25 Jun 1836 Limestone Co, AL by Samuel LENTZ, JP <Mfolkner@aol.com>
* Thomas PARKER to Telitha TOOTEN 24 Feb 1838 Limestone Co, AL by Samuel LENTZ, JP <Mfolkner@aol.com>
* William M. PARKER married Lilly A. GRIFFIN 5-5-1910 by F.J. Dean, Judge, From Book E. Marriages 1908-1916 Conecuh Co, AL. <FindMyKin@aol.com>
* Philemon PARKER married Eliza MONTGOMERY on 3 Feb 1828 in Jefferson Co., AL <martha@arc.net>
* Thomas E. PARKER married Susan TOMLINSON abt 1893 in Madison County, AL. <eparker03@sprynet.com>
* William David PARKER married to Frances Malinda CHAMBERLAIN, July 22, 1841, p.30, by James

Allums - RUSSELL CO. AL <NitaUno@aol.com>
* William S. PARKER - Lucinda YEILDING - 23 Sep 1854 - Morgan Co., AL.
* Wm. S. PARKER to Vicey HORTON 9th November 1873. Thompson Reeves, Justice of the Peace. Clay County, Alabama. Copy of actual marriage license. <JHEND64@aol.com>
* W. S. PARKER to Miss Emma MORRISON 30th December 1897. E.A. Phillips, Judge of Probate. Clay County, Alabama. Copy of actual marriage license. <JHEND64@aol.com>

Covington Co. Alabama Agricultural Census 1850
Parker, Benjamin - value of farming implements and machinery $5, 5 milk cows, 5 other cattle, value of livestock $40, 75 lbs. of butter, value of home-made manufactures $30, value of animals slaughtered $40

More About BENJAMIN PARKER and WINNEY:
Marriage: Married

Children of BENJAMIN PARKER and WINNEY are:
     i.   WILLIAM[4] PARKER, b. either 4/12 yrs of age not knwn for sure..
6.   ii. DANIEL C. PARKER, b. 1804, born in S. Carolina. 1850 Cens. Stewart Co., Ga.; d. 55 yrs old in 1860Census. Prec. 15, Butler Co. Ala.
    iii. MARY PARKER, b. 1843, Born Covington Co. Alabama.
    iv. JAMES PARKER, b. 1844, Born in Covington Co. Alabama.
    v. ALEXANDER PARKER, b. 1846, Born Covington Co. Alabama.
    vi. WINIFORD PARKER, b. 1857, Born Covington Co. Alabama.

4. JAMES[3] PARKER (*PETER*[2], *THE PARKER FAMILY*[1] *HISTORY*) was born 1810 in Born in Georgia 50 yrs old CovingtonCo. Alabama Census 1860, and died in Farmer. He married ELIZABETH in Married. She was born 1810 in Born in North Carolina.

Notes for JAMES PARKER:
1870 Mortalities Census of Covington Co. Alabama

James Parker age 61 born in Georgia
wife: Elizabeth age 56 born in North Carolina

More About JAMES PARKER and ELIZABETH:
Marriage: Married

Children of JAMES PARKER and ELIZABETH are:
    i. GABRIEL[4] PARKER, b. 1842, Farm Laborer 1860 Census CovingtonCo. Alabama.
    ii. LUCRETIA PARKER, b. 1844, 16 yrs old in 1860 Census Covington Co Alabama.
    iii. JAMES B. PARKER, b. 1846, 14 yrs old 1860 Census Covington Co Alabama.

        Notes for JAMES B. PARKER:
        40 214 190 Parker   J. B.   31 M X Grocerer   1,000 10,000 NC

        CENSUS YR: 1860 STATE: Alabama COUNTY: Montgomery DIVISION: Ramah REEL NO: M653-19 PAGE NO: 28
        REFERENCE: Enumerated by C. C. Wilkins on 17 July 1860, 2nd District

LN HN FN LAST NAME	FIRST NAME	AGE SEX RACE OCCUP.	REAL VAL. PERS VAL. BIRTHPLACE	MRD. SCH. R/W DDB
1 214 190 Parker	Louisa	24 F	GA	
2 214 190 Parker	Eugenia	27 F	AL	
3 214 190 Parker	Wm	4 M	AL	

5. WILLIAM[3] PARKER *(PETER[2], THE PARKER FAMILY[1] HISTORY)* was born 1820 in Parker Fam. found moving to Ala.around 1858. from S. Carolina, and died in Born S. Carolina; Died Alabama. He married EPSY in Married. She was born 1825 in Born S. Carolina; died Alabama.

More About WILLIAM PARKER:
Burial: Found in 1860 Census Covington Co., Alabama

More About WILLIAM PARKER and EPSY:
Marriage: Married

Children of WILLIAM PARKER and EPSY are:
  i.   FLORIDA[4] PARKER, b. 5 or 12 yrs of age unkn.
  ii. DARLI C. PARKER, b. 1845.
  iii. GEORGE L. PARKER, b. 1846, Born in Georgia..
  iv. SAMUEL PARKER, b. 1848, Born S. Carolina; died Alabama.
  v.   MARY JANE PARKER, b. 1853, Born in Georgia..
  vi. ELLEN PARKER, b. 1856.
  vii. MARTHA PARKER, b. 1858, Born in Alabama.

Generation No. 4

6. DANIEL C.[4] PARKER *(BENJAMIN[3], PETER[2], THE PARKER FAMILY[1] HISTORY)* was born 1804 in born in S. Carolina. 1850 Cens. Stewart Co., Ga., and died in 55 yrs old in 1860Census. Prec. 15, Butler Co. Ala. He married MARY MITCHELL 1825 in Jones County, Georgia Marriage, daughter of HENRY MITCHELL and MARY LASSITER. She was born 1809 in From Lumpkin Co. Ga. 50 yrs old 1860 Census Butler Co. ALA, and died in Caroline is from Stewart; meaning Mary Mitchell-not her Mother??.

Notes for DANIEL C. PARKER:
PARKER FAMILY RESEARCH

Two different WILLIAM PARKERS were in LUMPKIN CO. GA. Federal Census 1834
but NOT our Daniel C. Parker; he would have been too young to be head of household. Daniel Parker appeared on the US Census 1820 and 1830 Habersham Co. Georgia (I believe this is possibility a uncle of our Daniel C. Parker.

The man named on this family page; Daniel C. Parker born 1804; is found in the Lumpkin Co. Georgia 1840 Census as shown.
1840 CENSUS of LUMPKIN Co. Georgia Federal

Parker, Barnett	255a	CAPT. DAVIS'	GMD 935
Parker, Daniel	276a	CAPT. TURNER'S	GMD 836
Parker, Polly	274a	CAPT. WALKER'S	GMD 900
Parker, William	262a	CAPT. BARRETT'S	GMD 916

1850 LUMPKIN CO. Georgia CENSUS FEDERAL

64A	7	Parker	Benjamin	20 SC	pg0059B.txt
93A	4	Parker	Drury	1 GA	pg0090B.txt
64A	8	Parker	Elizabeth	19 GA	pg0059B.txt
65B	2	Parker	Juliann	16 GA	pg0059B.txt
65A	42	Parker	Margaret	37 Unknown	pg0059B.txt
107B	25	Parker	Milly	23 SC	pg0099B.txt
103B	11	Parker	Polly	50 GA	pg0099B.txt

65A	41	Parker	William	49 NC	pg0059B.txt
103B	13	Parker	William	13 GA	pg0099B.txt

Daniel C. Parker not found in the 1850 Census of Lumpkin County, Georgia.

LUMPKIN County, Georgia NOTE: This might explain why Daniel C. Parker left Lumpkin Co. Georgia.
6TH GEORGIA LAND LOTTERY - 1832 Lumpkin County, Georgia.
Georgia gave the Cherokee Nation East away in the 6th or 1832 Land Lottery.
Gold had been discovered in 1828 and some believe that the Indians and mixed bloods in the area had been aware of it and mined gold earlier than that. The State of Georgia divided the area where gold could exist into 40 acre lots and the rest into 160 acres. Scouts had been in the area looking out for where gold already had been found. Georgia had had troops in the area to try to stop the illegal poaching of the gold. The speculators had riders ready when the Lots were drawn and as soon as one of the "good" gold lots were drawn, the riders would be dispatched to the winners residence to purchase the lot. This was a race between the speculators fast horses and smooth talking buyers to see who could get there and close the deal before a competitor showed up.
Draws could be sold or mortgaged before the lottery even began and many people either gambled that they wouldn't win or that they wouldn't want the property and sold their draws. In Book A of the Deed Records of Forsyth County almost the entire book consists of assigned draws. Oliver Strickland was elected Clerk of the Superior Court of Cherokee County in the first election in February of 1832. When the counties were split, those officials who had been elected for all of Cherokee County assumed the office in the county of their residence. Oliver Strickland resided in Forsyth County and apparently kept the same book and just picked up with Forsyth County Deeds at that point. All early deeds in all of the ten counties will say for example, Land Lot "whatever", "whichever" Co., formerly Cherokee Co.
A lot of the people who drew, didn't want to move and just sold. People who owed money and were lucky in the draw had fines levied on them by their creditors and the lots were sold by the Sheriffs of the Counties. Many of the early sales will be recorded and indexed under the Sheriff's name. Of those people who decided to move and take up their land, if it didn't have gold, 40 acres of wooded hills and gullys wouldn't support a family. They had to buy extra land to farm. There were improved properties with houses or stores or taverns or mills or ferries. Some of these were sold back to the original owners and in some cases the new owner simply took possession and "disposed" the former owners. With the transfer of this much property there were lawsuits and lawsuits. Lawyers swarmed in to go where the cases were.
So as with any boom area you had an influx of speculators, lawyers, merchants with the addition on top of gold miners and "camp followers" and thieves. Add on top of this the preachers and teachers and the ordinary farmers and north Georgia started with a potpourri of people. Some stayed and some moved on, but it was an exciting time.

 Daniel C. Parker and his family left and moved to Butler Co. Alabama by 1855; as their son Henry Parker was born in Alabama, Butler County.   Daniel C. Parker and family are found on the Butler Co. Census Records in 1860. Daniel C. Parker and his wife had children in Lumpkin Ga. with the last one born in Alabama; as seen in Census records.

Our L. Reynolds Brightwell married Caroline Parker in Stewart Co. Ga. Sept. 13, 1846. (Box Ankel Dist. now Richland ga.)Since she got married in Stewart Co., Georgia it is a probability that the PARKER family members will be found in Stewart Co., Georgia.   When Len Reynold Brightwell and Caroline Parker were first married they were living in the home of Daniel C. Parker and family on the 1850 census of Stewart Co., Ga. Daniel C. Parker age 50; his wife - Mary age 38; their son-John age 15 years and then Elizabeth Caroline age 22 and her husband Reynolds age 25 are listed too.   There is a 10 year difference in the ages of Caroline and John. Daniel C. Parker served the County as Coroner of Stewart Co., Georgia from January 18, 1834 through January 13, 1836.

In the Census of 1860 of Butler Co. Alabama; Reynolds Brightwell is found living next door to William Brightwell and Daniel C. Parker is living down the road next door to Mary Mitchell (his mother-in-law).

Our Elizabeth Caroline (Parker) Brightwell and husband L. Reynolds Brightwell are found also and settling in Covington Co. Georgia.

DANIEL C PARKER
Land Office: GREENVILLE Alabama LAND RECORDS @ Ancestry.com
Document Number: 50864
Total Acres: 168.5
Issue Date: April 02, 1860
Signature: Yes
Canceled Document: No
Mineral Rights Reserved: No
Metes and Bounds: No
Statutory Reference: 3 Stat. 566
Multiple Warantee Names: No
Act or Treaty: April 24, 1820
Multiple Patentee Names: No
Entry Classification: Sale-Cash Entries
Legal Land Description: # Aliquot Parts Block # Base Line Fractional Section Township Range Section #
1 S½SE ST STEPHENS No 8N 15E 6
2 S½SW ST STEPHENS No 8N 15E 6

Federal Alabama Land Grants in BUTLER County lists:

Parker	Arthur		Butler	13E	9N	35	1837
Parker	Arthur		Butler	13E	9N	26	1837
Parker	Arthur		Butler	13E	9N	25	1837
Parker	Arthur		Butler	13E	9N	26	1858
Parker	Benjamin		Butler	13E	8N	8	1838
Parker	Benjamin		Butler	13E	8N	9	1838
Parker	Benjamin		Butler	13E	8N	4	1838
Parker	Daniel	C	Butler	15E	8N	6	1860
Parker	David		Butler	12E	8N	11	1837
Parker	Eldridge		Butler	13E	8N	7	1838
Parker	Gardner	G	Butler	16E	10N	34	1861
Parker	Henry	E	Butler	15E	8N	9	1858
Parker	Henry	E	Butler	15E	8N	17	1858
Parker	Henry	E	Butler	15E	8N	8	1858
Parker	Henry	J	Butler	15E	8N	8	1861
Parker	Israel		Butler	14E	8N	24	1860
Parker	John		Butler	12E	9N	31	1837
Parker	John		Butler	12E	8N	5	1837
Parker	John		Butler	13E	7N	21	1858
Parker	Mason		Butler	13E	10N	28	1888
Parker	Noah		Butler	14E	7N	25	1858
Parker	Noah		Butler	14E	7N	26	1858
Parker	Noah		Butler	14E	7N	24	1858
Parker	Noah		Butler	12E	8N	35	1858
Parker	Noah		Butler	14E	7N	25	1858
Parker	Noah		Butler	12E	8N	35	1858
Parker	Samuel		Butler	14E	7N	33	1858
Parker	Samuel		Butler	13E	8N	24	1891
Parker	Sterling		Butler	12E	8N	14	1837
Parker	William		Butler	12E	8N	36	1837
Parker	William		Butler	12E	7N	1	1837

ID: I519
Name: Daniel C. Parker

Sex: M
Birth: ABT 1805 in SC
Note: 1860 census
Note: 1860 census: Name: D C Parker Age in 1860: 55 Birthplace: South Carolina Home in 1860: Precinct 15, Butler, Alabama Gender: Male Value of real estate: View image Post Office: Leon and Rainsville Roll: M653_3 Page: 5 Year: 1860 Head of Household: D C Parker Household: D C Parker Precinct 15, Butler, AL 55 1804 South Carolina Male Mary Parker Precinct 15, Butler, AL 50 1809 Georgia Female John L Parker Precinct 15, Butler, AL 22 1837 Male Elander Parker Precinct 15, Butler, AL 20 1839 Female S Parker Precinct 15, Butler, AL 18 1841 Female Alfred Parker Precinct 15, Butler, AL 12 1847 Male M Parker Precinct 15, Butler, AL 10 1849 Female Henry Parker Precinct 15, Butler, AL 4 1855 Alabama Male
Change Date: 15 SEP 2004

Marriage 1 Mary Mitchell
Children
 Elizabeth Caroline Parker b: ABT 1827 in GA
 John L. Parker b: ABT 1838
 Elander Parker b: ABT 1840
 S. Parker b: ABT 1842
 Alfred Parker b: ABT 1848
 M. Parker b: ABT 1850
 Henry Parker b: ABT 1856

Notes for MARY MITCHELL:
THE MITCHELL family is found in the Covington County, Alabama 1860 Census records. Verified.

Mary (Mitchell) would have been 16 years old; when Caroline was born. A barbara Lang (Descendant of MaryMitchell's brother - Henry Michell) stated that Henry Mitchell married L. Reynold Brightwell's sister - Nancy Brightwell.

ID: I520
Name: Mary Mitchell
Sex: F
Note: 1860 census lists her as 50 yr old wife of D. C. Parker, Butler Co., AL
Change Date: 15 SEP 2004

Father: Mitchell
Mother: Mary

Marriage 1 Daniel C. Parker b: ABT 1805 in SC
Children
 Elizabeth Caroline Parker b: ABT 1827 in GA
 John L. Parker b: ABT 1838
 Elander Parker b: ABT 1840
 S. Parker b: ABT 1842
 Alfred Parker b: ABT 1848
 M. Parker b: ABT 1850

More About DANIEL PARKER and MARY MITCHELL:
Marriage: 1825, Jones County, Georgia Marriage

Children of DANIEL PARKER and MARY MITCHELL are:
7.   i.   ELIZABETH CAROLINE[5] PARKER, b. 1828, 1880 Census Sandy Ridge, Lowndes Co.,Ala. she was 52

yrs. old.; d. Aft. 1900, Liv in 1900 Crenshaw Co., Ala Census..
- ii. JOHN L. PARKER, b. 1837, Shown as 22 yrs old in 1860 Butler Co. Alabama Census.
- iii. ELANDER PARKER, b. 1839, Shown as 20, female, in 1860, Butler Co. AL Census.
- iv. S. PARKER, b. 1841, Shown 18 yrs old in 1860, Butler Co Census AL Census.
- v. ALFRED PARKER, b. 1847, Shn as 12 yrs in 1860 Butler Co AL Census.
- vi. M. PARKER, b. 1849, Shn as 10 yrs old Butler Co. AL Census.
- vii. HENRY PARKER, b. 1855, Shown 4 years old; born in ALABAMA Butler Co. 1860 Census.

Generation No. 5

7. ELIZABETH CAROLINE[5] PARKER *(DANIEL C.[4], BENJAMIN[3], PETER[2], THE PARKER FAMILY[1] HISTORY)* was born 1828 in 1880 Census Sandy Ridge, Lowndes Co.,Ala. she was 52 yrs. old., and died Aft. 1900 in Liv in 1900 Crenshaw Co., Ala Census.. She married LEN REYNOLDS BRIGHTWELL 13 Sep 1846 in Md Stewart Co., Ga. Box Ankel Dist/Now Richland Co. Ga., son of WILLIAM BRIGHTWELL and SARAH WINDSOR/WINDZER. He was born 1825 in Bn. Barnwell, S.C. Conf. Soldier/ Co. C. Ala. - 37th CIVIL WAR, and died 20 May 1863 in Believed buried Covington Co., Alabama - due to Civil War.

Notes for ELIZABETH CAROLINE PARKER:

CAROLINE BRIGHTWELL

ID: I267
Name: Elizabeth Caroline Parker
Sex: F
Birth: ABT 1827 in GA
Note: 1860 census
Note: 1850 census: Name: Elizabeth Brightwell Age: 22 Estimated Birth Year: 1827 Birth Place: Georgia Gender: Female Home in 1850 (City,County,State): Box Ankle, Stewart, Georgia Page: 63 Roll: M432_82 Caroline Elizabeth Parker Brightwell (wife of L.R. Brightwell)was daughter of Daniel C. Parker and Mary Mitchell.(see 1850 census of Stewart co. Ga.)& Butler co. al. census 1860.--Widow Caroline Brightwell & children on 1866 census of Covington co. al. & Crenshaw co. al. Census 1870. 1860 census: Name: E C Brightwell Age in 1860: 30 Birthplace: Georgia Home in 1860: Precinct 15, Butler, Alabama Gender: Female Value of real estate: View image Post Office: Leon and Rainsville Roll: M653_3 Page: 7 Year: 1860 1870 census: BRIGHTWELL, CAROLINE (1870 U.S. Census) ALABAMA , CRENSHAW, RUTLEDGE P O Age: 42, Female, Race: WHITE, Born: GA Series: M593 Roll: 12 Page: 107 1870 Crenshaw Co. Census Records, Township-Eleven Family #4: Bright, Caroline.....42.....wf.....GA Sarah........20.....wf.....GA Martha.......19.....wf.....GA Mary.........17,,...wf...AL Missouri.....15.....wf.....AL Matilda....,,13.... wf.....AL Albert.......11.....wm.....AL James........08.....wm.....AL
Change Date: 18 SEP 2004

Father: Daniel C. Parker b: ABT 1805 in SC
Mother: Mary Mitchell

Our L. Reynolds Brightwell married Caroline Parker in Stewart Co. Ga. Sept. 13, 1846. (Box Ankel Dist. now Richland ga.)Since she got married in Stewart Co., Georgia it is a probability that the PARKER family members will be found in Stewart Co., Georgia. When Len Reynold Brightwell and Caroline Parker were first married they were living in the home of Daniel C. Parker and family on the 1850 census of Stewart Co., Ga. Daniel C. Parker age 50; his wife - Mary age 38; their son-John age 15 years and then Elizabeth Caroline age 22 and her husband Reynolds age 25 are listed too. There is a 10 year difference in the ages of Caroline and John. Daniel C. Parker served the County as Coroner of Stewart Co., Georgia from January 18, 1834 through January 13, 1836.

In the Census of 1860 of Butler Co. Alabama; Reynolds Brightwell is found living next door to William Brightwell and Daniel C. Parker is living down the road next door to Mary Mitchell (his mother-in-law).

Caroline Brightwell is shown head of household in 1866 Census of Covington County, Alabama census. The William Brightwell listed in Covington Co., Ala. is believed to be Len Reynold Brightwell's brother. William went back to Georgia and settled in the Colquitt Co. area (near Rodney Brightwell) and is buried in Georgia, in the 1870 Census. William Brightwell was in the Home guard during the civil War in Covington Co., Alabama before moving to Georgia.

Len Reynolds Brightwell had died by the time this census of 1866 was done; and Caroline is listed a Head of Household with her children; shown as widow.

She was widowed age 52 yrs living in Sandy Ridge, Lowndes Co. Alabama, shown keeping house. It shows her as a Widow in the Pension Files for her husband and she received the pension the rest of her life. It shows her family from Stewart Co., Ga. Her state of birth was discrepancy,, Georgia or S. Carolina listed. Familysearch.com

In her later years, widowed, she is found in Census records with her youngest son, James H. Brightwell still living at home.

Caroline is shown as a Widow in the 1866 Census of Covington Co., AL and Crenshaw Alabama Census of 1870.

L. (Len) Reynolds Brightwell b. 1825 Barnwell S.C. Son of William 1 Brightwell and Sarah Windsor (See will of Anderson Windsor, Barnwell SC.)-L.Reynolds Brightwell died May 1863 in Covington Co. al as result of the Civil War.Co c Ala. 37th.

Caroline Elizabeth Parker Brightwell (wife of L.R. Brightwell)was daughter of Daniel C. Parker and Mary Mitchell.(see 1850 census of Stewart co. Ga.)& Butler co. al. census 1860.--Widow Caroline Brightwell & children on 1866 census of Covington co. al. & Crenshaw co. al. Census 1870.

ID: I266
Name: L. (Len) Reynolds Brightwell
Sex: M
Birth: 1825 in Barnwell, SC
Death: MAY 1863 in Covington Co., AL
Note: 1850 US Census: Brightwell, Reynolds (links to incorrect image) State: Georgia Year: 1850 County: Stewart Roll: M432_82 Township: Box Ankle District Page: 63 Image: 128 1860 census: BRIGHTWELL, L R (1860 U.S. Census) ALABAMA , BUTLER, 15-PCT Age: 33, Male, Race: WHITE, Series: M653 Roll: 3 Page: 7 Household: L R Brightwell Precinct 15, Butler, AL 33 1826 Male E C Brightwell Precinct 15, Butler, AL 30 1829 Georgia Female S J Brightwell Precinct 15, Butler, AL 11 1848 Female M A Brightwell Precinct 15, Butler, AL 9 1850 Female M E Brightwell Precinct 15, Butler, AL 7 1852 Alabama Female M E Brightwell Precinct 15, Butler, AL 5 1854 Female M C Brightwell Precinct 15, Butler, AL 3 1856 Female H A Brightwell Precinct 15, Butler, AL 1 1858 Male died as result of the Civil War. Co c Ala. 37th. Brightwell, Len Reynolds (sic Burnel) Private Company C Age at Enlistment: 38 Enlisted 31 March 1862 at Leon AL for a period of three years; Appears on Muster Roll of Company C dated 13 May 1862 at Auburn AL; Believed WIA in unknown action and died of his wounds at home while in service; Died 20 May 1863 and claim for deceased soldier filed 27 May 1863 by Caroline Brightwell, widow, at Covington AL (speed by which claim was filed supports belief that he was home at time of death); Appears on Pay Roll dated 31 Oct 1863 at Montgomery AL with notation "Died in Covington County, Alabama" (during the pay period); He was son of William Brightwell and Sara Windsor Brightwell of Barnwell SC; Wife/widow Caroline E. Parker Brightwell was daughter of Daniel C. Parker and Mary Mitchell; Included in report of Covington Rifles, SCV Camp #1586 of Andalusia, Alabama entitled "Known Gravesites of Confederate Soldiers and Sailors Buried in Covington County, Alabama" as one of "... buried on the battlefields or believed to be buried in unmarked graves in Covington County" with this entry: "Brightwell, L. Reynolds. Died in service 20 May 1863. Co. C, 37th Alabama Infantry. Believed to have died at home while on furlough. Wife Caroline."; Record in AL Archives for "Burnel Brightwell" contains identical information and is clearly a misread of "Reynolds" for "Burnel" by an unknown copyist
Change Date: 16 SEP 2004

Father: William Brightwell
Mother: Sarah Windsor

Marriage 1 Elizabeth Caroline Parker b: ABT 1827 in GA
Children
 Sarah Jane Brightwell b: 30 AUG 1849 in Stewart Co., GA
 Martha A. Brightwell b: ABT 1850
 Mary E. Brightwell b: ABT 1853
 Missouri E. Brightwell b: MAY 1854 in AL
 Matilda C. Brightwell b: ABT 1857
 Hilery Albert Brightwell b: ABT 1859
 James H. Brightwell b: 1861 in Butler Co., AL

More About ELIZABETH CAROLINE PARKER:
Burial: Sawyer Cemetery, Sandy Ridge, Alabama
Census: 1900, 73 yrs old in home of son James H. Brightwell in 1900 Cen Alabama/Crenshaw Co.

Descendants of *PERDUE FAMILY HISTORY*

Generation No. 1

1. PERDUE FAMILY[1] HISTORY was born in See notes..

Notes for PERDUE FAMILY HISTORY:

The Perdue family research and notes.
PERDUE RESEARCH NOTES
Information Found on Webpage 2/3/04 http://www.ideaworx.com/genealogy/aqwg01.htm#1
Pierre PERDEUX was born 1563 in France. He died 1631 in Maryland. Pierre PERDEUX married Anne
DES JARDINES.
Pierre PERDEUX
Birth: ABT. 1583 in Angers of Anjou, France
Death: 1631
Note:
Pierre Perduex, a native of Angers of Anjou, was many years advocate to Parliament of Paris, Master of
request to the Duke of Anjou, and chief magistrate of the Criminal Court of Angers. The tradition is that the
early Perdues were Huguenots and that they left France for England and Ireland before coming to America.
It is not known who was the first Perdue to come to America. Dr. William Perdue , a descendant of Pierre,
came to Pennsylvania from County Antrim, Ireland in April, 1737. The following is an exact quotation
from the records of Herman E. Perdue, attorney of Salisbury, Maryland.
"An elaborate manuscript compiled and emblazoned in the College of Arms containing "Sundrie Ancient
Remembrance of Arms, Genealogies and other notes of Gentility belonging to the Worshipful name and
families of Perduex." In the first reign of the Normans there flourished two noble families of the surname
Perduex, and that they were of like noble lineage or offspring of "The Dutchy of Normandy". This is from
the book "Early Settlers of Upper Sumner County Tennessee". These information was compiled by Lee
Alton Absher, M. D. of Knoxville, TN in 1966.
Debra Poole and Lewis Williams family
Entries: 7613   Updated: Wed Mar 12 15:27:04 2003   Contact: Debra Poole Williams
Second Generation
Henri PERDUE was born 1625. He married Marie LOISSON
Henri PERDUE
ID: I0897
Name: Henri PERDEUX
Sex: M
Birth: 1625
Occupation: Bell Founder
Note: Henri Perduex was born in the year 1625. He is the progenitor of the Perdue family in America. He
married Marie Loisson , herself a descendant of a noble French family. With a desire to worship according
to the faith of the Huguenots, he left France leaving considerable property, with a chateau in the country,
and a mansion in what is now called Rue St, Honore in Paris. He arrived in Bristol, England, in 1655 and
became associated with the Indies Company. At Bristol, his first child, Dean, was born September 6, 1656.
In 1657 Henri was appointed resident factor of the Indies Company, for martinique and on October 20,
1657, he sailed from Bristol, England on the brig, Thistle, Captain William Stackpool, master. See bristol
and America Vol. 3. He arrived at Fort de France, Martinque, December 1, 1657. His second son Rene, was
born at Fort de France June 12, 1658. At Fort de France was also born a daughter , Marie, November 7,
1660. This is taken from a book called " Early Settlers of Upper Sumner County, Tennessee, compiled
information on the Perdue family by Lee Alton Absher, M. D. written in 1966.
THIRD GENERATION
John_or Richard1 Prideaux {MR} was born in Accomac Co., VA about 1670.

He married an unknown person.

John_or Richard Prideaux MR had the following children:

+ 2 i. John2 Perdue was born 1695.

3 ii. Margaret Perdue was born in Maryland about 1705/1710. She married Thomas Berry in Duck Creek, Sussex Co., MD, March 17, 1731. Thomas was born in Maryland about 1705. \i0 Duck Creek monthly meeting records Duck Creek monthly meeting records

FOURTH Generation

John William PERDUE was born 1695 in 1673? in Worchester County, Maryland. He died 1743 in Worchester Co., MD. John William PERDUE married Mary LINGO about 1719 in Worchester Co., MD. John William PERDUE   may have been spelled Perdieu.

FIFTH Generation

John W. Jr. PERDUE was born 1725 in Worchester Co., MD. He died about 12 Aug 1802 in Worchester Co., MD. John W. Jr. PERDUE married Arcadia WALKER about 1753 in Worchester Co., MD.

129. Arcadia WALKER was born about 1732 in Worchester Co., MD.

Child: John3 Perdue (John2, John_or Richard1 Prideaux) was born in Worchester Co., MD 1725. John died about August 12, 1802 in Worchester Co., MD, at approximately 77 years of age.

He married twice. He married Arcadia Walker in Worchester Co., MD, about 1753. Arcadia was born in of, Worchester Co., MD about 1732. Arcadia and John Perdue were sealed May 23, 1987. Temple Code: JR. Arcadia was baptized a member of The Church of Jesus Christ of Latter-day Saints July 1, 1993. Temple Code: SLAKE. She was endowed October 13, 1993. Temple Code: SLAKE. He married Sabrough Fooks in Worchester Co., MD, 1773. Sabrough was born in of, Worchester Co., MD 1735. Sabrough died 1800 in Worchester Co., MD, at 65 years of age. Sabrough and John Perdue were sealed February 13, 1987. Temple Code: JR. Sabrough was baptized a member of The Church of Jesus Christ of Latter-day Saints July 1, 1993. Temple Code: SLAKE. She was endowed October 13, 1993. Temple Code: SLAKE.

John and Sabrough Fooks were sealed February 13, 1987. Temple Code: JR. John was baptized a member of The Church of Jesus Christ of Latter-day Saints March 17, 1987. Temple Code: JR. He was endowed March 20, 1987. Temple Code: JR. He was sealed to his parents May 22, 1987. Temple Code: JR. John and Arcadia Walker were sealed May 23, 1987. Temple Code: JR. Fooks Family History, "Perdue Descendents"; Worchester Co., MD Wills of John Perdue 1802 and James Perdue, 1802; Hancock Co., GA Census and Land Recs.

John Perdue and Arcadia Walker had the following children:

6 i. James4 Perdue was born in Worchester Co., MD about 1754. James died about October 27, 1802 in Worchester Co., MD, at approximately 48 years of age. He married Susanna.

James was baptized a member of The Church of Jesus Christ of Latter-day Saints March 17, 1987. Temple Code: JR. He was endowed March 20, 1987. Temple Code: JR. He was sealed to his parents May 23, 1987. Temple Code: JR.

+ 7 ii. George Perdue was born 1757.

8 iii. John Perdue Jr. was born in Worchester Co., MD 1760. John died 1830 at 70 years of age. John was baptized a member of The Church of Jesus Christ of Latter-day Saints March 17, 1987. Temple Code: JR. He was endowed March 20, 1987. Temple Code: JR. He was sealed to his parents May 23, 1987. Temple Code: JR.

9 iv. Eli Louden Perdue was born in Worchester Co., MD 1765. Eli was baptized a member of The Church of Jesus Christ of Latter-day Saints March 17, 1987. Temple Code: JR. He was endowed March 20, 1987. Temple Code: JR. He was sealed to his parents May 22, 1987. Temple Code: JR.

John Perdue and Sabrough Fooks had the following children:

10 v. Sabra F. Perdue was born in Worchester Co., MD 1775. Sabra was baptized a member of The Church of Jesus Christ of Latter-day Saints February 13, 1987. Temple Code: JR. She was endowed March 14, 1987. Temple Code: JR. She was sealed to her parents May 22, 1987. Temple Code: JR.

11 vi. Martha F. Perdue was born in Worchester Co., MD 1778. Martha was baptized a member of The Church of Jesus Christ of Latter-day Saints February 13, 1987. Temple Code: JR. She was endowed March 14, 1987. Temple Code: JR. She was sealed to her parents May 22, 1987. Temple Code: JR.

SIXTH GENERATION

John W. Perdue, Jr. and Arcadia Walker Perdue's Child:

George PERDUE was born 1757 in Worchester Co., MD. He died about 1840 in Lowndes County, AL.

George PERDUE married Edith TAYLOR about 1783 in Worchester Co., MD. [Parents]
   65. Edith TAYLOR was born about 1756 in Worchester Co., MD. She died before 1803 in Worchester Co., MD.
George4 Perdue (John3, John2, John_or Richard1 Prideaux) was born in Worchester Co., MD 1757. George died in Lowndes Co., AL.
He married twice. He married Edith Taylor in Worchester Co., MD, about 1783. Edith was born in of, Worchester Co., MD about 1756. Edith was the daughter of Thomas Taylor. Edith died before 1803 in Worchester Co., MD. Edith was baptized a member of The Church of Jesus Christ of Latter-day Saints March 13, 1987. Temple Code: JR. She was endowed May 19, 1987. Temple Code: JR. Edith and George Perdue were sealed May 23, 1987. Temple Code: JR. He married Elizabeth Dixon in of Worchester Co, MD, 1803. Elizabeth and George Perdue were sealed October 6, 1994. Temple Code: SLAKE.
George was baptized a member of The Church of Jesus Christ of Latter-day Saints March 17, 1987. Temple Code: JR. He was endowed March 26, 1987. Temple Code: JR. He was sealed to his parents May 22, 1987. Temple Code: JR. George and Edith Taylor were sealed May 23, 1987. Temple Code: JR. George and Elizabeth Dixon were sealed October 6, 1994. Temple Code: SLAKE. Kathryn Morey Yarborough research, Murphy-Perdue Society Research;Family Records in possession of Margaret Perdue Bell; Fooks Family History; Ala. and Md. Census Records.

George Perdue and Edith Taylor had the following child:
SEVENTH GENERATION
Child of George Perdue and Edith Taylor is:
John Hamilton PERDUE was born 5 Apr 1784 in Maryland. He died 26 Sep 1861 in Farmersville, Lowndes Co., AL and was buried in Sawyer Cemetery, Lowndes Co., AL. John Hamilton PERDUE married Mary MURPHY on 1827 in Monroe Co., AL. [Parents]
   33. Mary MURPHY was born Mar 1808 in South Carolina. She died 2 Feb 1892 in Champagnolle, Union County, Arkansas and was buried in Ebenezer Methodist Cemetery, Union County, Arkansas

EIGHTH GENERATION
Son of John Hamilton Perdue and Mary Murphy:
James Hilliand PERDUE was born 1828 in Lowndes County, Alabama. He died 1901 in Butler County, Alabama and was buried in Magnolia Cemetery, Greenville, Butler Co., AL. James Hilliand PERDUE married Jane FRANKLIN.
   17. Jane FRANKLIN.
J. H. Perdue served the Confederacy during the Civil War as a Private; Co. C 17th Alabama Infantry M374 Roll 5.
NINETH GENERATION
Son of James Hilliard Perdue and Jane Franklin Perdue:
Dr. James Lewis PERDUE was born 19 Feb 1851 in Butler County Alabama. He died 17 Dec 1932 in Greenville Ala and was buried 21 Dec 1932 in Greenville Ala. Dr. James Lewis PERDUE married Eva WRIGHT.
   9. Eva WRIGHT.

The 1850 Census of Lowndes Co. Slave Owners lists only one PERDUE:
   George Perdue owning (1) Slave.

PERDUE FAMILY RESEARCH:
LITTLE SANDY RIDGE CEMETERY
in Sandy Ridge, Lowndes Co., Alabama
Between I 65 and Highway 31, one mile south of Highway 185 on County Road #
79
Original survey compiled by Lewis A. Easterly and Alice M. Lee, published
by the Lowndes County Historical Society, 1977.

PERDUE, Dasnel B., son of J. L. & J. E. PERDUE, January 17, 1880, April 13, 1883
PERDUE, J. J., age 17 years, , October 30, 1862
PERDUE, Infant of G. W. & M. F. PERDUE
PERDUE, Alice Adonia, daughter of J. M. & L. F. PERDUE, March 24, 1871, June 29, 1895
NO BRIGHTWELLS listed in this cemetery.

Payne Cemetery, Sandy Ridge, Lowndes County, Alabama
January 1998
PERDUE, Estelle, 1879-1879
PERDUE, Eugenia, 1877-1879
PERDUE, David Greely, 'Buddy', 1872-1909
PERDUE, George Taylor, 1839-1915
PERDUE, Jesse Davis, 1875-1879
PERDUE, Julia Reeves, 1848-1932
PERDUE, Lydia R., 1870-1874
PERDUE, Robert, son of J. H. and Jane Perdue, 7-31-1850, 1-8-1861
NO BRIGHTWELLS listed in this cemetery.

Sawyer Cemetery, Sandy Ridge, Lowndes County, Alabama
April 1998
BRIGHTWELL, Charles M., son of J. H. and M. E. Brightwell, 2-8-1886, d. 6-26-1889
BRIGHTWELL, Ira, 7-21-1897, 1-22-1908
BRIGHTWELL, Mary E., 4-19-1861, d. 10-4-1914
BRIGHTWELL, Sarahe, daughter of J. H. and M. E. Brightwell, 10-31-1888, d. 9-12-1889
PERDUE, Alice T., 1866-1956, double stone with Jacob C.
PERDUE, Clara A. Stone, 1864-1942, wife of Issac
PERDUE, infant of J. C. and A. T. Perdue, born and died 1-11-1894
PERDUE, Issac, 1859-1925
PERDUE, Jacob C., 1860-1915
PERDUE, James Leonard, son of T. and N. Perdue, 6-31-1870, d. 11-2-1898
PERDUE, Rev. John B., 4-5-1788, 9-26-1860
PERDUE, Nancy, 1835-1915, wife of Thomas Perdue
PERDUE, Nancy E., youngest dau. of G. T. and Anna Perdue, 9-15-1854, 11-15-1861
PERDUE, Thomas, Jr., son of Thomas and Nancy Perdue, 10-23-1873, 9-25-1896
PERDUE, Thomas, 1833-1899
PERDUE, Thomas I., 2-1-1908, 9-24-1962
PERDUE, William S., son of Thomas and Nancy Perdue, 12-26-1870, 12-16-1889

168B 9	Perdue	A J	25	Ala	pg0158b.txt
143A 5	Perdue	Adelia	17	Ala	pg0136a.txt
131A 17	Perdue	Alexander	3	Ala	pg0125a.txt
129B 28	Perdue	Amand J	7	Ala	pg0125a.txt
131A 6	Perdue	Andrew W	19	Ala	pg0125a.txt
129B 22	Perdue	Ann	38	Georgia	pg0125a.txt
143A 4	Perdue	Arthur R	19	Ala	pg0136a.txt
131A 14	Perdue	Caroline	8	Ala	pg0125a.txt
131A 7	Perdue	Catharine	17	Ala	pg0125a.txt
143A 3	Perdue	Clara	36	S Carolina	pg0136a.txt
168B 10	Perdue	Eliza	18	Ala	pg0158b.txt
131A 15	Perdue	Ellen	7	Ala	pg0125a.txt
129B 21	Perdue	Geo T	38	Georgia	pg0125a.txt
129B 26	Perdue	George	10	Ala	pg0125a.txt
131A 4	Perdue	James	22	Ala	pg0125a.txt
129B 29	Perdue	James P	4	Ala	pg0125a.txt

131A 8	Perdue	Jane	16	Ala	pg0125a.txt
129B 25	Perdue	Jesse	16	Ala	pg0125a.txt
131A 5	Perdue	Jesse	21	Ala	pg0125a.txt
131A 2	Perdue	John	66	Maryland	pg0125a.txt
168B 14	Perdue	John	1	Ala	pg0158b.txt
168B 12	Perdue	John B	25	Ala	pg0158b.txt
184B 9	Perdue	John B F	16	Ala	pg0181b.txt
184B 8	Perdue	John B.	62	Maryland	pg0181b.txt
131A 12	Perdue	Margaret	11	Ala	pg0125a.txt
131A 18	Perdue	Marina	1	Ala	pg0125a.txt
131A 9	Perdue	Martha	14	Ala	pg0125a.txt
131A 3	Perdue	Mary	42	S Carolina	pg0125a.txt
131A 16	Perdue	Mary A	5	Ala	pg0125a.txt
131A 11	Perdue	Morris	12	Ala	pg0125a.txt
143A 6	Perdue	Nancy	15	Ala	pg0136a.txt
168B 11	Perdue	Nancy	8/12	Ala	pg0158b.txt
143A 7	Perdue	Orrin	12	Ala	pg0136a.txt
168B 13	Perdue	Rachael	18	S Carolina	pg0158b.txt
129B 27	Perdue	Rebecca A	8	Ala	pg0125a.txt
129B 30	Perdue	Seaborn J	4/12	Ala	pg0125a.txt
131A 13	Perdue	Seldon	9	Ala	pg0125a.txt
129B 23	Perdue	Thomas	17	Ala	pg0125a.txt
131A 10	Perdue	William	15	Ala	pg0125a.txt
129B 24	Perdue	William T	14	Ala	pg0125a.txt

pg 125a.txt about PERDUE Family:

21	408	408	Perdue	Geo T	38	M	Mechanic	500	Georgia
22	408	408	Perdue	Ann	38	F			Georgia
23	408	408	Perdue	Thomas	17	M	Planter		Ala
24	408	408	Perdue	William T	14	M			Ala X
25	408	408	Perdue	Jesse	16	M	Planter		Ala
26	408	408	Perdue	George	10	M			Ala X
27	408	408	Perdue	Rebecca A	8	F			Ala X
28	408	408	Perdue	Amand J	7	F			Ala X
29	408	408	Perdue	James P	4	M			Ala
30	408	408	Perdue	Seaborn J	4/12	M			Ala
3	427	427	Perdue	Mary	42	F			S Carolina
4	427	427	Perdue	James	22	M	Planter		Ala
5	427	427	Perdue	Jesse	21	M	Planter		Ala
6	427	427	Perdue	Andrew W	19	M	Planter		Ala
7	427	427	Perdue	Catharine	17	F			Ala X
8	427	427	Perdue	Jane	16	F			Ala
9	427	427	Perdue	Martha	14	F			Ala X
10	427	427	Perdue	William	15	M			Ala X
11	427	427	Perdue	Morris	12	M			Ala
12	427	427	Perdue	Margaret	11	F			Ala
13	427	427	Perdue	Seldon	9	M			Ala
14	427	427	Perdue	Caroline	8	F			Ala
15	427	427	Perdue	Ellen	7	F			Ala
16	427	427	Perdue	Mary A	5	F			Ala
17	427	427	Perdue	Alexander	3	M			Ala
18	427	427	Perdue	Marina	1	F			Ala

pg 158b.txt about PERDUE family:

```
9   1023 1023 Perdue   A J        25  M    Planter      100     Ala
10  1023 1023 Perdue   Eliza      18  F                          Ala
11  1023 1023 Perdue   Nancy      8/12 F                         Ala
12  1024 1024 Perdue   John B     25  M    Planter              Ala
13  1024 1024 Perdue   Rachael    18  F                          S Carolina
14  1024 1024 Perdue   John       1   M                          Ala
```

pg 136a.txt PERDUE FAMILY

```
3   613 613 Perdue    Clara      36  F                           S Carolina
4   613 613 Perdue    Arthur R   19  M    Planter               Ala
5   613 613 Perdue    Adelia     17  F                           Ala
6   613 613 Perdue    Nancy      15  F                           Ala
7   613 613 Perdue    Orrin      12  M                           Ala
```

pg 181b.txt PERDUE FAMILY

```
35  132 132 Per***    L. S.        50  M    Planter    1,224   Maryland
        REMARKS: Last name illegible; index has Perdue
36  132 132 Per***    Elizabeth    44  F                         * Car
        REMARKS: Last name illegible; index has Perdue
37  132 132 Per***    William W.   25  M    Planter             Ala
        REMARKS: Last name illegible; index has Perdue
38  132 132 Per***    Permelia     22  F                         Ala
        REMARKS: Last name illegible; index has Perdue
39  132 132 Per***    Matilda      20  F                         Ala
        REMARKS: Last name illegible; index has Perdue
40  132 132 Per***    Munroe       17  M                         Ala
        REMARKS: Last name illegible; index has Perdue
41  132 132 Per***    Narcissa     12  F                         Ala
        REMARKS: Last name illegible; index has Perdue
42  132 132 Per***    Southern T.  12  M                         Ala
        REMARKS: Last name illegible; index has Perdue;name may be Lonthem
8   136 136 Perdue    John B.      62  M    Meth. Clergyman 1,600  Maryland
9   136 136 Perdue    John B F     16  M    Planter             Ala
```

MARRIAGE RECORD FOUND:
Benjamin Joseph PERRY married Lucinda Caroline PERDUE on 26 Aug 186? in Sandy Ridge, Alabama.
<LAAYMEDLEY@aol.com> Click here to visit submitter's site

PERDUE,M.W. Crenshaw County, Alabama WILLS
Will filed the 06th day of March 1913,Book A page 199-201,He was at the
time of death was an inhabitant of this County.
I do hereby appoint ,choose and designate my son W.B.Perdue and my
son-in-law W.E.Gafford to be the executors of this will without bond.
I give devise and bequeath to my daughter Mrs.Sallie Herlong one-forth of
my property both real and personal.
I give devise and bequeath to my daughter Mrs.Abbie Gafford one-forth of
my property both real and personal.
I give devise and bequeath to my son W.B.Perdue one-forth of my property
both real and personal.
I give devise and bequeath to the children of my deceased son M.M.Perdue
who are,Virgil Perdue,Leland Perdue and Nellie Perdue all three together
one-forth of my property both real and personal.
It is my will and desire that Tallulah? G.Perdue the widow of my son
M.M.Perdue,shall hold and care for and safety keep the portion and share

of the children of my son M.M.Perdue.   Signed Dec.09,1911

FEDERAL LAND GRANTS IN ALABAMA, BUTLER COUNTY lists:

Perdue	James	E	Butler	16E	11N	31	1850
Perdue	James	E	Butler	16E	11N	20	1852
Perdue	James	H	Butler	16E	11N	32	1852
Perdue	James	H	Butler	16E	11N	31	1852
Perdue	James		Butler	16E	11N	5	1841
Perdue	John		Butler	14E	10N	27	1823
Perdue	John		Butler	14E	10N	22	1823
Perdue	Joshua	A	Butler	16E	10N	8	1848
Perdue	Joshua	A	Butler	16E	10N	8	1858
Perdue	Joshua	A	Butler	16E	10N	5	1858
Perdue	Sovereign	T	Butler	16E	11N	9	1852
Perdue	Sovereign		Butler	16E	11N	9	1843
Perdue	William	E	Butler	16E	11N	32	1843

Butler Co. Alabama Cemetery Records:

Perdue	Calvin R.	Perdue Cemetery
Perdue	Challie Russell	Perdue Cemetery
Perdue	David Foster	Perdue Cemetery
Perdue	Fannie M.	Perdue Cemetery
Perdue	Felon J.	Perdue Cemetery
Perdue	Foster W.	Perdue Cemetery
Perdue	Inf. dau. of Zell & Fannie	Perdue Cemetery
Perdue	Irby Conrad	Perdue Cemetery
Perdue	J. E. W.	Perdue Cemetery
Perdue	J. F.	Perdue Cemetery
Perdue	James L.	Perdue Cemetery
Perdue	Joshua A.	Perdue Cemetery
Perdue	Margie	Perdue Cemetery
Perdue	Martha A. W.	Perdue Cemetery
Perdue	Martha A. W.	Perdue Cemetery
Perdue	Mary Emily	Perdue Cemetery
Perdue	Mary Louese	Perdue Cemetery
Perdue	Minie Lee	Perdue Cemetery
Perdue	Osburn M. (?)	Perdue Cemetery
Perdue	Payton	Perdue Cemetery
Perdue	Webb A.	Perdue Cemetery
Perdue	William Peyton	Perdue Cemetery

PERDUE CEMETERY BUTLER CO. Alabama:
Butler County, Alabama
Go out Highway 31 North. Take right at "The Highlands" toward Spring Hill Community. This road is also known as the Steiner Store Road. Go past the Tom Gregory place and just beyond what is now known as the Harrison place take a dirt road to the right. This cemetery is about 1/4 mile on this dirt road on the right."

J. E. W. Perdue b. March 5, 1823   d. August 10, 1889

Martha A. W. Perdue, wife of J. A. Perdue
b. February 13, 1821   d. February 6, 1891

Foster W. Perdue, son of J. A. a nd M.A.W. Perdue
b. October 1, 1846   d. June 21, 1864

111

Aged 16 yrs. 8 mos. 20 ds.

David Foster Perdue, son of P. and F. Perdue
b. October 18, 1876   d. August 29, 1886

Martha A. W. Perdue
b. February 13, 1821   d. February 6, 1891

Joshua A. Perdue
b. November 19, 1817   d. January 23, 1894

Osburn M. (?), son of J. F. and M. Perdue
b. May 19, 1889   d. November 20, 1896

J. F. Perdue
b. November 2, 1850   d. November 30, 1896

Margie, wife of J. F. Perdue
b. December 29, 1859   d. March 23, 1929

Minie Lee, wife of Felon Perdue
b. October 2, 1885   d. March 10, 1917

Felon J. Perdue
b. December 2, 1876   d. September 18, 1927

Webb A. Perdue
b. August 26, 1881   d. January 23, 1954

Mary Emily Perdue
b. July 28, 1846   d. August 1, 1884

James L., son of L. B. and Mary E. Perdue
b. June 15, 1876   d. July 9, 1896

Challie Russell, inf. son of W. O. and A. Perdue
b. August 7, 1917   d. November 15, 1917

William Peyton, inf. son of W. O. and A. Perdue
b. June 7, 1916   d. October 11, 1917

Irby Conrad, son of Peyton and Fannie Perdue
b. December 24, 1881   d. November 8, 1914

Inf. dau. of Zell and Fannie Perdue
b. July 2, 1915   d. July 21, 1915

Inf. dau. of Zell and Fannie Perdue
b. August 7, 1918   d. August 8, 1918

Mary Louese, dau. of Zell and Fannie Perdue
b. December 28, 1923   d. February 23, 1927

Mary Perdue, wife of Llewellyn E. Gregory
b. February 22, 1883   d. June 11, 1942

NOTE: James Hilliand PERDUE was born 1828 in Lowndes County, Alabama. He died 1901 in Butler County, Alabama and was buried in Magnolia Cemetery, Greenville, Butler Co., AL. James Hilliand PERDUE married Jane FRANKLIN. [Parents]
  17. Jane FRANKLIN.

Child of PERDUE FAMILY HISTORY is:
2.   i.   JAMES E. W.[2] PERDUE, b. 05 Mar 1823, 10/30/1836 EnltdCo. C 17th Ala. Infantry Priv. M374 Roll 35 Civil War Records; d. 10 Aug 1889, Perdue Cem./Butler Co. Ala.-Did he die in Civil War?.

Generation No. 2

2. JAMES E. W.[2] PERDUE *(PERDUE FAMILY[1] HISTORY)* was born 05 Mar 1823 in 10/30/1836 EnltdCo. C 17th Ala. Infantry Priv. M374 Roll 35 Civil War Records, and died 10 Aug 1889 in Perdue Cem./Butler Co. Ala.-Did he die in Civil War?. He married MARTHA A. E.. She was born 13 Feb 1821, and died 06 Feb 1891 in Perdue Cemetery/Butler Co. Alabama.

Notes for JAMES E. W. PERDUE:

James E. W. Perdue is the father of James Larkin Perdue as reported in the Crenshaw History Book, Alabama by Mr. Styron of North Carolina. This information he stated was found at the Lowndes County Courthouse.

PERDUE - Confederate Alabama listed were:

J. H. PERDUE Confederate; Co. C. Private; M374 Roll 5; 17th Alabama Infantry
James E. W. PERDUE; 17th Regiment Alabama; Private, M374 Roll 35

Others:
Foster PERDUE
ALEX T. PERDUE
L. P. PERDUE
Lorenzo B. PERDUE
Morris W. PERDUE
Payton PERDUE
W. PERDUE
W. E. PERDUE

James E.W. Perdue (First_Last)
Regiment Name 17 Alabama Infantry
Side Confederate
Company K
Soldier's Rank_In Private
Soldier's Rank_Out Private
Alternate Name
Notes
Film Number M374 roll 35
Confederate Soldier

J.H. Perdue (First_Last)
Regiment Name 17 Alabama Infantry
Side Confederate
Company C
Soldier's Rank_In Private
Soldier's Rank_Out Private
Alternate Name
Notes
Film Number M374 roll 35

OTHER Confederate PERDUE Soldiers in the Co. C; 17th Alabama Infantry:
Foster Perdue   Alex T. Perdue   L. P. Perdue   Lorenzo B. Perdue
Morris W. PerduePayton Perdue   W. Perdue   W. E. Perdue

17th Alabama Infantry Regiment
The 17th Alabama Infantry Regiment was organized at Montgomery in August, 1861. In November, it moved to Pensacola and was present at the bombardment there that month and again in January. In March 1862, the regiment was sent to western Tennessee where it was brigaded under J. K. Jackson of Georgia, with the 18th, 21st, and 24th Alabama regiments. The unit fought at Shiloh and lost 125 k and w. A month later, it was in the fight at Framington, with few casualties. In the autumn, when Gen'l Braxton Bragg moved into Kentucky, the 17th, weakened by illness, was left at Mobile. It was there drilled as heavy artillery and had charge of eight batteries on the shore of the bay. It remained at that post until March 1864 when it was ordered to Rome, GA. The brigade consisted of the 17th and 29th Alabama regiments, and the 1st and 26th Alabama and 37th Mississippi regiments were soon after added. The brigade was commanded at different times by Gen'l Cantey of Russell, Col. Murphey of Montgomery, Col. O'Neal of Lauderdale, and Gen'l Shelley of Talladega. The regiment was engaged at the Oostenaula bridge and in the three days' battle of Resaca, with severe loss. The 17th had its full share of the campaigning from Dalton to Jonesboro, fighting almost daily, especially at Cassville, New Hope, Kennesaw, Lost Mountain, and Atlanta. In the battle of Peachtree Creek, it lost 130 k and w, and on the 28th of July, 180 k and w. The entire loss from Resaca to Lovejoy's Station was 586, but few of whom were captured. The regiment moved into Tennessee with Gen'l John Bell Hood and lost two-thirds of its force at Franklin; a number of the remainder were captured at Nashville. A remnant moved into North Carolina and a part fought at Bentonville. It was then consolidated with the 29th and 33rd Alabama regiments, with E. P. Holcombe of Lowndes as colonel, J. F. Tate of Russell as lieutenant colonel, and Willis J. Milner of Butler as major. The regiment surrendered at Greensboro, NC, in April, 1865.
Field officers: Cols. Thomas H. Watts (Montgomery, resigned); R. C. Fariss (Montgomery, resigned); and Virgil S. Murphey (Montgomery, captured at Franklin); Lt. Cols. R. C. Fariss (promoted); Virgil S. Murphey (promoted); and Edward P. Holcombe (Lowndes, wounded at Resaca); and Majors Virgil S. Murphey (promoted) and Thomas J. Burnett (Butler, wounded at Atlanta).

Company "C" 17th Alabama Infantry Regiment, organized in Butler Co., AL, was also called the "Blue Rifles". I went to the Alabama Archives on 16 Mar 2000 and found the muster roll for this company. J. M typed it. There was no last name for J. M. I have footnote numbers beside some names in the newspaper article. The footnotes refer to additional information or different information that was in the muster roll at the Archives. At the end of the article I added names that were on the muster roll but not in the newspaper article. The muster roll states that the Company was organized on 14 Sep 1861.

The Greenville Advocate
April 30, 1903

SAWYER CEMETERY, Sandy Ridge Alabama:
PERDUE, Alice T., 1866-1956, double stone with Jacob C.
PERDUE, Clara A. Stone, 1864-1942, wife of Issac
PERDUE, infant of J. C. and A. T. Perdue, born and died 1-11-1894
PERDUE, Issac, 1859-1925
PERDUE, Jacob C., 1860-1915
PERDUE, James Leonard, son of T. and N. Perdue, 6-31-1870, d. 11-2-1898
PERDUE, Rev. John B., 4-5-1788, 9-26-1860
PERDUE, Nancy, 1835-1915, wife of Thomas Perdue
PERDUE, Nancy E., youngest dau. of G. T. and Anna Perdue, 9-15-1854, 11-15-1861
PERDUE, Thomas, Jr., son of Thomas and Nancy Perdue, 10-23-1873, 9-25-1896
PERDUE, Thomas, 1833-1899
PERDUE, Thomas I., 2-1-1908, 9-24-1962
PERDUE, William S., son of Thomas and Nancy Perdue, 12-26-1870, 12-16-1889

More About JAMES E. W. PERDUE:
Burial: Who was his wife?

Child of JAMES PERDUE and MARTHA E. is:
3.   i.   JAMES LARKIN[3] PERDUE, b. 20 Oct 1859, Born Little Sandy Ridge Cem. Lowndes Co. AL; d. 30 Mar
                    1917, Perdue Cemetery/Butler Co. AL/Died in Influenza Epidemic. 58 years old. His sons were
                    farmers..

Generation No. 3

3. JAMES LARKIN[3] PERDUE *(JAMES E. W.[2], PERDUE FAMILY[1] HISTORY)* was born 20 Oct 1859 in Born
Little Sandy Ridge Cem. Lowndes Co. AL, and died 30 Mar 1917 in Perdue Cemetery/Butler Co. AL/Died
in Influenza Epidemic. 58 years old. His sons were farmers.. He married JANE ELIZABETH STYRON 04 Jul
1877 in Lowndes Co., Ga. Had eleven children., daughter of LEWIS STYRON and MARY CAIN. She was
born 13 Dec 1857 in Had Eleven Children.Sandy Ridge Com. Ala Lowndes Co. AL, and died 04 Dec 1951
in Died age 93 yrs. see notes..

Notes for JAMES LARKIN PERDUE:
James Larkin Perdue - - - - - -

He was living with Josiah Fields on he 1870 Census of Crenshaw Co., Ala. Older members say Larkin's
father left his son Larkin Perdue with Joe Fields.
Question: Did father die in Civil War? Research being done on this.
Question: Where was the wife and mother?

More About JAMES LARKIN PERDUE:
Burial: Buried Ivy CreekCemetery, near Rutledge Comm.

Notes for JANE ELIZABETH STYRON:
Jane Eleizabeth Styron; was 93 years of age when she died. since 1938, she had made her home with her
daughter and son-in-law; Ruby Lillian (1900-1994) and William Ashley gibson. (1898-1965). She is
buried beside her husband. Ivy CreekCemetery,near Rutledge Crenshaw Co., AL.

More About JANE ELIZABETH STYRON:
Burial: Buried Ivy CreekCemetery, near Rutledge Comm.

More About JAMES PERDUE and JANE STYRON:
Marriage: 04 Jul 1877, Lowndes Co., Ga.   Had eleven children.

Children of JAMES PERDUE and JANE STYRON are:

      i.   BUFORD[4] PERDUE, b. an infant..
     ii.   CAREY LLOYD PERDUE.
    iii.   MATTIE SEE "DOLLY" PERDUE, b. Bet. 1881 - 1953; m. JOHN FRANK KILLOUGH; b. Bet. 1878 - 1949.
    iv.   JOSEPH C. PERDUE, b. Bet. 1885 - 1960; m. EULA MAE KILOUGH; b. Bet. 1893 - 1974.
     v.   CARRIE BELL PERDUE, b. Bet. 1885 - 1968; m. HENRY KILLOUGH; b. Bet. 1881 - 1956.
4.   vi.   WILLIAM FLETCHER (FUTURE) "BUD" PERDUE, b. Bet. 1885 - 1969, Rutledge Alabama..
   vii.   JAMES RILEY PERDUE, b. Bet. 1888 - 1964; m. GUSSIE WHITEHEAD; b. Bet. 1899 - 1981.
  viii.   MESHAC HAMMOND PERDUE, b. Bet. 1890 - 1976, Served in U.S. Military in France during World War I.; m. VERLA MISSLETINE, Married.

        More About MESHAC PERDUE and VERLA MISSLETINE:
        Marriage: Married

    ix.   ELLEN PERDUE, b. Bet. 1892 - 1978; m. CHARLIE CLEVELAND STYRON; b. Bet. 1890 - 1978.
     x.   OLA MAE PERDUE, b. Bet. 1893 - 1977; m. JAMES W. ROWELL; b. Bet. 1891 - 1954, World War I Veteran..

Generation No. 4

4. WILLIAM FLETCHER (FUTURE) "BUD"[4] PERDUE *(JAMES LARKIN[3], JAMES E. W.[2], PERDUE FAMILY[1] HISTORY)* was born Bet. 1885 - 1969 in Rutledge Alabama.. He married (1) IDA R. SULA STAGGERS in Married Had 7 children only two lived., daughter of WADE STAGGERS and MARY. She was born in of Rutledge Alabama., and died in She died and he remarried again.. He married (2) JACKIE BURGINS.

Notes for WILLIAM FLETCHER (FUTURE) "BUD" PERDUE:

More About WILLIAM FLETCHER (FUTURE) "BUD" PERDUE:
Burial: Buried Ivy Creek Cemetery, near Rutledge, Crenshaw Co. AL

More About WILLIAM PERDUE and IDA STAGGERS:
Marriage: Married Had 7 children only two lived.

Children of WILLIAM PERDUE and IDA STAGGERS are:
      i.   CUMI[5] PERDUE, m. HOMER KILLOUGH.
5.   ii.   EVA LUCILLE PERDUE, b. 21 Apr 1915, Eva was married once before this marriage.; d. Jun 1981, SS# 416-66-7927-Montgomery, Ala./Mag. Bapt Ch Cemetery w/husband Leroy..

Generation No. 5

5. EVA LUCILLE[5] PERDUE *(WILLIAM FLETCHER (FUTURE) "BUD"[4], JAMES LARKIN[3], JAMES E. W.[2], PERDUE FAMILY[1] HISTORY)* was born 21 Apr 1915 in Eva was married once before this marriage.[1], and died Jun 1981 in SS# 416-66-7927-Montgomery, Ala./Mag. Bapt Ch Cemetery w/husband Leroy.. She married LEROY BRIGHTWELL in Married at the home of her parents., son of JAMES BRIGHTWELL and MARY BEDGOOD. He was born 25 Mar 1908 in Born Crenshaw Co. Ala./1910 cens. shows him 5 yrs. old- yr. 1905 (???), and died 07 Apr 1955 in Laverne, Crenshaw Co., Ala.Death Cert. # 6797[2].

Notes for EVA LUCILLE PERDUE:
FamilySearch™ U.S. Social Security Death Index
30 September 2000

Select record to download - Maximum: 50

Eva BRIGHTWELL
Birth Date: 21 Apr 1915
Death Date: Jun 1981
Social Security Number: 416-66-7927
State or Territory Where Number Was Issued: Alabama

Death Residence Localities
ZIP Code: 36107
Localities: Montgomery, Montgomery, Alabama

A Daniel Perdue is buried at Little Sandy Ridge Cemetery as follows in Alabama:
PERDUE, Dasnel B., son of J. L. & J. E. PERDUE, January 17, 1880, April 13, 1883
PERDUE, Samuel Elijah, son of John J. & Mary M. PERDUE, aged 11 years, 10 months, , October 4,
1853, mother was Mary M. Gingles PERDUE
PERDUE, J. J., age 17 years, , October 30, 1862
PERDUE, Infant of G. W. & M. F. PERDUE
PERDUE, Alice Adonia, daughter of J. M. & L. F. PERDUE, March 24, 1871, June 29, 1895
PERDUE, Estelle, 1879-1879
PERDUE, Eugenia, 1877-1879
PERDUE, David Greely, 'Buddy', 1872-1909
PERDUE, George Taylor, 1839-1915
PERDUE, Jesse Davis, 1875-1879
PERDUE, Julia Reeves, 1848-1932
PERDUE, Lydia R., 1870-1874
PERDUE, Robert, son of J. H. and Jane Perdue, 7-31-1850, 1-8-1861
PERDUE, Alice T., 1866-1956, double stone with Jacob C.
PERDUE, Clara A. Stone, 1864-1942, wife of Issac
PERDUE, infant of J. C. and A. T. Perdue, born and died 1-11-1894
PERDUE, Issac, 1859-1925
PERDUE, Jacob C., 1860-1915
PERDUE, James Leonard, son of T. and N. Perdue, 6-31-1870, d. 11-2-1898
PERDUE, Rev. John B., 4-5-1788, 9-26-1860
PERDUE, Nancy, 1835-1915, wife of Thomas Perdue
PERDUE, Nancy E., youngest dau. of G. T. and Anna Perdue, 9-15-1854, 11-15-1861
PERDUE, Thomas, Jr., son of Thomas and Nancy Perdue, 10-23-1873, 9-25-1896
PERDUE, Thomas, 1833-1899
PERDUE, Thomas I., 2-1-1908, 9-24-1962
PERDUE, William S., son of Thomas and Nancy Perdue, 12-26-1870, 12-16-1889

More About EVA LUCILLE PERDUE:
Burial: Buried Magnolia Baptist Church, Crenshaw, Ala.

Notes for LEROY BRIGHTWELL:

Leroy Brightwell's first marriage was to a part Native Indian American. But the children of this line are not
known at this time by researcher.

Leroy BRIGHTWELL
Birth Date: 25 Mar 1908
Death Date: Aug 1984

Social Security Number: 217-10-0806
State or Territory Where Number Was Issued: Maryland

Death Residence Localities
  ZIP Code: 21701
  Localities: Frederick, Frederick, Maryland
Harmony Grove, Frederick, Maryland
Hood College, Frederick, Maryland
Hopeland, Frederick, Maryland
Lewistown, Frederick, Maryland
Lime Kiln, Frederick, Maryland
Oak Acres, Frederick, Maryland
Pine Cliff, Frederick, Maryland
Tulip Hill, Frederick, Maryland

Children: Eva Purdue was married before she married Leroy and had two step-children. Then marrying Leroy, she had twelve more children of their own.

Leroy Brightwell
Age: 24
Estimated birth year: 1905
Birthplace: Alabama
Relation to Head-of-house: Head
Race: White
Home in 1930: Luverne, Crenshaw, Alabama
Year: 1930; Census Place: Luverne, Crenshaw, Alabama; Roll: T626_11; Page: 4B; Enumeration District: 19; Image: 0424.

Troy is located in Pik County, Alabama. a bit of important informatin. There IS NO RECORD OF ANY BRIGHTWELLS LIVING IN PIKE CO.AL. BEFORE THE Civil War and it WAS SOME TIME AFTER THE CW
BEFORE A BRIGHTWELL FAMILY MOVED IN TO PIKE CO. AL. There are NO SLAVE RECORDS ON ANY BRIGHTWELLS in Pike Co. Al.

Brightwell's that married in Pike County. Alabama
Brightwell E. E. married Gertrude Hurley 4-4-1895
Brightwell G.F. married Hilda M. Rhodes 2-27-1898
Brightwell J. F. married S. E. Darby 5-1-1879

At Family Reunion in Anadulsia Alabama August 19 & 20th, 2005; the following Children of James H. Brightwell and wife Mary Elizabeth "Mollie" were present:

Huey Brightwell; Bruce Brightwell; Ted Brightwell; Robert Brightwell; Ed Brightwell, Horace Brightwell; Betty Brightwell and Bobby Brightwell

    Lots of pictures of this group are shown in scrapbook.

More About LEROY BRIGHTWELL:
Burial: Buried Magnolia Baptist Church Cem. Crenshaw, Ala.
Death Information: 17 Apr 1955, 51 years old at death.

More About LEROY BRIGHTWELL and EVA PERDUE:
Marriage: Married at the home of her parents.

Children of EVA PERDUE and LEROY BRIGHTWELL are:

6.	i.	BOBBY RAY[6] BRIGHTWELL.

6. i. BOBBY RAY[6] BRIGHTWELL.

7. ii. HORACE GREGORY BRIGHTWELL, b. Lives in Semmes/Mobile Alabama 251-645-2471.

8. iii. HUEY LANE BRIGHTWELL, b. Live in Highland Home, Alabama 334-537-9710.

9. iv. JAMES EDWARD "ED" BRIGHTWELL, b. 334-222-0501/Brantley Alabama.

10. v. MARGARET "PEGGY" IRENE BRIGHTWELL, d. 2003, Deceased.

 vi. MARY LOUISE BRIGHTWELL, d. Died at 6 mths of Whooping Cough.

11. vii. ROBERT WAYNE BRIGHTWELL.

 viii. JAMES WILLIAM "MOSCOE" [SGT. BRIGHTWELL, b. Abt. 1930, Born Vernledge/Crenshaw Co. Alabama; d. Buried/Magnolia Bapt. Ch. Cemetery; m. VIRGINIA PETTY, Married/Divorced.

Notes for JAMES WILLIAM "MOSCOE" [SGT. BRIGHTWELL:
James was the FIRST child of his parents. He grew up and joined the ARMY then served in Germany. He was born in Crenshaw Co. Alabama.

 After coming home from the service; he worked in the logging business. He passed away in bed at Brantley, Alabama. There were reports of a truck accident the day before. The insurance company paid money to his mother Eva Purdue Brightwell. She used the money to purchase the home of her father Fletcher [Future} Perdue in Crenshaw Creek, Alabama near Ivy Creek.

 Moscoe was the name he was referred by; and he was married only once to Virginia Petty but later they divorced. It is believed that he had a son named James William Brightwell but not known for sure. At the time of James death they were divorced.
He is buried at Magnolia Baptist Church Cemetery in Crenshaw Cem. Alabama

More About JAMES BRIGHTWELL and VIRGINIA PETTY:
Marriage: Married/Divorced

 ix. THURMAN "TED" BRIGHTWELL, b. 26 May 1942, 256/353-1803/11612 Wadsworth St. SE,Decatur Ala.35601; m. SUE ANN ALDRIDGE, 16 Jan 1970, Married no children.; b. 11 Aug 1943, Decatur , Ala..

More About THURMAN BRIGHTWELL and SUE ALDRIDGE:
Marriage: 16 Jan 1970, Married no children.

12. x. BRUCE "JIMMY" BRIGHTWELL, b. 21 Jul 1944, Brantley, Ala./now Fredericksburg, Virginia; d. phone# 540-891-6344.

13. xi. BETTY JOYCE BRIGHTWELL, b. 22 Sep 1948, Alabama.

I shall pass through this world but once,
Any good, therefore, that I can do,
Or, any kindness that I can show,
To any human being,
Let me do it now.
Let me not defer it, or neglect it,
I shall not pass this way again.

Message by the Author Lanette Hill

A Family Story never ends.....it continues
to grow as more babies are added to our
families. My wish is that you take this
information, add your family information
to it. Let it continue to grow for you and
your descendants. You will treasure this
information and so will your descendants
for years to come.